Long Walk Through War

TEXAS A&M UNIVERSITY
MILITARY HISTORY SERIES
4

Klaus H. Huebner

Long Walk Through War

A COMBAT DOCTOR'S DIARY

TEXAS A&M UNIVERSITY PRESS : COLLEGE STATION

Frontispiece: Men of the 88th Infantry Division approaching Itri through fields from the south. Courtesy U.S. Army Signal Corps

Library of Congress Cataloging-in-Publication Data

Huebner, Klaus H., 1916–
   Long walk through war.

   (Texas A & M University military history series ; 4)
   Includes index.
   1. Huebner, Klaus H., 1916– —Diaries. 2. World
War, 1939–1945—Personal narratives, American.
3. World War, 1939–1945—Campaigns. 4. United States.
Army—Biography. 5. Physicians—United States—
Biography. I. Title. II. Series.
D811.H749 1987   940.54'7573'0924   86-30103
ISBN 0-89096-320-7 (alk. paper)

To all Blue Devils, who fought so valiantly in Italy

Contents

List of Illustrations   *page ix*
List of Maps   *xi*
Preface   *xiii*
Introduction: September 15, 1943–December 3, 1943   *3*
Wartime Troop Train Comfort:
    December 3, 1943–December 7, 1943   *6*
Awaiting Shipment to Places Unknown:
    December 7, 1943–December 16, 1943   *8*
On the *Empress of Scotland* to Casablanca:
    December 16, 1943–December 25, 1943   *10*
A Night in the Casbah:
    December 25, 1943–December 27, 1943   *12*
Casablanca to Magenta, Algeria:
    December 27, 1943–December 30, 1943   *14*
War Games Continue:
    December 30, 1943–February 1, 1944   *16*
On the *Neuralia* to Naples, Italy:
    February 1, 1944–February 12, 1944   *29*
War Games and Mountain Climbing in Italy:
    February 12, 1944–March 3, 1944   *32*
On the Front Line: March 3, 1944–May 11, 1944   *42*
Breakthrough of the Gustav Line:
    May 11, 1944–June 13, 1944   *61*
Albano, Rome, Tarquinia: June 13, 1944–July 5, 1944   *98*
Push to the Arno River: July 5, 1944–July 28, 1944   *107*
Return to Rome for Relaxation:
    July 28, 1944–September 17, 1944   *117*
The Apennine Campaign and the Gothic Line:
    September 17, 1944–November 8, 1944   *122*
Rome Revisited and Montecatini:
    November 8, 1944–April 15, 1945   *155*
Slaughter in the Po Valley: April 15, 1945–May 3, 1945   *172*
Epilogue: Before and After   *197*
Index   *203*

List of Illustrations

Approaching Itri from the south   *frontispiece*
Klaus Huebner, Villamagna, Italy,
     September, 1944   *following page 42*
Officers of 3d Battalion with captured swastika flag
Forced night march
Troops in review
Practice in lowering a casualty down a cliff
Garigliano front line, Minturno area
Front-line terrain, Garigliano River area
Pallazzo Reale in Caserta

Mopping up in Santa Maria Infante   *following page 90*
Town Square in Itri
Amaseno River Valley during a lull
Approaching the outskirts of Rome
Entering Rome
Klaus Huebner, 1944
German-held stronghold of Volterra
Rest area near Villamagna
Orchards and fields on the way to the Arno River

Troops being relieved, near Mount Altuzzo   *following page 140*
Following fleeing Germans, near Castel del Rio
Mud deep on a road near Sassoleone
Gen. Mark Clark visits San Clemente
Mule train bringing up supplies
Relieving troops on mountain in the Apennines
Short nap in hole, near Manzuno
Village of Loiano
Regimental assembly, near Florence
Stroll between shellings, near Livergnano

Monterumici Hill Mass and Furcoli Ridge   *following page 176*
Monterumici Hill Mass and Mount Adone
Litter case borne down road near Monterumici

Cave on Furcoli Ridge
Surrendered Germans, Monterumici Hill Mass
Moving off Monterumici Hill Mass toward Bologna
Heading downhill into Po Valley
Captured Germans, Po Valley
Crossing the Po River in ducks
Captured Germans, near Cornuda
Bivouac near Mezzano the morning peace was declared

List of Maps

Route of the 3d Battalion, 349th Infantry Regiment:
  Arrival in Naples, February 12, 1944, and the Long Walk
  into the Alps   *page 55*
The Push to Rome from the Garigliano River   *64*
The Push from Rome to the Arno River   *109*
The Apennine Campaign: Breakthrough of the Gothic Line and
  the Shifting Winter Line   *123*
The Po Valley Campaign: Route of the 3d Battalion
  into the Po Valley and the Alps   *175*

Preface

Long Walk Through War is an account of my experiences as a front-line doctor during World War II. I joined an infantry battalion in Texas, helped ready it medically for combat, accompanied it to northern Africa for more training, and finally walked along with it as it fought its way from just north of Naples, Italy, to the Brenner Pass in Austria.

A doctor who served with an infantry battalion was called the battalion surgeon. However, I was never a surgeon in the true sense of the word. What I expected was not what I experienced. Not all doctors saved lives in hospitals. During combat, my aid station was any location with some defilade, a farmhouse, a cave, or a barn, or only the reverse slope of a hill. Casualties of many descriptions suffered both by my troops and by the enemy were treated on the run.

After the war people assumed that just because a doctor served in the armed forces he was more competent than a doctor who did not. This was not so. Those on the front lines learned more military tactics than medicine, since facilities to treat casualties were limited. Constant attention to self-preservation was also essential, since medical officers could not be replaced as quickly as infantry officers. A battalion surgeon learned to remain calm in any situation and show no emotion no matter how severe the casualty; he also learned that by his presence alone he gave moral support needed by all casualties. Living with and observing the same men for two years led to a better understanding of the miseries and emotions experienced by infantry soldiers in combat. Their valor was unpredictable; their resourcefulness often astounding; during lulls in activity their pleasures were intense and often basic, since death in the near future was always a possibility.

For obvious security reasons, combat personnel were not permitted to keep a diary on the front line. At fairly regular intervals, however, I managed to scribble my experiences on the back of campaign maps and hide these in my aid kit. Considering the possibility of being captured, I never mentioned units or individuals or places by name in my notes but filled these in later when rotated to a rear area for a rest. Here I also stuffed all my accumulated notes into my barracks bag for safekeeping. In 1947, while events were still fresh in my mind, I pieced all my notes together in a manuscript in diary form.

Besides the names of Section 8 discharges, nothing in my diary is fiction. Boredom, excitement, agony, fear, revulsion, hate, and self-pity were common.

My description of combat events and the medical treatment rendered were from a vantage point just behind the fighting companies of my infantry battalion. I did not witness hand-to-hand combat or grenades being tossed, but I received detailed descriptions of such events from my litter bearers as they returned with casualties and from the walking wounded who gave eyewitness accounts of the combat just in front of us. We often listened to small-arms and machine-gun fire, but the only danger to aid station personnel was from mortar shells, artillery shells, airbursts, shoe mines, booby traps, and sometimes sniper fire.

To understand fully many passages in my account, the reader needs to know the components of an infantry division with emphasis on the battalion. During World War II an infantry division consisted of a fighting nucleus of three infantry regiments and such rear-echelon units as the medical battalion, a quartermaster company, an ordnance company, a counter intelligence corps detachment, a military police platoon, a division band, and special headquarters troops. Also belonging to the division and often called to duty forward were a reconnaissance troop, a signal company, a division artillery with its battalions, and a combat engineer battalion.

The three infantry regiments were always numbered. To the 88th Division belonged the 349th Infantry Regiment, the 350th Infantry Regiment, and the 351st Infantry Regiment. Each infantry regiment consisted of three battalions, the 1st, the 2d, and the 3d. Each battalion had three rifle companies, a heavy weapons company, and a headquarters company.

Each company of a battalion except Headquarters Company was identified by a capital letter of the alphabet. The companies belonging to the 1st battalion were therefore A, B, C, D, and those of the 2d battalion, E, F, G, H, and those of the 3d battalion, I, K, L, M. The last letter always identified the heavy weapons company, and this company carried heavy but still portable weapons such as heavy machine guns, mortars, and bazookas.

Headquarters Company was the command, supply, and intelligence and communications center of the battalion. Without it, the other companies of the battalion would have no direction. Consequently, a headquarters company was considered to be one of the least expendable.

To Headquarters Company was attached a medical detachment consisting of two physicians, a staff sergeant, several technical sergeants, a clerk, a jeep driver, litter bearers, and aid men. The aid men were attached to each of the four companies; here, they slept and walked with the riflemen. Their only defense was a Red Cross armband and their gear, an aid kit. They were the first to treat any casualty while bullets whizzed by and shells whirred overhead. The job of the litter bearers was to pick up those casualties too severely injured to walk and carry them to the battalion aid station, where a physician and his technical sergeants were located. During combat, the aid station tried to locate itself as close to Headquarters Company as possible and was any spot of temporary refuge to which the wounded could be taken and given emergency first aid until they were picked up by rear-echelon personnel for evacuation to the rear.

Long Walk Through War

Introduction

SEPTEMBER 15, 1943–DECEMBER 3, 1943

I was the doctor with an infantry battalion. I walked with the men who carried guns and slugged it out on foot. I treated the wounded where they fell. All my combat days were spent in Italy.

I was prepared to enter the Army. I elected to join the medical Reserve Officers' Training Corps while still a freshman in medical school. Consequently, after my graduation and internship and two well-rounded Medical Field Service School courses, I felt reasonably well prepared for Army service. When called to duty, I expected either a responsible Army hospital assignment or an assignment to a cadre to teach others. At least, we had been promised something to that effect when we elected to join the Reserve Officers' Training Corps (ROTC). However, when in September, 1943, my orders came to report for duty, they read 88th Infantry Division. This was somewhat of a blow. It was at this time that I first realized that one's Army assignment as a physician was not determined by one's background or IQ, but by a little file clerk in Washington who pulled one's file card when it suited him. At any rate, my dreams of a hospital vanished rapidly. An infantry division it would be.

The 88th Infantry Division was an all–Selective Service division. It had already completed its maneuvers and basic training and was now quartered at Fort Sam Houston, San Antonio, Texas.

My fate was to be Assistant Battalion Surgeon, 3d Battalion, 349th Infantry Regiment. The title sounded impressive. I hoped that my duties would be the same. I had doubts, however, for when I translated the title into simple words, it meant a doctor who just walked along with the foot troops. At least I had adventure in store for me, though the "surgeon" in my title could not be taken literally.

My stay in Texas was rather brief. The 88th Division was rumored to go overseas shortly. I shall give a brief résumé of my two months in Texas, for it is of some interest of how an infantry division readies itself for combat, not only physically and tactically, but also medically.

I arrived at Fort Sam Houston on September 15, 1943. It was a most impressive Army camp, and it swarmed with troops. Fort Sam was a city within a city. Here were paved streets, traffic lights, at least five motion picture theaters, self-service cafeterias, a large officers' club complete with swimming pool, post exchanges, clubs for noncommissioned officers, bright-looking family homes surrounded by beautiful lawns and tropical trees. Troops lived in large brick barracks and officers in comfortable bachelor or family quarters.

As is usual in the Army, when things look too good, something

is wrong. I soon learned that we would spend only one week out of
every three in Fort Sam Houston. The other two weeks we would spend
in continuing infantry training in the barren hills of nearby Camp
Bullis and Cibalo. Here the men fired on the target ranges, practiced
mine and grenade detonations, raided simulated enemy villages, and
enacted house-to-house and hand-to-hand combat. Night tactical problems were held frequently. My duties at all of these activities were
simply to be around to treat accidents as they occurred, usually minor
stab wounds, minor burns, sprains and bruises, and, occasionally, a
stray bullet wound. I treated from my aid kit, and anything serious
I sent off to Fort Sam. In addition to these occasional first-aid treat-
ments, I walked from one rifle company's training area to another and
gave scheduled lectures, all part of the infantry boys' precombat medical education. My hour-long speeches dealt with malaria prevention,
mosquito control, fly control, louse control, water purification, mess
kit sanitation, garbage pit and grease trap construction, venereal disease control, war gases, artificial respiration, and first-aid demonstrations in bandaging, splinting, and methods of carrying the various
types of wounded. I became an authority on latrines and could expound for hours on the simple trench latrine, the two-holer, four-holer,
and the deluxe eight-holer with lid covers to boot. Even the shallow
cat hole received honorable mention.

In the battalion bivouac area the men slept in pup tents on dirt
floors. In this area sick call was held once daily. From our pyramidal
tent aid station, which contained two first-aid chests, we treated anything and everything—the usual assortment of foot blisters, aching
backs, spider bites, common colds, diarrheas, minor burns, gonorrhea,
and crab lice. My medical knowledge was not strained.

Living with the men daily, treating them, and moving among them
in their training did, however, give me a profound knowledge of their
character, ability, and mental stability, factors that later were most
important in treating them under combat conditions. In less than a
month I learned how to distinguish the goldbrick from the sick man
without the help of x-rays, blood counts, or elaborate laboratory pro-
cedures. I learned many other things, too, things that were not medical but later most useful, such as a good knowledge of the M-1 rifle,
carbine, Browning automatic rifle, bazooka, and 60-mm mortar. I also
learned to sleep on a mud floor. Soon I could take a complete bath
and shave from a helmet full of cold water. I no longer needed a mirror to shave but could do so by feel. I also learned how to go without
a bath for two weeks, to eat standing, and to hike 22 miles in less
than twelve hours; I arose at 5:00 A.M. and crawled into my sleeping

bag at 8:00 P.M. I suffered and cursed, but since misery loves company, I soon became very fond of all my medical charges, a robust, rough, well-disciplined, fearless, and well-conditioned battalion of troops.

The occasional one week out of three we spent in Fort Sam was always very busy for me. While the troops were out on passes, I, as medical officer, remained in the battalion's medical barracks from morning to night. Company commanders were becoming serious about their personnel, and since it was rumored that we were to leave the States shortly, each officer wanted only the best men to remain in his outfit. The chronic complainers, those always hitting the sick book, the old men, the mentally unstable, these had to go. And these men were problems. Bed-wetting, sleepwalking, backaches, and chronic headaches were frequent complaints. The answer to our problems was discharge from the Army under Sections 8 and 10. A Section 8 discharge meant that the man was either a true psychopath or had a psychological problem. A Section 10 discharge meant that the individual had a physical defect rendering him unfit for duty.

I shall always remember a few outstanding Section 8 cases. Harry Forbes was an example. He seemed perfectly sound except that after each shower he insisted on drying himself only with toilet paper. He consistently ignored all towels. He appeared in formation with one shoe off and the other on, or with tie missing or turned backward, or all his clothes turned inside out. All punitive measures and extra-heavy work details failed to cure his habits. Section 8 relieved us of him. James Kress was another problem. He consistently answered the telephone by holding the earpiece to his mouth. No urging could change his habit. He too became a Section 8. Bed wetters were threatened with cystoscopies, headache complainers with spinal taps and ventriculograms, and many suddenly became asymptomatic. I often felt that many of the men we were discharging under Section 8 were really not psychopaths at all. Many were probably excellent actors with more endurance than their medical officer or company commander. Since one rotten apple, however, can spoil a barrel, we got rid of all problem cases.

The Section 10 candidates were less of a headache. Pronouced flat feet and herniated intervertebral disks were easily diagnosed. I shall never see so many flat feet again. Someday I will make the suggestion through proper channels that induction centers look at feet first before assigning a recruit to the infantry.

Final inspections during the last few days before entraining for the port of embarkation were numerous and more rapid, and I often felt that on occasion I established records. By this time I knew the corporal features of my men better than their faces. The last battalion short-arm inspection of eight hundred men was completed in two hours.

On December 3, 1943, the troops were up to strength and physically ready to move overseas. No one knew where to. Individual units were broken up, to be reassembled later at the port of embarkation.

Wartime Troop Train Comfort

DECEMBER 3, 1943–DECEMBER 7, 1943

This is December 3, 1943. Last night was my last night in San Antonio. I knew that today I would go somewhere, but where? Somebody knows but no one will tell us. Seldom have I had such a headache! It was a perfect evening shot to hell. For the first time since in Texas, I had a date, and today I can't even remember who she was, what she looked like, or how I crawled to my bed in the bachelor quarters. But then, it was the last night in Texas, thank God for that. This is the day. This is it. I only wish my poor head would stop aching. Since 8:00 A.M. we have been waiting on the cement-paved barracks courtyard ready to move out to the train headed for the port of embarkation. Which port? New York? New Orleans? San Francisco? No one will tell us. What a ridiculous uniform we are wearing, dress olive drab (OD) blouse, usual OD trousers, steel helmet, and barracks bag or val-pack (military-issue canvas garment bag). I suppose one must look good to go to a port of embarkation. It is 2:00 P.M. and we are still waiting. My stomach cannot stand lunch anyway. I would like to know the name of the joker who ordered us out at 8:00 A.M.

At last we are all set to move out, but wait, there is a little excitement in the lines of M Company. The usual troublemaker is at it again. This time he has knifed the man ahead of him, arguing over a bottle of whiskey. The wound is only a laceration of the chest wall without lung involvement, so that a simple dressing is sufficient. No infection will occur, since the man is overloaded with shots. I only hope that these two jokers are just as sharp in combat as they are today. Now off to the train in a column of fours. Camp workers stand about and wish us luck. In fifteen minutes we reach the fourteen-car passenger train. This looks too good to be true; something must be wrong. I am assigned to car fourteen, am the only M.D. on board, and hence am automatically train surgeon. Car fourteen is occupied by division headquarters officers so that I shall really live high. As train surgeon I suppose I am to hold sick call daily, inspect the mess car, and tour the washrooms. Just what else I am to do, I do not know. No one has told me anything. The greater portion of my own battalion has left a few hours earlier on another train, but I shall rejoin it at the port of embarkation, wherever that will be. The coaches are comfortable. Meals are served at your seat, mess personnel passing through the aisles serving hot food from metal inserts. The seats can be converted to bunks at night, and since breakfast is unusually early, most of us enjoy it in bed. This is the softest life I have had in three months.

Blackjack is played incessantly from 9:00 A.M. to midnight. Stakes are high, one to ten dollars a card. Such fervent gambling is still completely foreign to me. As I watch, I wonder how some captain's wife would react to seeing her captain lose several hundred dollars so recklessly. But then you can't take it with you, and with this type of gambling, time races by. Guzeman, Schockman, Peterson, all platoon leaders and second lieutenants, are great chaps. I enjoy their company. How does a lawyer fit into the infantry as a lieutenant? Lieutenant Pierson looks too gentle a schoolteacher to be sent out to kill. Captain Young, however, a 200-pound strongman, is the ideal type and should distinguish himself well. I wish them all luck, for I have learned to like them all.

The scenery along our route through the southern states has left me unimpressed. As the train rolls slowly through West Virginia and Virginia, I am astounded by the beauty of these states and can see why the men who hail from here speak so fondly of them. We pass through miniature Grand Canyons, tunnels, and winding draws, lined by sharply rising cliffs. The hills and mountains all look fresh, clean, and majestic; nothing is barren as in Texas. I promise myself to visit these states someday, provided I come back. I now regret not having seen enough of the United States and rapidly dismiss the thought from my mind that this might be my last opportunity. As we approach Richmond, Virginia, the train rolls past the house of little Joe, I Company's medic, and the poor kid points to it with a longing in his heart. He is only eighteen and very homesick. If his parents only knew that he just passed by! The episode is quickly forgotten—no time for sentimentality at this stage of the game.

Sick call is held to a minimum on this trip. Diarrhea is the most frequent complaint, and most of the men refuse to seek medical attention. They have long since learned that all they need do is stop eating, and nature will take care of the rest. Foreign bodies in the eye are removed with the patient standing in the aisle, weaving back and forth with the train's motion as it jostles over its roadbed.

After three days we arrive at Camp Patrick Henry, and we finally know that we are in Virginia, near Hampton Roads, a well-known port of embarkation. We now also realize that we are probably destined to go to Europe. England? Italy? It might also be Africa or even India.

On my arrival at Camp Patrick Henry, I snafu immediately. The train has just stopped. There are no lights. I imagine it is just another one of our numerous layover stops that have been so frequent along our entire route. I have no inkling that we have arrived at our destination. My duties on arrival are to leave the train immediately and, accompanying the train commander, Colonel Kielty, report on the double to the regimental commander awaiting us. Colonel Kielty and I just sit and wait. After a few moments the coach door is practically torn from its hinges and the regimental commander storms toward Colonel Kielty shouting, "What the hell's the matter, get out and report!" There is much puffing and blowing, and I feel rather uncomfortable. A few words about our recently acquired and therefore new regimental commander. I know that I shall not like him! He is over-polished, too conceited, talks too much, and brags incessantly. I try hard not to judge a man until he has had a chance to prove his worth. But why does he carry a swagger stick? A showman, no doubt. I recall his last lecture at Fort Sam, in which he remarked, "You must first be blooded before you can be called a man." I thought this to be an asinine remark. He has never seen combat. His shining swagger stick only distracts attention from his red nose and fat hind quarters.

Awaiting Shipment to Places Unknown

DECEMBER 7, 1943–DECEMBER 16, 1943

So this is Camp Patrick Henry. There is complete blackout, which seems ridiculous, since we are thousands of miles from the war zone. The Army must be crazy. After detraining, we march in a column of twos to assigned barracks. The night is very cold. In the darkness the land appears flat and dotted with prefabricated Army barracks. I cannot see too well. It is too dark. Tall, dark pines line the camp roads and surround the barracks. A quarter moon occasionally breaks through the clouds, and I think of nurse Betty. I suddenly realize that stopping to see her just because I knew I was headed for overseas duty was unfair. Her letters would now help tremendously. However, I want my life to remain uncomplicated at this stage of the war.

I rejoin my battalion at Camp Patrick Henry. Sick call is held in a centrally located barracks building, and all the medical officers work in shifts to take care of all the battalions. A rather serious diarrhea outbreak hospitalizes five hundred men. Most of them, however, recover in several days. Only a few goldbricks are persistent, but by this time I am completely immune to all the symptoms suggesting gang-plank fever.

Mail censorship is enforced. In his letter home Captain Felts cannot even ask his wife how his son Patrick is, since the word *Patrick* is censored. All we can write is that we are well. Most letters home are empty indeed.

Training continues at Patrick Henry. We check and recheck baggage and equipment. Gas mask drills continue. We climb down nets slung over billboards and into land-anchored lifeboats.

All living quarters are the same, rectangular barracks with double-tiered bunks. Crap games for small fortunes last long into the night.

I spend most of my evenings in the officers' club of the camp's station hospital. My first brief contact with army nurses begins. These girls have been around! They are calloused to hard-luck stories and are not in the mood to comfort homesick souls. To win their favors, a carefree and devil-may-care attitude is the method of approach. Most are good company even though in their late twenties or early thirties, provided you remember that they, too, have their problems and have no desire to listen to yours. Whiskey quickens the pace of conversation, and a tactfully planned method of attack is often successful. Drinking and dancing continue late into the night, and I seldom return to the barracks before 3:00 A.M. Dance and be merry, for tomorrow ye die! The tactics of the married officers must be far superior to mine, for some do not return to their quarters until daybreak.

Soon I am only too anxious to leave Camp Patrick Henry. I long for action. The suspense of the future is mounting. On the evening of December 16, 1943, after a two-hour wait in formation carrying full musette bag, val-pack, and blanket roll, and wearing a steel helmet, we finally march off to entrain for Hampton Roads. The night is freezing cold. My back aches under the burden of equipment. We rapidly climb aboard the train, but sitting is impossible. The shoulder straps of my bag cut into my skin, and my arms are numb. Lieutenant Savage keeps repeating that this is it. I am glad that it is. I am completely fed up with hurrying and waiting, of complaining and lamenting, and of being herded like cattle from here to there. At Hampton Roads, Red Cross ladies await us at the pier serving doughnuts and hot coffee. Gray-haired ladies cheerfully serve us at midnight! In my thoughts I deeply respect them. The satisfaction of helping is their reward. A huge black mass, her portholes blacked out, looms ahead of me. I can hardly wait to climb aboard. As my name is called, I clamber up the gangplank. We are to sail at dawn.

On the *Empress of Scotland* to Casablanca

DECEMBER 16, 1943–DECEMBER 25, 1943

I am in a stateroom midships. Twenty Air Corps officers, all destined for India, are my bunk mates. Will India be my destination? I now recall General Sloan's mentioning sacred white cows in one of his speeches while at Fort Sam.

At the crack of dawn I have my first opportunity to look about on board. In the hallway midships hangs a picture identifying our large paint-camouflaged ship. It is the *Empress of Scotland*, formerly the *Empress of Japan*. I now assume that we shall travel unescorted, since the *Empress* runs fast and can readily outdistance enemy submarines. I immediately take a strong liking to the *Empress*, but then I have always loved ships—any ship. She is a much better ship than the 7,000-ton molasses tanker I worked on during college vacation in 1936.

As the sun rises we are already under way. We have all been issued Mae West belts with which you must eat, walk, and sleep. Occasionally I leave mine in another stateroom and, suddenly remembering it, dash madly back to retrieve it. I walk the sundeck at least once daily, even though it is bitter cold. Here on deck is the only place where daylight smoking is permitted. Smoking within the holds or staterooms, or smoking at night, is unlawful for obvious security reasons. On deck, you can watch occasional schools of porpoises and scan the horizon for ships that never appear. The *Empress* changes its course every seven minutes, and a sudden 45-degree lurch is clearly felt. The reason for this soon becomes obvious—traveling unescorted, the *Empress* stays out of the path of any object detected by her radar, friend or foe. With each change of course, the same thought runs through all of our minds—enemy submarine?

Days pass rapidly. The Army Transportation Corps insists on daily abandon-ship drills, and justifiably so. Carrying five thousand troops on board is a tremendous responsibility. Should the *Empress* ever receive a direct torpedo, I am sure that at least half of the troops would perish. It takes at least forty-five minutes for all men to assemble on deck in abandon-ship formation. Enlisted men pour from deep holds and cramped nooks and corners. Some Joes never will learn the difference between an "Up" stairway and a "Down" stairway, and are therefore creating crucial traffic jams. The maneuver for "battle stations," in case of attack, is also practiced daily. Designated units man machine-gun turrets and antiaircraft positions, and decks are rapidly cleared of all personnel. My battle station is in the ship's hospital. Will a real battle-station alert ever come to pass?

The food is excellent, at least for the officers. Mess inspection is not one of my duties, and I have no knowledge of the type of food consumed by the enlisted men. Meals are served all day in continuous shifts, the dining rooms being too small to accommodate all personnel at one time. I am scheduled for breakfast at the early hour of 6:00 A.M., lunch at 10:30 A.M., and supper at 4:00 P.M. Chess on a miniature chess board is my chief diversion, and the hours pass rapidly. Pappy Felts, my superior medical officer, is my most bitter opponent. Pappy never loses his sense of humor. At least five times daily he opens his porthole and repeats the same comment, "Oh, what do I see, I see the sea, and that's all I see." After this profound remark, he again concentrates on his next chess move.

The Red Cross distributes its literature faithfully. For the first time, pamphlets describing North Africa appear. This gives me my first clue to our destination.

My medical duties on board last only one hour daily. Sick call for my portion of troops is held in a small square midships. Most cases are sore throats and, since we have only three bottles of standard pills, my T/3 sergeants (technician, grade 3) recommend the simplest treatment: ". . . just gargle with salt water; there's plenty of it." The seasick are plentiful, but there is no cure. The worst are sent to the ship's hospital, which is out of my jurisdiction. Major Shutzky, the division psychiatrist, is truly seasick. His bunk mates insist that his symptoms are only mental, but he continues to emese the entire trip. The color of the enlisted personnel is light pastel, often a light green, as they emerge from their holds into which they are packed like sardines, one hammock jostling against the other. I feel truly sorry for GI Joe. The dark, poorly ventilated holds reek of sweat and vomitus. Men have lost their identity, and seem to be only numbers. No wonder that some soon become bitter. Out of curiosity, I venture into an enlisted men's mess. The mixed odor of spilled mess-gear water, disposed food, and perspiration rapidly chases me back on deck, where I inhale deeply. This time, the men's complaints of upset stomach are truly justifiable. Men who had pink cheeks at Camp Patrick Henry now look like ghosts.

At dusk, the strict order "Black out, now" blares over the megaphone. In seconds, the Empress is a black monster plowing through the Atlantic. Activity within the ship, however, continues. In total darkness the day's garbage goes overboard. Should any enemy submarine find it at daybreak, we are already hundreds of miles away. Crap games are held in the staterooms and in the holds under dim-lit bulbs. Where light can be turned on, some men read, others snore, some just lie and think. At midnight a routine personnel check is made. Are the Mae Wests on hand? Are your clothes on? The lights go off. Many men say a silent prayer, hoping that the *Empress* will still be afloat by morning.

On the morning of Christmas Eve an airplane carrier and two destroyers suddenly appear on the horizon. They are apparently friendly, for signals are exchanged. The *Empress* fires all its rockets for practice, or could it be to salute? These ships are the first sign of life in six days. Are we approaching land?

Christmas Eve, 1943, is a memorable occasion. The celebration lasts all of five minutes. At 9:00 P.M. the ship's megaphones suddenly announce the president's Christmas message. A few paragraphs of good cheer and our splendid devotion to duty are read, a short Christmas carol follows, and then the cheerful ending, "that is all." We had all forgotten Christmas.

On December 25, 1943, land is sighted. We are told that we will soon be in Casablanca, Morocco, North Africa.

A Night in the Casbah

DECEMBER 25, 1943–DECEMBER 27, 1943

From off shore Casablanca looks like a small toy village of bright white houses set against a background of gray dunes and having a lawn of blue water. Were it not for the few tall buildings, one would never guess it to be a large city. As we approach closer, the sprawling suburbs come into view, and the illusion that Casablanca is only a hamlet disappears. The *Empress* docks along a bare pier. After standing on deck in formation for at least two hours, we finally disembark by being herded down the gangplank and into waiting trucks. For some reason I think of the Chicago stockyards. Our next destination is nearby Camp Don Passage, and our trucks must pass through Casablanca. The streets are moderately wide and lined with low, flat-roofed stone houses. These appear to be all front and no back. Their roofs frequently extend over the sidewalks and are supported by narrow cement columns. Pooled water stagnates in the streets' nondraining gutters. Native troops wearing beards and red caps sit on curb stones. Many of the native Arabs walk barefoot, even though it is December. They are wrapped in dirty gray sheets. The women are veiled, and seeing the dirty gray color of their drapes, I lose all curiosity about what may be hidden beneath. We pass small, blue-colored native buses loaded with laundry bags, but I am told the bags are live Arabs. Small donkeys half the size of our Missouri mules walk slowly along the streets, either overloaded with bundles or carrying a human barracks bag.

Whenever the animal hesitates, its herder whips it unmercifully. At larger street intersections are the open-air sidewalk cafes, but all the iron wrought chairs are empty. Dirty Arab cherubs run alongside our trucks shouting for chewing gum, chocolate, and cigarette butts. In ten minutes we have passed through the city and are approaching Camp Don B. Passage.

Camp Don B. Passage lies on a flat hill overlooking the Atlantic Ocean. Hundreds of pyramidal tents, row after row, lined up in perfect formation, without cots but with wooden floors, stretch for city blocks. I together with three other officers from Headquarters Company, Captain Bellmont, Lieutenant Melcher, and the "Moose," toss our musette bags, val-packs, and blankets into the respective corners of our assigned tent. The temperature is near freezing. While still on the *Empress*, I read in my pamphlet on Africa warnings of the African heat and of sun stroke. Nothing ever seems as described.

At sundown we have Christmas dinner—cold salmon, cold C rations, and a Hershey bar for dessert. The C rations consist of canned foods that require no cooking, packed in a five-inch by eight-inch cardboard box. We are restricted to camp and can do nothing but attend the camp movie held in an abandoned horseshoe-shaped quarry. Benches have been set into the steep slopes. The show is *Mortal Storm*. The sky is clear, stars shine brightly, and the air is bitter cold. Capt. Pappy Felts shivers and his teeth chatter and he does not enjoy the love scenes. With each Hollywood kiss, the GIs cheer and howl and embrace the cold air and smack their lips. After the show we crawl between our two blankets spread over the floor and sleep very little. Africa is too damn cold—something the Army forgot to mention.

The next morning we are permitted to cable home but cannot state where we are. I send the standard permitted message, "All well and safe. Best wishes for the New Year." Our blue-seal dollars are exchanged for gold seal. Gold-seal dollars are in turn exchanged for francs. We are still restricted to camp, but after dark four of us manage to slip away in a supply truck. Our hope is one evening of fun in the Casbah.

Strict blackout is still being observed in Casablanca, although there has been no enemy air attack for over a week. I won't remember the streets through which we wander; it is too dark. The gutters smell of sewage and excreta. The night club we are looking for is located in the basement of a large apartment house. We descend a spiral wooden stairway and enter a long, narrow, smoke-filled room. The floor is covered with sawdust. We are greeted by laughter and Dixieland jazz. Red-checkered cloths cover the tables. They are filled with native French girls, officers of the Free French, the Air Corps, and the Merchant Marine. A five-piece Negro brass band sits on a low stage along the middle of the long wall of the room. We are ushered to a table immediately in front of the bandstand. The sound of the brass is deafening, and we cannot hear ourselves talk. The band is wearing red caps with blue tassels. Cigarettes hang from the mouths of the middle-aged piano and bass players. The favorite tunes are "Pistol Packin Mamma" and "The Music Goes Round and Round and Comes Out Here." We are served native burgundy, and with each bottle the waiter remarks, "Three dollars per bottle, tip not included." Having consumed three bottles of the native brew, we feel easier and begin to enjoy ourselves. At a single table behind us is a petty officer of the Swedish Merchant Marine. His head rests on one outstretched arm, the other hangs limply down his side, and his eyes are very glassy. He continues to consume burgundy. He bothers no one and no one annoys him. He is oblivious to everything. I wonder how he will ever find his way home tonight, especially with Arab rabble lurking in dark doorways. Any foreign agent could readily pump him for information. French women sit on the laps of our Air Corpsmen. Lingering embraces attract my attention. Black-haired, olive-skinned French prostitutes with fancy coiffures, strong perfume, long earrings, and jangling bracelets walk from table to table. Low cut, half-open blouses reveal most of bosoms. They stop at your table, run their fingers through your hair, and press their soft breasts against your cheek. Twenty dollars for the night is their price. They are already a great temptation. We cannot afford to be hijacked on our second day overseas and must therefore, ruefully, decline their wares. Yet the Air Corps accepts all comers. Most of the boys are too drunk to remember the venereal consequences.

At midnight we return to camp. We remain close together, walking the center of the street, thus avoiding the possible danger lurking behind dark corners and doorways. We do, however, step into the excreta from mules, natives, and GIs. Toilets are either missing or not being used. I think of Hedy Lamarr and the Casbah, but somehow we seem to have missed the Hollywood-pictured Casablanca. Soon we hail a passing supply truck and ride back to Camp Don B. Passage.

Casablanca to Magenta, Algeria

DECEMBER 27, 1943–DECEMBER 30, 1943

On the morning of December 27, 1943, begins our trip through French Morocco by way of Rabat and Fez, thence into Algeria to the Magenta-Bedeau area, training site of the French Foreign Legion. We are again herded into two-and-a-half-ton trucks, which take us to the freight yards. En route we repeat tossing our cigarette butts and chewing gum to waiting Arab children. I see my first haggard camels. They appear very malnourished. Our train consists of twenty-four cars, one compartment car for officers, the other twenty-three cars being 40-and-8s, World War I–vintage freight cars that would hold forty men or eight horses. I had heard about 40-and-8s and thought that they were long extinct. The cars remind me of "Toonerville trolleys." I wonder how the Army will manage to pack forty men with full equipment into each of these four-wheeled antiques. It is done, however. The cars are swept out, straw placed on the floor, and a Lyster bag (a portable bag used for supplying disinfected drinking water to troops) full of water hung from the ceiling in the middle of each car. While half of the men sleep, the other half remain standing. The Lyster bag usually leaks, and the poor fellow sleeping under it often awakens soaking wet. Most men shun its immediate vicinity. Cold canned C rations are the only food. We sterilize our forks by passing them through the flame of a candle. No one washes or shaves. The weather remains bitter cold. The nights are very long for those men who spend them standing and shivering as the wind whips through the sliding doors of the box cars. The slow-moving train purposely stops approximately every four hours, usually on flat land and away from villages. Men swarm from their cars armed with shovels. Cat holes are dug in the pasture and bowels evacuated. Each man carries an ample supply of toilet paper in his helmet liner. As the train begins to move, those men handicapped by having diarrhea are forced to hurry and make a frantic dash for the last car, leaving shovel and helmet behind. Bladder evacuations are simpler, men rapidly learning to judge the train's speed and take accurate note of wind directions.

The roadbed is littered with tin cans for hundreds of miles, evidence of previous trains having passed before us. From Casablanca to Rabat and Fez, we pass through many dirty, ill-kept villages and around sandy mountains or through them via long curved tunnels. After Fez the scenery changes. The train rolls through large canyons and around greener mountains, their steep slopes terraced, on which grow orange trees loaded with ripe fruit. Large waterfalls tumble down dangerous cliffs. This part of Africa is nature's wonderland.

The officers' car is hardly more comfortable than the 40-and-8s. Each compartment has two wooden benches. The Army, however, manages to pack six of us with full equipment into space meant for four. The seats, window sills, and floor are covered with dirt. I learn to sleep with feet to the ceiling and head resting on the bench. Some men can actually sleep standing. Periodically I string my shelter halves of my pup tent to the ceiling and thus manage to catch a few hours of comfortable sleep.

We arrive in Magenta dusty, unshaven, and unkempt. From here it is six miles to our camp. Our order is to walk. There are many Army vehicles available at the railroad station, but we march. Why should a physician walk six miles with full musette bag, gas mask, three blankets, and two shelter halves when empty vehicles trail our column? However, when our regimental colonel says walk, you walk. The colonel is beginning to irritate me. It is dark when we begin our six-mile march. After three miles, all my San Antonio-incurred foot blisters recur. All I can think of is a lettuce-and-tomato sandwich. The more my blisters rub, the sorrier I feel for myself and the hungrier I become. After two and one half hours of silent cursing, the sound of the division band echoes through the dark night. It is lined up along the road welcoming the 3d Battalion of the 349th Infantry. Its march music is very patriotic. Most of the men mumble something about blowing it out of their barracks bag, and their welcome is not at all appreciated. We are shown to our tent city, and a heavy rain begins to fall. The tents are not equipped; that is, they contain nothing except a dirt floor; no lights and no cots. Weary and dog-tired, I drop to the wet floor and sleep soundly, rolled into my three blankets and two shelter halves.

War Games Continue

DECEMBER 30, 1943–FEBRUARY 1, 1944

Another month of training begins in Magenta, Algeria. Our camp lies on a plateau, the Atlas Mountain range to our south. Our battalion's pup tents form a large rectangle, field kitchens to the front of the tent city and latrines to the rear. Officers sleep in a small camp of pyramidal tents a few hundred yards away. A large recreation tent stands alone to one side of the bivouac area. A single pyramidal tent serves as our aid station.

The nights are still bitter cold. Water in your canteen or helmet freezes overnight. I try to hold sick call at 8:00 A.M. but must discontinue the practice. It is too cold for a man to strip down for examination. He shivers and shakes, and as the ice-cold stethoscope touches his skin, he jumps with a start. Sick call is held at 4:00 P.M. instead. Most of the complaints are minor, the same sort of ailments as encountered in the field in Texas. Only one new illness apears, hepatitis. The most I can do is diagnose. For treatment, the man is evacuated to the division clearing station. From there he will probably be sent to the nearest station hospital approximately forty miles away. I speak little of the practice of medicine since arriving in North Africa, for the simple reason that there is no opportunity to practice. My job becomes clearer to me each day. I diagnose. A man is either sick or well. If really sick, he goes to the rear; if well or only mildly ill, he stays. Any man requiring more than three days' treatment for illness is evacuated. My daily routine inspections, however, continue. We still have kitchens, grease traps, mess gear, and latrines. Since the latter are located to the rear of the tent city, they are the most quiet spot. I enjoy the way the latrine orderly snaps to salute. His job is really an intelligent one. For fifty dollars a month, he sits all day to see that the latrine covers are closed. He is the most contented man in camp. He sits on the latrine all day, thinks, and writes letters home. I conjecture on the sentimental beginning of his letters: "I sit here thinking of you," etc. I hope the lad's imagination is superior to mine. My inspections last less than an hour. I often stroll off into the hills for a brief walk and just meditate. From the top of a small hill our tent city looks small, neat, and clean. A large rolling field lies below me, and the Atlas Mountains loom majestically in the distance. Far away a donkey and Arab wind their way along a lonely trail. The hills and mountains are covered with low shrubs seldom over four feet high. No lush tropical vegetation or tall trees, as I expected to find in Africa. Water freezes during the night, but during my mid-day walks, the sun is hot and the temperature at times reaches 80 degrees. Lizards basking in the sun scurry hurriedly from my path into the shadows of the shrubs.

On January 2, 1944, our Christmas turkey arrives. Even though eaten from mess kits, it is a pleasant change from C rations.

The *Stars and Stripes* makes its first appearance and is truly a novelty. For the first time in weeks we hear of what is happening in other parts of the world.

Demolition demonstrations, mountain climbing, tactical night problems, and more intensive first-aid instructions take up most of my time for the next thirty days. In a small area away from camp, live hand grenades explode and shrapnel whines. White phosphorus shells and mortars are fired. We become indoctrinated to the sounds of war.

For several days each week I lead my medical detachment along a mountain trail to its very top. We walk slowly and learn to twist our way over rocks and brush. We hand-carry our medical equipment. Where we will eventually be going, we shall probably not be able to use jeeps. Soon that damn mountain becomes quite a nuisance. It never changes. It's up in the morning and down in the afternoon.

Achilles tendons begin to hurt; a new ailment, mountain climber's disease. Muscles at the calf and tendons of the heel begin to swell and throb, and many men are disabled for days. Others just hobble along, their legs strapped with adhesive. We are slowly becoming conditioned to mountainous terrain. One morning two mules make their appearance at my aid station. I am told to load them with medical chests, litters, and splints, and take them along on our climbing expeditions. The animals are very sure-footed but slower than we are, and their stubbornness is pronounced. Soon, however, we become quite accustomed to the two additions to our medical staff and treat them like comrades, for they are in just as much misery as we are. Two years ago, while still interning, I never dreamed that today I would be leading two mules up an African mountain trail. I always had higher aspirations.

Tactical night problems are truly a nightmare. We leave camp at 3:00 P.M. and follow the battalion of troops in a column of ducks, five yards' interval between men. The rifle companies lead, Headquarters Company is next in line, and we follow it, thus bringing up the rear. Two of my aid men walk with each infantry company. My other nineteen enlisted men, twelve of them carrying litters, walk with me. We all carry first-aid pouches and blanket rolls. The single column of men stretches out for over one mile. After six hours it is dark, and we are climbing mountains. The infantry companies disperse into the hills and assume imaginary tactical positions. I am ordered to set up an imaginary first-aid station approximately fifty yards from Headquarters Company, which serves as battalion command post. I don't quite understand exactly what is going on. I suppose I don't have to. The battalion command post will tell me if and when I am to move. I must learn never to think for myself, for this is the Army. The battalion command post is just a location, just a ditch or a gully immediately behind a hill. Portable radios hum and squeak, and I have no idea whom we are supposedly annihilating. Men sit about their buzzing radios in total darkness, heads held in their hands, blankets thrown over their shoulders, shivering and fighting off sleep. The headquarters commandant occasionally looks at his maps and relays orders to the companies.

My aid station exists in name only. In total darkness we dig holes. We are really digging our bed for the night. The colder it gets, the deeper we dig. After several hours we all have holes to fit any elaborate coffin. We climb in, cover ourselves with a blanket, and try to sleep. For me this is an impossibility. First my buttocks are cold, and then my feet become numb, and finally my neck and back begin to ache. Hunger pains ensue next. I am beginning to feel sorry for myself and wonder what I have done to deserve punishment like this. At other times in the past, whenever I felt discouraged or down and out, I would look back upon my life searching for reasons that would justify my indulging in self-pity. Such lengthy recall would also always put me to sleep, and that is just what I need tonight as I lie shivering in this miserable foxhole.

I think of when I came to the United States in 1926 at the age of eleven and of some of the memorable events since then. Some occurrences, even though minor, had a great influence on how I planned my future.

My father and mother both came from affluent families; their parents had been owners of industrial drilling and mining firms. After World War I, however, because of inflation and currency devaluations, all accumulated riches except real estate went down the drain. My father had inherited some real estate but had unfortunately sold it. Now the only money available to my father was that he earned as a chemist employed by the German chemical giant I. G. Farben. In 1924 United States firms enticed German chemists with patents in their heads to come to the United States and work for them. Thus my parents, one sister, and I came to the United States at the expense of my father's new employer, a chemical concern in Philadelphia, Pennsylvania. This employer was most generous and paid for everything. Steamship passage was in first class; he shipped all our furniture as well as a Dachshund; he also placed us in a newly built house in the suburbs of Philadelphia.

Leaving Germany was not a painful emotional experience. Even to a child of eleven, the existing economic turmoil was disturbing. I recall never yet having tasted real butter and having only eaten lard. I also often stood in line at the railroad depot for as long as six hours waiting to buy a twenty-five-pound bag of potatoes I would then cart home in my little wagon.

Coming to the United States seemed like an exciting adventure. I had already read about thirty novels by a chap named Karl May, who described himself as an adventurous traveler and spent most of his time out west with the Indians. My first glimpse of the new land when I awoke on board ship one morning was Hoboken, New Jersey. I had expected to see mostly forests and prairies and Indians, but instead I saw skyscrapers and, later, paved streets on which ran huge trolley cars. However, I adjusted quickly and soon learned that there was much more to the United States than unattractive big cities.

I recall my father's salary being seventy-five dollars per week, which in 1927 was considered excellent. In those days, a trolley-car ride cost ten cents, a gallon of gasoline twenty-five cents, to mail a letter two cents, and an admission to an evening movie show, twenty-five cents. A new Chevrolet automobile cost eight hundred dollars.

A golf course was located about a thirty-minute walk from our home, the path to it going over fields and some woods. I soon learned from other boys that one could make money there. My first caddying job was for a disgruntled old man who paid me the minimum amount of seventy-five cents for eighteen holes. I had the impression that the caddy-master despised German kids, since he never assigned a golf bag to me until all other waiting caddies were out on the course. Many days, I made no money at all. I just sat and waited and hoped, but it was never my turn. I shall never forget one beautiful lady. She and her husband arrived at the parking lot of the club in a maroon Buick roadster. Her husband received the last experienced caddy, and the lady's bag was assigned to me. I thought she was the kindest and best-looking lady I had ever encountered. She seemed terribly worried that a skinny little fellow like me was carrying such a big golf bag. However, I did not have a problem doing so. At the end of eighteen holes she had a brief whispering conference with her husband and then gave me a crisp one-dollar bill and a twenty-five-cent coin. This meant a fifty-cent tip. It was the most money I had ever made in my life. All the way home I clutched the dollar bill tightly in my fist, sang to myself, and wished that I had given that lovely lady a thank-you kiss. I hoped that from now on I would get only ladies to caddy for.

To learn English rapidly I was sent to a two-room Lutheran church school in downtown Philadelphia, where American children learned German but I could learn English. For four hours every Saturday morning may parents hired a private tutor for my sister and me. After two years I spoke fluent English and was told that I no longer had an accent.

All went well in our new country, the United States, until the Great Depression of 1929 to 1931. My father's plant closed, and he was out of a job with no prospects in the near future for another. My father had a Ph.D. in chemistry and considered it degrading to work in any other capacity but chemistry, no matter if we starved. It was then that my mother took charge. She had always been a lady of leisure in Germany, but now she took the initiative to keep bread on the table and a roof over our heads. She rented a large house on the campus of the University of Pennsylvania and sublet six of the rooms to students. Some of the students were medical students, and it was my lengthy conversations with them that aroused my interest in medicine.

My interest in medicine now established, my goal was to become a physician. As a doctor I would always be my own boss and never lose my job, as my father just did. Also, if I ever accumulated money, I would buy real estate, since this will not depreciate. To be able to go to college and then medical school would require money, of which we had none. Tuition fees could probably be scraped together or borrowed, but not money for room and board. The solution to this problem was to be accepted by the University of Pennsylvania, only two blocks away from home. To make certain that I would be accepted, I had to aim for a least a B + or A average in high school because I had no "pull" to get in by any other method than good grades. This I accomplished by all work and little play. I never had a date in high school and often longed for one. One of my diversions was making both the track team and the cross-country team. However, during three years I never won a race or even finished in the money, but I never quit and finished every race, and this satisfied my ego. The track coach always thought that I would make it one day and thus kept me on the team. Once I placed fourth in a field of twelve.

I worked and saved money. I washed cars, walked dogs, and sold programs during football games on Saturday afternoons in Franklin Field. I also sold Christmas trees, magazines, and insecticide. I always hoped that when I knocked on a door, a woman would answer because then I would usually make a sale. This was not because of my gift of gab but because women seemed to have more sympathy, and I still looked thin and malnourished. Before prohibition came to an end I also made homebrew. This activity was most remunerative. My father had taught me the technique of brewing beer. I had at least five families for customers for whom I brewed weekly. I received five dollars for each five gallons brewed and bottled. Making twenty-five dollars per week, I was stashing bucks aside.

After I was graduated from high school cum laude and with a few special honors, I had no problem gaining entrance to the College of the University of Pennsylvania and taking a premedical course. My next goal was to finish college as rapidly as possible in order to save on expenses but at the same time achieve grades good enough to be accepted by the medical school, the chances of which were about 1 in 40. Again it would be years of all work and little play. I crammed in enough major subjects to be able to finish college in three and one-half years instead of four but had to study every weekday night from six to midnight. On Saturdays I helped my mother clean house. During one summer vacation I worked as deckhand on a German molasses tanker running between Philadelphia and Cuba. It was in a small town in Cuba and at the urging of my fellow seamen that I lost my virginity in a whore house. With that experience out of the way, I imagined myself more adult or mature. During the other summer vacations I worked as a bartender in a camp for young men and women in the Pocono Mountains of Pennsylvania at Delaware Water Gap. All the waitresses were college girls. I had one long-lasting friendship with one of them but did not permit it to become more than that, since marriage and studying for a career in medicine were, for a man in my position, not compatible. With female guests, whom we were also expected to entertain, it was a different situation. I had an intimate relationship with only one of the guests, whom I liked very much. During every heavy midnight petting session she would say, "Undo me." I finally did.

All my hard studying paid off. When I was graduated from college with a Phi Beta Kappa key, I was readily accepted by the Medical School of the University of Pennsylvania. During these four years I worked one summer in my usual bartender's job, another summer in the Medical Field Service School in Carlisle, Pennsylvania, and during the third summer took a junior internship in the Lankenau Hospital in Philadelphia. To make a little extra change I worked as telephone operator for the campus police several nights a week. Hard study had become a habit and was now easy. I dated several student nurses but purposely avoided any lasting relationships. My goal was to finish my internship and then establish myself in practice before even thinking of marriage. Several of my fraternity brothers were already married. Their life seemed complicated already. They were expected home at definite times; their wives demanded more attention than they could afford to give them. Marriage definitely interfered with their studies.

On December 7, 1941, during my fourth year in medical school I was the attending student at my first obstetrical case. During periods that the patient was sedated and quiet, I listened to the radio in the doctor's room. The air attack on Pearl Harbor was announced. I knew then that any future planning on my part would be just wishful thinking. The Army would plan things for me.

I finished medical school without a hitch and was accepted for my internship by the hospital of my choice in Philadelphia. Thus far I had achieved all my goals. We were rushed through nine months of internship instead of twelve so that we would be Army material three months sooner. The staff of interns was also cut from twelve to six, and we did double duty. Again, it was all work and little play. I was too tired to establish any significant relationship with any one of the many attractive student nurses. Only once did I have a one-night stand with one of the girls on one of the ancillary services. She was an attractive girl, and her motives were the same as mine, a one-night fling to get it out of your system with no strings attached. I would have like to become better acquainted with this girl but my uncertain future did not permit this. I was already following the saying, "Live and be merry for tomorrow ye may die."

I had basic training early. When I entered medical school in 1938, I was told that if I volunteered to take medical Reserve Officers' Corps training starting in my freshman year, I would when graduated, and in the case of war, be already trained and would then probably draw cadre duty to train other physicians just drafted. All this sounded like a marvelous idea and smart planning. I fell for the program. As part of the course I would be required to attend the Medical Field Service School in Carlisle, Pennsylvania, for six weeks at the end of my second year of medical school, and again for another six weeks at the end of my internship. This I did. From then on, however, what had been promised never occurred. Instead of being assigned to a cadre, I was assigned to an infantry division. I really goofed when I volunteered in 1938. That is why I am now sitting in this hole. I have no one to blame but myself. However, I have learned my lesson: while in the Army never volunteer for anything again!

I never do go to sleep. Sergeant Fertig can sleep anywhere. He is from Brooklyn. While I shake and shiver, he rests comfortably, back leaning against a rock, blanket thrown over his head, and snoring so loudly that he must be awakened routinely so as not to disclose our position to our imaginary enemy. The monotony of this cold night is broken only a few times by casualties drifting to us from the hills. A company aid man has directed them to our position. They are mostly anxiety neuroses. Private Lark, just a young kid, has thrown his rifle away and wants somebody to shoot him. His heart pounds and he is wet with perspiration. A sedative, a blanket, and rest for the night on a litter is all that I can offer him. He will soon become indoctrinated. Steadier nerves and more self-control are all he needs. As the morning sun rises and its rays take the chill out of my bones, life suddenly seems again worth while living. I might make it. Mules appear loaded with hot food. After a warm breakfast, the six-mile hike back to camp begins. I wonder who won the battle.

After our return to camp, the regimental commander, the man I dislike, expresses his opinions on the night's problem in a picturesque, elaborate critique to his officers. I soon become convinced that the colonel is a psychopath. I believe he has a precombat neurosis. His lectures are always filled with colorful and violent curses. He is displeased with last night's problem. We must repeat it tonight. Men violated blackout; he saw cigarettes burning a mile away. Someone had built a fire; he is convinced it was not an Arab sheepherder, although it really was. The following lecture serves as an example of his intelligent comments: "You stink! You and your God damned maneuvers in Louisiana! Last night you were lousy and you always will be lousy. All your sergeants are three-striped privates. You yourself have no right to call yourselves officers. You will carry out orders exactly as I issue them, and if you don't, I shall club you into the ground with my both fistes." (He never says fists.) "I specialize in incorrigibles. Send your problem children to me. If you can't use your fistes use a club. If I say 'take that objective' you will take it even if it costs the life of every man. I shall be on top long before you will, but I need men to follow me and not boys. If you feel a hand up your ass it is I reaching for your guts. I want no yellow bastards!" To me the colonel appears either drunk or mentally deranged. I am sure the division commander is unaware of this man's behavior. His courage lies in words. I doubt seriously that he is a West Point graduate. How did he ever become a full colonel? However, he is the most colorful man I have met in the Army to date.

Camp life in North Africa also has its brighter moments. Since scattered Arab sheepherders and nomads occasionally wander into our camp, guards are posted all night to prevent looting. We are told that no Arab is to be trusted. Anything dressed in white and not promptly responding to the password is an Arab intruder. Some guards soon become trigger happy. One night a white Lyster bag gently swaying from a tree branch is bayonetted, and water flows like blood. GI Joe hesitates running to the latrine at night in his long underwear. On several occasions he is mistaken for an Arab, and bullets almost find their mark.

When night problems are not scheduled, movies are shown in the recreation tent. We sit on the ground and look up at small 8-mm films. The pictures are at least ten years old; the reels are only partial and tear approximately every five minutes, followed by ten-minute delays for repair. Hollywood beauties receive recognition by howls and jeers, and one man shouts, "Give me a piece, lady." Another GI loudly sighing at a love scene, is reminded by another to "blow it out your homesick ass."

Pappy Felts and I are now buying muscatel in five-gallon cans. The nights seem shorter when we are under the influence of wine. Pappy recites the poem "Dangerous Dan MacGrew" far into the night. Lieutenant Hollis from Tennessee sings hillbilly songs to his guitar, strange notes to be heard in North Africa. Before crawling into my sack, I step to the outside of my tent. The African moon is so bright it lights up our entire camp as though it were an arc lamp. I think of home and the girls I once knew. I am not sorry not to be married. I have no responsibility and no longing for wife and child. I do not await mail call as anxiously as the others and am not despondent when no mail arrives. A few moments of silent thought under the bright moon and

I reenter the tent, drink a few more cups of muscatel, and, trying to forget it all, fall promptly off to sleep.

GI Joe always amazes me. He is ingenious. He can accomplish the impossible. We are forty miles from the next town. I have not seen a single Arab hut since arriving here. One morning Private Roark reports to the aid station and desires a prophylactic. He states he was exposed two hours ago and seems smug, carefree, and content. He reveals nothing of his adventure. I shall never know where he found that woman in this wilderness.

One Sunday morning I receive a pass to the nearest city, Sidi Bel Abbès, forty miles distant. My duty is to be responsible for twenty enlisted men also on pass. I must see that they behave properly in town and be certain that all return home. After a two-hour ride over winding, bumpy dirt roads in a three-quarter-ton truck, we arrive in Sidi Bel Abbès. The enlisted men are released to roam as they please, with orders to return to the trucks by 8:00 P.M. I decide to reconnoiter the city. The town is rather primitive, even though the streets are paved. The houses are long and low, with wide, bare doors and windows. They remind me of the ones in the smaller towns of Cuba. There is no traffic on the streets, and it is a very quiet Sunday. The first garrison of the French Foreign Legion is still in use. It consists of low stone barracks built many years ago along a narrow stone paved street. I do not inspect the barracks but simply walk by. I see a few Legionnaires, who look like any other Army personnel in foreign uniform and not at all like incorrigibles. Fooled again by Hollywood. I venture to a nearby park which, too, is deserted. Paved walks wind their way around circles of date, fig, and orange trees and a variety of strange shrubs. Two French officers and their wives out on a Sunday stroll are the only people to be seen. Finding little life in the park, I decide to visit the local officers' clubs in town.

The British officers' club is in the middle of town on the second floor of a simple, square, unimpressive family dwelling. The club's walls are bare. The furniture is dusty and antique. An old phonograph, dating back to 1918, furnishes the music. The bar is a long wooden counter devoid of all decoration. The French barmaids are middle-aged and speak only French. Vermouth and cognac are the only choice of beverage. I had expected to eat dinner here but find that food is not available. I am able to purchase several hard-boiled eggs and wash these down with cognac. This is my Sunday dinner. No officers are here, no entertainment is offered, and I leave. Perhaps the French officers' club is the center of activity. It, too, however, is only a large bare room, has wooden floors and bare walls, hard chairs around small square tables, and an undecorated circular bar stands in the middle of the room. Food is again unobtainable, and I am starved. I eat dark rye bread and drink muscatel. Not much life here either. A half-dozen French officers with their native wives sit glumly at the bar or at the tables looking very bored. I pay in francs and still can't tell one franc note from the other. Having had only muscatel, cognac, vermouth, hard-boiled eggs, and rye bread since breakfast, I am ravenously hungry. One GI tells me that the U.S. 64th Station Hospital is in this town. Locating it, I finally have a satisfactory supper in the officers' mess. You actually sit at tables to eat, eat from plates, and have ice cream for dessert. I wish that I had never come here, for seeing the comforts the medical officers have here only makes me jealous, and I am now more dissatisfied than ever. I wonder how some men rate a station hospital assignment. Life here must be a picnic. At 8:00 P.M. I help comb the streets of all military personnel, count off the command for which I am responsible, and head back to camp with a heavy heart, having spent a nonexciting day in Sidi-Bel-Abbès, a cold, lifeless, empty, and bare town.

On January 27, 1944, our tent city folds. We are pulling out to a new location. The time—5:00 A.M. Why so early I don't know. Our last night is spent sleeping in the open, all gear having been packed and tents torn down. At midnight I roll into my blankets and look up into the clear sky. The stars are brighter than I have ever seen them before. I feel extremely despondent. Thus far, I have been nothing more than a first-aid man with lieutenant bars. My medical knowl-edge is becoming rusty for lack of a true challenge and facilities. I only follow orders, am herded about, eat standing, dig holes, and am uncomfortable and cold wherever I am. I am becoming bored. Thus far, it has been all training and no action. I am ready to go anywhere at anytime. All I desire is the real thing. The suspense of the un-known is mounting. I am anxious to experience actual combat and to get it over with. I am tired of preparing and pretending. Perhaps all this is part of Army psychology, keep men expecting, keep them bored, and when the real time comes they are ready to do anything, for they are desperate. I can't sleep on my last night in Magenta. At 3:00 A.M. a strong wind arises, and I smoke cigarettes until dawn. The sound of baggage trucks accompanies the sunrise. Soon the order to move out in a column of twos is given. Just before we march, I treat a few cases of diarrhea, issuing tablets of bismuth and of ipecac and opium from my aid kit. These men would probably get well without treatment, but I suppose I am doing something worthwhile anyway. Now comes that six-mile hike again with full packs. However, I have learned. I have not been issued direct orders to walk; therefore, I am not walking. I am learning fast. There is room on the truck with the baggage detail, and this time I arrive at the Magenta railroad station sitting on top of my equipment instead of carrying it. Poor GI Joe, however, walks. He will always walk even though trucks are everywhere. Can't let GI Joe get out of practice. At the station those 40-and-8s greet us again. They still look the same, and it is still forty men to a car, Lyster bag swaying in the middle, half the men reclining and snoring with their necks twisted and feet curled in all positions while the other half stand. C rations are the menu for the trip. The cars are dustier than ever. They apparently carried flour and sand on their last trip, and our ODs are soon a mess of spotted white. After a three-hour wait at the station the train finally pulls out. I wonder why we arose at 5:00 A.M. and have now waited for three hours. No one will ever know. Some things in the Army just cannot be explained. They occur all the time, and not a soul seems to come up with the right answer.

It is an eight-hour trip to wherever we are going. To where, no one again seems to know. That's what I like about the Army; you never know anything. You are just a serial number, you do what you are told, and it's as simple as that. I decide to stand up on this trip, since it is a daylight trip and probably my last chance to see Africa. I might as well see as much of the country as I can. The train rolls along the edge of a large valley. I can see across an endless green meadow with a mountain range as its background. A dirt road winds through the green valley, and I see a four-horse Arab coach, a cloud of dust behind it. From the distance it has the appearance of a miniature toy. The scene reminds me of a picture I always had hanging over my bed as a small child, a red and yellow four-horse mail coach driving along a dirt road running through a green field. I always loved that coach, it seemed so small and colorful and the surrounding mountains so large. A herd of sheep graze on a distant slope. Here is a field of white, purple, and yellow flowers in full bloom in January. They suddenly seem very beautiful. A poem I learned in junior high school suddenly flashes through my mind. "I wandered lonely as a cloud that floats on high o'er hills and dales, when suddenly I saw a crowd, a host of golden daffodils." The author I have long forgotten. Here are well-kept vineyards, orange groves, and well-tilled fields. I long for peacetime so that I could stop here and really enjoy this glorious panorama. The air is cold, the 40-and-8 rattles, my feet are tired standing, and my daydreaming ends abruptly.

Near midnight our cattle train of humans pulls into a large freight yard and stops. All is blacked out. An Army railroad worker walks by and is bombarded with questions. Where are we? "Oran," says the corporal. He has been here for the past eighteen months loading and unloading troops and supplies. He hopes to go home shortly. To me, eighteen months seem like a lifetime. I am already bored after one month and have only just arrived. We wait at least forty-five minutes in total darkness for the order to detrain. I sit on the edge of the car, my feet dangling over its side, my pack thus resting on the car's floor and not cutting into my flesh at the shoulders.

After unloading, we again pile into trucks and drive along a puzzle of dirt roads worn into deep ruts, so that men and equipment are jolted about unmercifully. It is too dark to see anything. In thirty minutes we reach a barren, muddy camping site, where pyramidal tents are pitched on slanting knolls. The tents have cots. Wonders will never cease. I am quartered with a chaplain, the "Moose," and a bearded Red Cross man. The latter reminds me of Robinson Crusoe. Mosquitoes abound, and I use my repellent liberally. I am very tired and soon fall asleep. We must be near the Mediterranean Sea, for it is warmer and much more comfortable.

In the morning I study the surrounding terrain. I am in another large tent city erected on a series of knolls. Foxholes have been dug into the slopes of the surrounding sand dunes. The holes are filled with empty cartridges. We are near the Mediterranean port of Oran, and these foxholes were occupied by the Vichy French and their colonial troops during their defense of the North African shores against the British and American Rangers coming from Britain and landing near here on D day of Operation Torch on November 8, 1942. That was over fifteen months ago. We are, however, getting closer. At least we are on terrain actually fought over. I wonder why the holes are not deeper and why so many are V-shaped. I imagine most were occupied by machine-gunners. When in combat I must remember to dig my hole deep—these seem too inadequate. Perhaps I am too conscious of self-protection.

We spend only four days near the shores of Oran. I hold a brief sick call daily. All our medical equipment is packed away, and we treat all ailments from musette bags. Medical supplies seem to be very scarce. My sergeant finally obtains a few bottles of tablets and dressings from a nearby medical depot so that each man can at least refill his aid kit. The most impressive event to occur is an outdoor shower for everyone. A small square area is fenced in with canvas, and a fluttering pump delivers cold, rusty water at irregular intervals. Even though ice cold, it is much better than a helmet bath.

The night of January 31, 1944, is our last in North Africa. I walk over to Lieutenant Callahan's quarters. He is a second lieutenant, infantry, and platoon leader. He has built a small fire in front of his tent and is writing a letter home. A bottle of cognac stands on the ground beside him. I join him and also write a brief note. I remember little of the rest of the night. Staring into the flames and talking, we empty the bottle of raw cognac.

On the *Neuralia* to Naples, Italy

FEBRUARY 1, 1944–FEBRUARY 12, 1944

Early in the morning of February 1, 1944, we pile into trucks and shortly arrive at the harbor of Oran. It is a beehive of activity. Supply depots are everywhere. All types of equipment is stacked in huge piles. Barrage balloons fill the sky, anchored from both shore and ships. The harbor is full of tankers, cruisers, liberty ships, cargo vessels, and troop carriers. This time we are probably going in a convoy. I wonder which will be my ship.

The *Neuralia* is a wonderful ship. I imagine she is about 8,000 tons. I am quartered mid-ships in a two-bunk room on a balcony overlooking the main dining room. We have electric lights, running water, sheets, and blankets. I have not had such luxury in over two months.

On board the *Neuralia* I feel like a king. Hindu personnel are in the dining room and also double as room stewards. They are dressed in long, black shining robes and wear wide-brimmed black plate-like head gear. They walk about silently and seldom speak. When their chores in the dining room are completed, they sit on the floor along the wall or in corners with legs crossed and are hardly noticeable. Their facial expressions never change. I imagine they are quite proud of their race and probably look upon our carefree attitude with contempt. My Hindu room steward awakens me each morning with, "Wake up maaster, it's haalf paast *height*." Perhaps he is a former Oxford scholar. His English is perfect.

Except for lack of decorations, the ship's dining room is probably just as it was in peacetime. All meals are quite an event. We are eight men to a round table. Never before have I seen so little food served on so many plates. Each meal consists of many courses, and each course is served under separate glistening aluminum cover. The anticipation as each dish is uncovered is always a highlight. The portions of food served are always a trifle compared to the size of the dish. Seven courses could easily fill a single mess kit plate. After a few meals we all agree that more food and less display would be welcomed. However, small bits of food just keep coming under large dishes. Mutton is served endlessly. The British must have saved their mutton for years, just for us. Each piece is never larger than a small child's palm, and the supply is never exhausted. I would give a month's salary for a steak. Lieutenant Hollis keeps pleading, "Please just pour the food over my head, as long as it is food, and please skip all the fancy plates."

Tea time is at 4:00 P.M. daily. No war can possibly stop tea time on a British ship. The small porcelain demitasse disappears in Captain Potter's large palm. He cannot pick it up by the handle. His fingers are too bulky. It just vanishes in his grip and he drinks all the tea with one gulp. We would all prefer a plain canteen cup. A plate of cake is on each table, one small piece for each man. One day Lieutenant Schockman reaches the table first and eats all the cake. Captain Potter is furious, and a tremendous verbal battle ensues. Small things in life are becoming important. Two officers are practically coming to blows over several pieces of stale baked goods. I think that this display of emotion, however, will assure each man his share of cake for the rest of the trip.

The British ship's surgeon is my medical adviser while on board the *Neuralia*. I hold sick call for one hour daily in the bow hold of the ship but have very few customers, since the sea is rough and the bow is the worst place to be. I treat minor sore throats, and callouses and blisters still not healed from marches in North Africa. I ask the surgeon if I should enforce any precautions necessary to prevent outbreaks of diarrhea. He is not too concerned about my problem. He is typically British, about thirty-five years old, bored with life at sea, bored with the ship and all its patients. However, I am sure he will always love England. He looks the type. His answer to my questions is, "Don't worry about diarrhea, old chap, we always have a bit of a go at it." After this remark I worry little and spend most of my time in my bunk engrossed in *The General Died At Dawn, A Maid and a Million Men, The Great Impersonation,* and *To Walk the Night.*

Our first day at sea is already eventful. We are a large convoy of ships, I judge at least sixty. Each ship floats its barrage balloon to safeguard against strafing. At 9:00 P.M. on the night of February 1, 1944, the alarm of "active stations" sounds through the *Neuralia*. I suppose we are again practicing. Soon, however, I hear unfamiliar thuds hitting the water and suddenly realize that we are apparently under Nazi plane attack. We all follow orders previously issued to lie on the floor in our rooms, Mae Wests in place, helmets on, and hands folded across our neck. The distant thud of bombs hitting the water continues for about forty-five minutes. They must be falling at least a mile away, for the ship is not even jolted. At first my heart beats a little rapidly, and I feel ashamed. During a lull, curiosity overwhelms me and I rush on deck. As medical officer I can always use the excuse that I am checking for casualties. Tracer bullets from all ships light the sky. It looks like a glorious Fourth of July. After fifteen minutes, all firing stops and the all clear is sounded. I am informed by the ship's surgeon that our convoy has been attacked by a fleet of Nazi planes, one ship in another group has been sunk, but none of the vessels carrying 88th personnel has been hit during the raid. For some reason, I feel better. At long last I have been under some enemy action, even though minimal.

Our convoy runs slowly. From Oran past Algiers, Bizerte, and Cape Bon. The latter were captured by the Allies only sixteen months ago, in May, 1942. Battles here are only recent. We pass Malta on our starboard side, and the Neuralia really begins to rock. The Mediterranean Sea is much rougher than the Atlantic Ocean. Plates slide off our tables, and walking is impossible without grasping the rails. Most men are seasick and remain in their bunks. A Liberty ship on our starboard side rolls, dips, and rises with each wave. A large locomotive is anchored on its foredeck, and each time the ship dips the entire engine is completely inundated with water. We pass around the southeast corner of Sicily and run up the eastern coast, anchoring in Augusta harbor for thirty-six hours, waiting to be joined by another convoy. From a mile off shore the town looks ghost-like. Through field glasses I see buildings shorn in half, heaps of stone rubble, and empty windowless houses. This is my first view of a war-torn, bombed-out city. We move on up the Sicilian coast and see Mount Aetna on our left—huge, stately, and snow covered. The sea is calmer as we approach the Straits of Messina. It is night and very quiet on deck. A bright moon illuminates our large convoy so that each ship looks like a large shadow gliding over a dark mirror. By morning we are in the straits. The current is swift and the winds strong. The shoreline is intriguing. Mountains are on both sides of us, with isolated towns nestled into the recesses of steep slopes. With the Straits of Messina behind us, we enter the Tyrrhenian Sea, pass to the east of Stromboli and along the western shore of Italy into the Gulf of Salerno, past the Isle of Capri and into the Gulf of Naples. The Isle of Capri looks just like any other mountain except that it has two distinct humps and juts out of the sea. Mount Vesuvius with Pompeii at its base is unmistakable. We edge into Naples harbor. The sky is overcast and very cloudy. It is an excellent day to land. It is too overcast for enemy air attack, and we are a profitable target. The date is February 12, 1944.

War Games and Mountain Climbing in Italy

FEBRUARY 12, 1944–MARCH 3, 1944

We remain on board ship for several hours before disembarking. I have a good opportunity to view the harbor. Barrage balloons are everywhere. The water is littered with sunken ships, and only parts of their hulls are visible. The stern of one wreck lies here and the smoke stack of another there. A few ships have capsized at their moorings. I can't tell whether the wrecks are Allied or German. The piers and docks are wrecked, and only large sections of concrete remain standing. All the houses along the waterfront show the effects of recent bombings. They are in ruins. All windows have been blown out. Some houses are completely sheared in half. Other houses have only one floor intact. Naples harbor is apparently bombed quite often. I feel somewhat uncomfortable after viewing all the surrounding destruction and wish that I were off the ship. The longer I remain on board, the more I feel like a sitting duck.

At dusk the patients in the sick bay are unloaded first. I only have one very seriously ill soldier. He has some type of purpura, either Henoch's or Schoenlein's.

It is dark by the time the troops disembark. We are herded off the gangplank and assemble in a vacant lot approximately two hundred yards from the dock. Surrounding us are bombed ruins and rubble. We sit on the ground and await orders. There is complete blackout. No cigarettes are lit. No light shines. Finally comes the order to move out in a column of twos. We march through a labyrinth of dark, deserted, and crooked streets. Only the footsteps and coughing of the men echo from the walls of the deserted dwellings and ruins. After thirty minutes we arrive at a railroad station. It, too, is in shambles. At one time it boasted a magnificent arched glass roof, but now only the steel frame remains. The glass has been blown to bits. After we wait in total darkness for at least another half-hour, a train pulls into the station. We load rapidly. Again, no one knows where to. We are sandwiched into compartments with wooden seats. It is very dark, and I cannot tell who is sitting beside me. After an hour's slow ride in total darkness, the train stops. We unload, walk for another half-hour, and arrive at a U-shaped group of tall, white buildings. I am told we are in Bagnoli, and that these buildings compose the Italian Collegio Costanza Ciano, and were the German staff headquarters prior to the fall of Naples. We are to remain here for the night, then move on to a permanent bivouac area. I can see very little in the total darkness. We follow a guide into one of the four-story buildings and are led along wide hallways and up four flights of marble stairs. The spacious rooms off each hallway have bare walls and terrazzo floors. All rooms are devoid of furniture but are filled with snoring GIs rolled on the floor in blankets in a twisted puzzle of legs, arms, and heads. My medical detachment and I finally find ourselves together again in the same room. We break out K rations (a bar of concentrated food resembling a candy bar), and soon thereafter, all men are asleep. I remain wide awake, for I am very curious to see more of this place. I wander through all the hallways and down the stairs from the top of the building to the bottom. Reaching the basement, I hear voices. No troops should be here. I slowly grope my way toward a thin streak of light coming through a crack of a door. Slowly opening this door to what appears to be a stockroom, I am confronted by four ragged and dirty Italian urchins, all between the ages of six and ten, sitting before a smoldering fire built on the cement floor and eating U.S. Army C rations. At my sight they burst forth into "Pistol-Packing Mama" and deluge me with requests for chocolate, gum, and cigarettes. After giving them all the articles in my possession, I grope my way back to my quarters for a well-deserved night's rest.

At daybreak the next morning I have a better chance to look about. We are in a cluster of beautiful four-story white buildings arranged in the shape of a horseshoe. Each floor has a large balcony facing a common courtyard. The buildings are well camouflaged, the white paint being covered with bands of yellow, orange, and green. Painted cardboard shrubs and trees close in each balcony. Troops resting on these camouflaged balconies cannot possibly be observed from the air. Captured German water tanks stand in the courtyard. At one end of the horseshoe is a tunnel leading to an air-raid shelter several stories underground. The toilets in the College are unique. Toilet bowls are absent. Instead, there are square open stalls with footrests only. Being a latrine expert, I feel that more comfortable toilets would fit in better with the rest of the buildings. What intrigues me most about this place, however, is that we are actually occupying buildings the enemy held not too long ago.

The dirt highway running parallel to the College is heavily traveled. Trucks run north and south, and most are bound north, the direction to the front. Across the highway lies the small town of Bagnoli. It is rumored that we shall leave the College at dusk. It is now noon, and Chaplain Crowley and I decide to visit Bagnoli for the afternoon. We cross the highway along which Italian civilians have erected crude wooden stands and are selling figs, nuts, necklaces, and charms. As we walk across a field and approach the village, a group of Italian children hail us, shouting, "Hey, Joe, wanna see my sister?" One shabbily dressed youngster says, "Hey, Joe, wanna go to my house and eat?" It is starting to drizzle, and we accept his offer, for we are tired of both rain and C rations. Any home-cooked dinner would be worth any price. The youngster leads us to a shabby Italian home in the middle of town. We are ushered into the family dining room and wait. Girls are giggling in the next room. Perhaps we are in a whore house. The padre is undisturbed. After approximately five minutes, the man of the house enters and says, "What you like to have, Joe?" The padre introduces himself as a Catholic chaplain and draws immediate respect. The giggling in the next room ceases abruptly, and two teen-aged girls show their faces, then excuse themselves. We are apparently really after food only. The padre asks for wine and spaghetti. We are led into a warm kitchen and sit at the table with Mama and Papa and the youngster who has led us here. We are served two huge plates of spaghetti and drink much red wine. It tastes delicious. The usual number of flies sit on the bread and table, and I suddenly wonder how the spaghetti was made. The padre, however, is unconcerned about the sanitary conditions, trusts in the Lord, and asks for a third plate. Our stomachs being full, we offer to pay five dollars each for our meal, which is accepted smilingly with many *multi grazias*. We bid the family goodbye, then stroll through the town in spite of the rain. It is not very exciting. We roam through narrow, dirty streets lined with small shops that have nothing to display. Junk jewelry shops and sloppy vino bars abound. By mid-afternoon we return to the College. On arriving, we find it empty of all troops. The order to move out must have been given very suddenly. Two days in Italy and I have already goofed, being left behind by my outfit. I race up four flights of stairs and to the room where I had been quartered. Only my equipment still lies on the floor; otherwise, the room is bare. I grab my blanket and musette bag, rush out of the building and to the highway, with hopes of flagging down any 88th Division vehicle. I am very fortunate, for soon a 349th Infantry Cannon Company truck passes by. It is not a 3d Battalion truck but it belongs to the same regiment, so that it will probably do. Having flagged down the driver, I climb into the cab. The driver says he does not know his destination except that a convoy of 88th Division trucks is somewhere ahead of us. He was part of a convoy once, but lost it gassing up. We race down the highway for approximately three miles and luckily soon join the tail-end of 88th Division vehicles. It looks as though we are safe. By now it is dark, and the steady rain has changed to a hard downpour. I wonder if the chaplain got a ride. I forgot all about him in my excitement. We drive through a section of war-torn Naples, then leave town on a prominent highway. An 88th Division artillery truck is ahead of us. I hope its driver knows the way. After fifteen minutes the driver of my truck

states he cannot go on. He must pull off the side of the road, for he
has diarrhea. That does it. We lose the convoy. All we can do now is
follow the main highway and ask MPs stationed in small towns in
what direction they have recently seen an 88th Division convoy go.
I wish the Army would issue maps or tell one something beforehand.
We roll through innumerable war-torn villages, but it is raining so hard
no military police (MPs) are out on the streets. The downpour is so
heavy you can see for approximately only ten yards. We just keep driving and guessing, taking the most logical road fork. The trip to me
seems endless, the driver stopping every few miles to evacuate his
bowels. After several hours we at long last catch up to a column of
tail lights moving very slowly. The trucks bear markings of 88th Division Artillery. Again, we feel much relieved. The convoy turns off the
highway on to a narrow dirt road. The mud is axle deep. The road winds
over hills and sharp curves. All the bridges are flooded by the downpour. One truck ahead of us capsizes into a small creekbed, but none
of the occupants are hurt. By midnight we arrive at an old broken-
down mansion on a hilltop. I am told we are at 88th Division Headquarters Command Post. I tell the driver to bed down for the night
with the artillery unit. In the morning I shall get a map and inquire
for the location of the 349th Infantry, which should be somewhere
in this vicinity.

The broken-down mansion is a former summer hotel. All its windows are shattered. Its walls and plaster are cracked. The rooms are
damp and dusty. The basement serves as Army kitchen. After asking
the artillery commander for permission to remain here for the night,
I am invited to go down to the basement for some food. We have Spam
sandwiches and hot coffee. At 1:00 A.M. I find a bedspring in a vacant
third story room and roll into my blankets for the night.

Breakfast at 7:00 A.M. is in the former hotel's dining room. The room
is somewhat airy, the cold wind blowing through paneless windows.
The artillery officers offer me a very satisfactory breakfast consisting
of Cream of Wheat, French toast, and coffee. The hotel's headwaiter
is still here and serves the food. He is probably not as cleanshaven
as he used to be, is not dressed in a tuxedo, but is wearing a dirty gray
apron and serving GI chow. After breakfast artillery headquarters lo-
cates the bivouac area of the 349th Infantry, and I draw a map that
should lead me to my troops. I imagine that I have been declared AWOL
by this time. However, when a driver develops diarrhea one has some
sort of an excuse. We spend six hours reaching our destination, hin-
dered by all types of obstacles. Most of the bridges along our route
are either flooded or washed away, and we detour and retrace our route
frequently. The wheels sink hub-deep into the mud, and water often

floods the motor. We detour through British, French, and Italian bivouac areas. Finally we see road signs directing us to the 349th Infantry Regimental Command Post. It is in Gioa, a small town of about
twenty houses. My cannon company truck has at last found its outfit. I hitch a jeep ride for three miles farther north to the 3d Battalion.
I find that I was not even missed. The troops spent all night on the
road and had arrived only a few hours before I did.

Our bivouac area, an extensive olive grove, is about five miles from
the town of Piedmonte d'Alife. Cassino lies twenty kilometers to the
northwest. At least we are getting closer. Our olive grove is at the base
of a large bare mountain with sharp, rising cliffs. The battalion troops
are quartered in pyramidal tents pitched under and between olive trees.
The ground is soft, muddy, and rain soaked. Straw is used on the tent
floors. There are no lights, stoves, or cots. Those who neglected to dig
drainage ditches around their tents are awakened during the night by
mud streams flowing into their blankets. The mud is so deep it runs
over and into your combat boots. I find it impossible to set up an adequate aid station under such conditions and am granted permission
to use an old tool shed along the dirt road running parallel to our bivouac area. The shed is full of manure, straw, and rubbish. In three
days it is cleaned out, swept and reswept, and sprayed with DDT powder. Two old wooden counters are used as dressing tables. We set up
our two medical chests and erect four cots. We acquire a pot-bellied
stove and candles. Soon I have the best medical setup I have had since
leaving the States. I can at least look at a man where it is reasonably
warm and can lay him on a cot and examine him adequately. I can
keep a man overnight for observation. I can read sitting on a cot and
even have candlelight. My medical sergeants Torres, T/3 Marceau, T/3
Fitzsimmons, as well as Pfc. Hurley, are all happy. Along one side of
our shed and acting as a reminder that this ground was also once
fought over is a lone grave. It bears a simple white cross on which
is inscribed the name "Feldwebel Sonnefeld."

We hold sick call just before supper time. To hold it during training
hours would invite goldbrick attendance. Sick call is always lighter
when held during off-duty hours. Bronchitis, sinusitis, tonsillitis, common colds, foot infections, diarrhea, scabies, impetigo, and backaches
make up all the ailments. I practice very little medicine, one hour
daily at the most. The men no longer hit the sick book. They are only
twenty-five minutes from the front, and most know that they have
been declared medically fit long ago.

For our meals we tramp through the mud to battalion headquar-
ter's kitchen. Italian civilians from surrounding farmhouses always
attend and bring up the rear of the chow lines. They pick up scraps

and leftovers. Small urchins search the garbage pits and pick up anything edible. Each ragged child clutches a small tin can waiting for someone to share his meal with him. Most leave with a full stomach and take more home. We are for the first time seeing the misery caused by war.

The nights are damp, cold, and windy. It rains every day and most of the night. We sleep very well in our aid station except for the mice. They jump onto my cot, crawl into my shoes, and chew on the cellophane-wrapped medical dressings. They are practically household pets, for when you flash a light on them they sit up on their hind quarters and stare back at you without scurrying. In my past two letters home I have requested mouse traps.

The only other nightly interruption is "Bed Check Charlie." This is a lone German plane that flies over the American rear areas nightly, hoping to spot some blackout violation and report that area for a likely target the next day. Bed Check Charlie's motor is unmistakable. It sounds like an old lumbering engine. Bed Check Charlie never drops any bombs but just drones overhead to remind us that the Luftwaffe is still somewhat active. Several times night fighters also fly over our area and drop flares, but never bomb. They are probably trying to gather information on a possible buildup of supplies. These planes, however, keep the troops on the alert. Those that have not dug foxholes around their tent dig them now, and those that have dug them dig them deeper.

The days drag by. I wish we were actually on the front. We continue playing war. The troops pursue their daily hikes, and fire machine guns and mortars into the cliffs of the mountain side. Night problems are still on the schedule. Not very far away stands an isolated, broken-down castle on a large hill with steep slopes. This castle we attack for several nights, digging an aid station into the slopes and gradually advancing until the castle is ours. Why are we taking a castle on such strategic heights? Could it be that we are practicing to take the Abbey at Cassino? The uncertainty of our near future is the most dreadful part of waiting.

I am told to attend a seven-day mountain-climbing school. I am happy to do anything that will alleviate the daily monotony of sitting and waiting for our move closer to the front. I, my sergeants, and corporals are ordered to practice climbing cliffs and lowering litters down steep grades. At 7:00 A.M. each day we entruck and drive to the marketplace of Piedmonte d'Alife. This town is about five miles distant, and the dirt road passes over many blown-out bridges that we have hastily reconstructed. The Germans have certainly been thorough in blowing bridges. Along the entire road I see only one not destroyed. I imagine that the German soldier who missed that one was demoted.

In the marketplace or town square of Piedmonte d'Alife we detruck. It is crowded with stands where Italians sell olives, nuts, and a few vegetables. They shout and clamor to advertise their wares. Leaving the truck behind, we march through Piedmonte in a column of twos toward a steep mountain just north of the town. Little ragged kids tag along, running in their bare feet. The smaller ones wear only thin cotton dresses or shirts, no underwear, their naked buttocks exposed to the wind and rain. Charcoal stoves sit on the doorsteps of most homes warming up, waiting to be carried indoors as a source of heat for cooking. These people certainly are still primitive and seem years behind American civilization. Charlie Williams, medical officer of the 2d Battalion, walks beside me. He is tall, gangly, thin and bald-headed, and most unmilitary. To the beat of our marching feet he sings a Fascist tune, and the Italian spectators stare open-mouthed at his audacity. Fascists are enemies. Charlie would probably be shot for his joke were he in the Italian Army. But then Americans are free to do what they want, and Charlie loves to sing. Reaching the out-skirts of town, we wind our way slowly up a mountain trail, up and up. We are constantly reminded to walk very slowly—our first lesson. It may take hours to reach the top, so don't blow all your energy the first half-mile. We reach the snow line and the breeze stiffens.

All sorts of thoughts run through my head along this trail. I bet the folks at home are thinking of me as a hard-working military sur-geon operating for many hours daily. However, here I am climbing up a mountain trail. This is certainly not a medical subject. It is of no use to complain; no one would listen anyway. Nothing makes sense anymore. I feel like a mountain goat. Why all this mountain training? Is Cassino so important? Are we going to attack Rome from the south? Will all the mountains be this high? How can men fight over terrain like this? We certainly won't be able to use tanks and cannon.

At the foot of a large, overhanging cliff approximately one-third from the top we stop. Alpini sergeants meet us here to be our dem-onstrators. The Alpini are the crack mountain troops of the Italian Army. Their uniform is green; they wear Tyrolean hats with goat's beard ornament. How they shape up as fighters I don't know, but they can certainly crawl up cliffs like flies crawl up a wall. First, we are taught footwork. Each foot must be securely placed, the looseness of the ground must always be tested, and it is most important to be able to change from one foot to the other with one sure hop. Use of hands is emphasized next. We must take advantage of each crack and crev-ice, in every rock. We learn to use ropes and how to anchor them. I enjoy fastening the rope to a large boulder on top of the cliff, then running it between my legs and over my shoulder and stepping off into the unknown, my body dangling in mid-air, my feet kicking to keep from striking the sides of the rocks. It's amazing all you can do with only a stout rope at your disposal. You feel strange dangling in mid-air looking down hundreds of feet. However, you learn to depend on yourself and your fellow men. Mountain climbing means team-work, and it can be great fun. It takes a great deal of time and training to lower wounded on a litter down any steep slope, and cliffs are ex-tremely difficult.

Doc Williams loses his enthusiasm after the first two days. He de-cides that this sort of training is not for him. After having witnessed the basic principles once, he lets his sergeants and corporals do all the practicing while he strolls off to the very top of the mountain. After my third day of training I follow him to satisfy my curiosity. What does Charlie do up there? Soon I see him sitting with his back against a huge rock, which protects him from the wind. He is enjoy-ing a beautiful view of the entire country below us. He just sits and philosophizes, the sun beating on his bald head. It is a wonderful place to hide, and we are never missed. The view is terrific. Here come hun-dreds of our planes heading north. They drone overhead in perfect for-mation, leaving long vapor trails behind them. Where are they going? To bomb Cassino? the Brenner Pass? the Po Valley? or Rumania? They certainly look impressive. Looking down and across a large draw we see another mountain. A mule pack train slowly makes its way to the top for a weekend bivouac in the snow. Through field glasses I recognize Lieutenant Melcher in the lead. The boys in this mule train must have mixed feelings too. In the States they were probably con-tented factory workers, garage mechanics, office boys, college boys, and perhaps even businessmen. They are carrying packboards up a snow-covered mountain and leading mules. Quite a change in occu-pation. An Italian peasant and his wife wander down another trail. The woman is carrying a huge bundle of kindling wood on her head. The man leads the way, and the woman with the heavy bundle trails behind him.

The slopes of all the surrounding hills are terraced. To build all these terraces must have been a job of centuries. Generations have prob-ably lived from the olives grown here during the past decades. On top of the largest mountain is a small, snow-covered village. It looks like a cozy haven. I hope it is untouched by war. I can imagine myself in one of its warm houses, sitting by a blazing fireplace sipping vino. It's only a dream, for Charlie reminds me that it is time to break out my C rations for lunch. I shall always remember the olive mountain in Piedmonte where I could sit and think for hours, wondering where I would be if there were no war and wishing that this damn war were

over. Will either of us still be around when it is? When are we moving up? Life is becoming boring. Time is dragging. It is already February, 1944, the Russians are throwing the Germans back, and we have
not even seen actual combat. What are we waiting for? An ocasional
post exchange boosts our morale a little. Kits for prophylaxis against
venereal disease are available. What for? We have not had leave for
over three months and are supposed to be moving up front and not
to the rear.

Toward the end of February, 1944, we are at last placed on alert orders. Three days pass and nothing happens. The suspense is mounting. Using the excuse that I need certain medical supplies, I ask my
jeep driver to drive from camp up the main highway north toward Cassino. Here lies the 38th Evacuation Hospital. It does my heart good
to see a hospital, even though it is just a group of large tents. Here,
however, men sleep on cots and have stoves, and meals are served on
plates. I ask permission to see the operating room tent. Here I see my
first war casualty just arrived. He is a British soldier, his right leg
missing, and he has many shrapnel wounds of the back. The patient
is calm as he is prepared for surgery. For him the war is over. I return
to camp with mixed feelings. I wish I could have remained in that tent.

Our move to the front is postponed daily. It rains constantly, and
the mud is now knee deep. We have been ordered to paint a large red
cross on a white background on all our helmets. Red Cross armbands
and combat clothes are issued.

On February 29, 1944, all tents are torn down and equipment packed.
That night we all have our own thoughts.

On March 1, 1944, at 8:00 A.M. we move north in convoy. It is raining, then sleeting. Occasionally we are pelted by hail. My two medical jeeps bring up the rear of the convoy. The roofs and windshields
of the jeeps are down, according to orders. Wind and rain beat my face.
We are on Highway 7 leading north to the front. We pass through many
small villages, mostly all rubble. British camps are scattered along
the road. After six hours of driving we arrive at the edge of a muddy
field and another olive grove. The order is to pitch tents. This beats
me. Is not today the big day? Apparently it is not. A latrine rumor
states that we will camp on this field for several days, then move up
at night. I look about and see many British vehicles. Most of our vehicles, once unloaded, disappear to the rear. Those that do remain are
devoid of all identification marks. They could belong to anyone. The
helmets which we so carefully painted with red crosses are taken away
from us. We are issued British helmets instead. I am told that we shall
relieve a British outfit and must look like British troops just in case
German scout planes should spot and photograph our campsite. From

now on we must also mislead any Italian civilians, who may be informers. For several weeks, anyway, we are supposed to be British. Shortly after an early supper on March 3, 1944, all tents are town down. I load all my medical equipment and supplies into my two jeeps. I am having a rather uncomfortable time. One hour ago I took three tablespoonfuls of Epsom salts, for I discovered that I had acquired pin worms. The laxative is now beginning to work. I would do something like this on the eve of our most important move to date. . . . At dusk the troops are loaded into English lorries and our convoy pulls out. The troop trucks move first; these are followed by three large truck-loads of ammunition; then come my two jeeps. I consider following ammunition trucks exactly not too sporting, for should a shell hit these, I too would be part of the big blow. However, I am having enough trouble holding back my diarrhea and the thought of the ammunition trucks in front of me increases the urge. After an hour's ride, road signs appear warning in large letters: "Lights Out — Under Enemy Observation." Military police along the road emphasize the warning verbally. The convoy proceeds slowly in total darkness. Soon bright flashes followed by ear-splitting explosions coming from both sides of the highway make us realize that we are apparently passing artillery positions. Occasionally a high-pitched whine, increasing steadily in intensity and concluding with a loud crash and whirring noise, tells us that a German shell has landed in retaliation. The convoy never stops, shells exploding left and right but none hitting the highway, although some sound awfully close. After another thirty minutes we leave the highway and follow a dirt road running parallel to a rail bed and soon arrive at a pontoon bridge crossing a river. I am told that the river's name is the Garigliano. The troops unload and rapidly cross the bridge on foot. I follow their column in my jeep. The shores along the bridgehead are pockmarked with huge craters. Really big shells must be hitting here, and I am anxious to get away from this potential hell hole. I breathe a sigh of relief when my jeeps have crossed and the bridge lies behind us. It should be a prime German target, probably earmarked nightly for time on target fire. It is an eerie feeling, wondering how soon the next shell will come in. All you do is hope you won't be around to greet it when it does. Once we are over the bridge and several miles distant, a large black wall looms ahead of us. It is apparently a mountain and our destination. Having just crossed a river, we must naturally be in a valley. This shadow of a mountain in the distance is the first mountain I am actually glad to see since in Italy. Its rear slope looks like the only safe place tonight. The pace of the troops is nerve-rackingly slow this first night under fire, and my vehicles following them are moving at a snail's pace. The

shadow of the mountain looms closer and closer. Our artillery fire
sounds less noisy. We must now be at least one mile in front of our
artillery positions. The only shells that can hit us now are mortars;
we are too close to the mountain for enemy artillery to curve down
on us. Suddenly I feel safer up front than in the rear. After a time that
seems endless the troops finally halt. A British corporal appears out
of the darkness and asks me to slowly follow him. We branch off on
to a small muddy road and soon arrive at a farmhouse snug against
the rear slope of that wonderful mountain. I am told that this is my
aid station. We enter the rear door through a series of blackout cur-
tains and enter a candle-lit room, filled with British medics dressed
and ready to move out. They waste no time. In several minutes all
my seventeen men have relieved the British. We are finally at the front
and on our own.

On the Front Line

MARCH 3, 1944–MAY 11, 1944

The aid station is a welcome haven after our first evening under scattered incoming artillery fire. It is a small, two-room farmhouse, the
walls built out of field stone and at least two feet thick. Sturdily built
field stone houses are a blessing on the front line. More assuring is
the fact that the departing British medical officer states that our house
is safe from artillery fire and that mortars will probably never score
a direct hit, since the mountain in front of us is too high. The entire
house consists of one room downstairs and one upstairs. Each room
is about fifteen by fifteen feet. We have a fireplace downstairs that
we obviously cannot use for security reasons. The upstairs room has
only a thin slate roof, its only disadvantage. Any shell can pierce it.
Consequently, only a few of my men sleep upstairs during the first
few days, the rest waiting until they have had a chance to study the
frequency of incoming shells. This first night no one knows exactly
how to behave, and if a man were frightened to death he would never
show it. The sounds of war are still new. Incoming shells sound entirely different from outgoing shells. All shells pass high over our
building—all we hear is the characteristic whine, whistle, and rustle.
Low, fast-traveling projectiles have a high-pitched whine that passes
rapidly. Larger projectiles have a low whistle, while the heavy stuff
only rustles. Seventeen of us sleep in the first-floor room that evening
—on the cement floor rolled into blankets or on our bedroll. Not knowing what to expect, some sleep wearing helmets. We have no casual-

Snapshot of Klaus Huebner in a rest area in Villamagna, Italy, September, 1944.

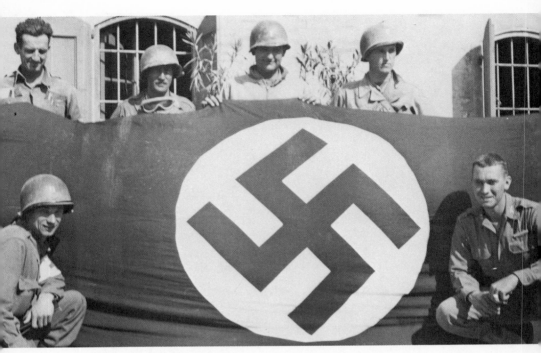

Officers of the 3d Battalion, 349th Infantry, with a captured swastika flag. *Kneeling, left to right:* Capt. Klaus Huebner, Capt. Ted Bellmont; *standing, left to right:* Maj. Knox, Capt. Peterson, Lt. Todd, Lt. Col. Henderson. Courtesy Eugene Engelen, Park Ridge, Ill. *Below:* Men of the 88th Division on twenty-two-mile forced night march. Courtesy U.S. Army Signal Corps.

88th Division troops in review at Fort Sam Houston, Texas. Courtesy U.S. Army Signal Corps. *Below:* Getting practice in lowering a casualty down a cliff. U.S. Army Signal Corps photo, courtesy Lt. Col. (Ret.) William Konze.

Left anchor of the Garigliano front line, Minturno area. *Below:* Front-line terrain when the 3d Battalion was first put into action, Garigliano River area. Courtesy U.S. Army Signal Corps.

Pallazzo Reale in Caserta (King's Palace). Courtesy Lt. Col. (Ret.) William Konze, 88th Infantry Division historian and property custodian.

ties that first night but fall asleep still studying the different sounds of incoming and outgoing shells.

The next morning is bright and sunny. I step outside of our house and closely inspect our surroundings. We are the middle of three houses just to the left of a small dirt road junction. The road in front of our house is about fifteen feet wide, runs east to west, and parallels the front line. Across the road begins the sharply rising mountain slope. One hundred yards up the slope are dug-in mortar positions; halfway up the slope infantry positions begin. Approximately thirty yards to the left of our station is another farmhouse. It is heavy weapons, M Company's, command post. Twenty yards to our right is a house not too sturdily built and hence uninhabited. At the road junction thirty yards to our right two heavy tanks stand guard. The few small windows and the front door of our station are heavily sandbagged and blacked out. The only exit from the station is through the first-floor rear door. Its outside approaches are also protected by a four-foot wall of sandbags. Our backyard or southern exposure is a small neglected vegetable garden. Several haystacks remain standing. Beyond our garden for a distance of about five miles lies the flat Garigliano River Valley. Approximately one quarter-mile to our right and also along the road is another group of three houses, housing the battalion command post. Approximately three miles to our right is the town of Castelforte, German occupied and nicknamed little Cassino, since it is a formidable town of rubble. The real Cassino with the abbey lies approximately ten air miles to our right. Seven miles to our left is the Gulf of Gaeta. Thus our division occupies a seven-mile sector, our left or west flank anchored at the Gulf of Gaeta just below the town of Minturno, thence running inland and east for about seven miles to German-held Castelforte. On our division right flank and dug in before Castelforte are British troops, and to their right the New Zealanders are still looking up at the abbey at Monte Cassino. We are the only American division along the entire Fifth Army southern front and the first all–Selective Service division to enter on any front in World War II. To hear this makes us all proud. Our duty is to hold and harass the enemy while the right flank of British and New Zealanders attempt to take Cassino, the commanding height over Highway 6, the central highway to Rome.

My aid station site is ideal, just as it should be and in accordance with the teachings at Carlisle. The steep mountain to our front is excellent defilade. We are along a road, and ambulances can come up at night. We are centrally located, battalion troops being on both sides and in front of us. However, we are not near a stream, as the books state we should be, but then the books were written before jeeps carrying water cans were in use. Unorthodox is the fact that we are located in the midst of a very desirable target area, since a heavy weapons company command post is on our left side, tanks are sitting on our right side, and mortars dug into the slopes are in front of us; but then our house is not under direct enemy observation, and if German shells hit us it will be pure luck for which the enemy cannot be blamed.

From March, 1944, to May, 1944, newspaper reports from the United States hardly ever mention Italy. It is the so-called quiet front. News flashes report routine patrol activity only. In one month, however, our sector experiences 99 dead, 252 wounded, and 36 missing. Even though it is the so-called quiet sector, men die daily. I see my first battalion casualty on the second day. A deserted building near the battalion command post is our morgue. No one inhabits this building, since it is on the road to Castelforte and under direct enemy observation. I venture to it cautiously, curious to inspect the mortal damage of mortars. I slowly open the creaking front door of the house; lying on the cement floor is a GI, his legs deformed by compound fractures, his skull fractured and brain exposed. A brown rat is feeding on the spilled brain and never stirs. One brief glance is enough; I close the door and walk away. The boy died a soldier. I am glad he had no inkling of his fate in this damp room. The graves registration detail will pick him up under cover of darkness tonight, put him in a mattress cover, then take him to the designated cemetery.

Our casualties are light but steady. Most occur at night and are suffered by boys on patrol. Daylight casualties are usually due to carelessness. During lulls of sporadic exchange fire, the men come out of their foxholes to take sun baths and reveal their positions. Jerry is very clever. He wastes no shells. He waits until a reasonable number of men show their disconcern and until enough are gathered in groups to make shelling worthwile. Then he opens up with several airbursts, and casualties result. Most wounds are shrapnel. They are puncture wounds of the back, legs and arms. GIs not quick enough to hit the dirt suffer penetrating abdominal wounds. Mortar wounds are more severe. Mortars are more accurate. Falling close to men, they cause extensive mutilation. It is not unusual for one man to have compound fractures of several extremities at one time as well as numerous penetrating wounds of the abdomen and face. Our system of evacuation is rapid. Our field telephone has direct contact with each company spread over the slopes in front of us. As soon as casualties occur, the company notifies us of their location. Our jeep starts off along the road as far as it dares to go. The litter bearers are met by the company aid man, who leads them to the casualty. A first-aid dressing to stop bleeding has already been applied. The victim is car-

ried down the slope on a litter, loaded into the jeep, and arrives at
the aid station. Here I remove the original bandage and inspect the
seriousness of the wound. The wound is cleansed of dirt and debris,
sulfanilamide powder is applied, and the wound is freshly dressed.
Plasma is given immediately to anyone showing the least signs of
shock. We have over fifty pints of plasma on hand and are very liberal
with its use. The casualty receives more morphine, which we have
on hand in syrettes, thus eliminating glass syringes and sterilization.
Unless he has an abdominal wound, he receives hot coffee and food.
We do not evacuate the casualties until dark, since the road to the
medical collecting company is under direct enemy observation. The
ambulance drives up to our station nightly to pick up casualties. If
a man is critical and needs surgery immediately because of hemorrhage from brain, lung, or abdominal injuries, the ambulance makes
the run in broad daylight. Traveling alone on the road and clearly
marked, the ambulance never draws intentional enemy fire.

A self-inflicted wound always poses somewhat of a problem. Is it
intentional or accidental? Carbine wounds through the web of toes,
through the heel, and through hands do occur now and then. I hate
to accuse a man of shooting himself in order to be evacuated. I suppose most are accidental, although I can never be too sure. It is not
my job to pass judgment, but only to treat. The company commander
makes the final decision.

The occasional stubborn civilian rummaging near the front lines
usually finds himself a casualty sooner or later. Wandering through
fields or over roads, civilians frequently step on mines. I see one small
twelve-year-old boy who found an unexploded grenade and decided
to take it apart. His right hand is blown off, all his fingers of his left
hand are mutilated, and a fragment has also penetrated his right eye.
He is a pitiful and miserable-looking sight. We render first aid and
evacuate him that night.

Any civilians who insist on roaming the front lines are in extreme
danger. They are a nuisance to us and the Germans, since either side
considers them possible spies. Thus if an Italian, caught between the
front lines, walks towards German lines, we shoot him; if he walks
toward our lines, the Germans fire. No matter what he does, he eventually winds up in some aid station with a bullet wound, and frequently it is a mortal one.

No matter how serious a situation is, there are always amusing in-
cidents. We have many. Most occur in total darkness. One night a soldier reports stabbing several Germans to death while keeping watch
in his foxhole on the forward slope. Inspection the next morning reveals that his story is only partially true. The rustle toward which

he crept was probably that of a rodent, and the Germans he stabbed had been dead for several months, dead so long that they were only skeletons but still fully dressed. The odor of death had long vanished. The areas occupied by the most forward platoons are well wired and booby trapped. In the dark men often trip over their own wires and set off flares, causing much commotion. Walking along the road in total darkness from one command post to the other can be most dangerous, especially if you have forgotten the password for the night. You are stopped by a sudden "Halt" and stammer for a word you do not remember. You only hope that the guard is not trigger happy. You say anything and say it fast and make it sound convincing. You give a sigh of relief as the guard cautiously approaches, recognizes you, and reminds you of the password. Axis Sally of Berlin has a better memory than you have. She is the Tokyo Rose of the Italian front. At times she broadcasts the correct password for the night. She also warns rear outfits to stop taking sitting-up exercises in broad daylight or else she will see to it that the habit is stopped by a few rounds of heavy stuff.

Booby-trapped houses frequently cause casualties. The Germans apparently know that GI Joe is very curious and inspects everything. Forsaken trunks, closets, or attics are their favorites. Never open a previously unopened door or pry open an old trunk, closet, or door. Everything might explode right into your face, resulting in the loss of both hands and eyesight.

Even though we are no longer playing war but actually on the front, latrine inspections continue. Once weekly at least, I climb to all company areas. Being on the reverse slope, I am naturally not under observation but still not safe from an unexpected airburst or mortar round. While I was on one of my rounds and approaching a latrine still fifty yards away, a mortar shell blew the entire slit trench to kingdom come. That latrine I won't have to inspect. I do not think latrine inspections are important enough to risk your life, but the Army apparently does. Dud shells convince men of their religion. One of the sergeants from I Company is ordered to come to the aid station for a checkup. I am told that his company received a mortar barrage, and one shell fell directly into his hole and buried itself halfway into the ground between his legs and failed to explode. It had been a dud. The sergeant is a good Catholic, but from now on he will be one of the best.

The Germans seldom waste ammunition. Whenever they shoot, they try to make their shells count. From their maps they must know what buildings we occupy, even though they cannot see us. They try for our buildings with high-arched mortars at regular intervals. At sundown we can always expect a barrage. Approximately one dozen shells explode at mortar time. Shrapnel whines and falls into our doorway, deflected by our sandbag wall. The plaster on our walls crumbles and falls. The walls shake, and there is a mad rush for misplaced helmets. Those caught on the outside hit the dirt and walk into the station later, somewhat pale but unhurt.

Jerry is on a higher mountain than the one in front of us. We can see his observation post distinctly by walking about twenty-five yards south in our backyard. Here is the location of our latrine. It is the only installation in my station that is under observation. Mortar time usually catches a few boys unaware. Consequently the latrine is used either earlier in the day or later at night.

On nights a combat patrol is not out we do very little, and life is boring. Playing chess with one of my sergeants is my chief diversion. I also censor all letters written. I write home twice weekly, but not being able to state where I am or what I am doing, all letters are very boring. We have an abundance of wine, but it tastes bitter and musty. Sergeant Torres finds fifty gallons of vino buried under a haystack in our backyard. Many of us do not drink any of it for several days, waiting to see how the others tolerate it. The Germans may have added a little poison. This, however, does not turn out to be the case, and the wine becomes a stock beverage. A quart of Old General rye whiskey is another stock item. I receive one bottle every three weeks to be given to the casualties. It boosts borale. A shot of liquor is often a reminder of the good old U.S.A. and acts almost as well as a hypodermic.

When patrols are out at night, suspense is the rule. Patrols are always in trouble. Their objective is to capture a German. For this they must attack German outposts or catch enemies napping in their holes. There is a small hill just beyond us that is called OP Hill, and we know that this is a German outpost. Our patrols reconnoiter this hill frequently. One of our first patrols sent out has this hill as its objective. The patrol leaves at 11:00 P.M. For two hours there is deadly silence. Suddenly, the rapid firing sound of German machine pistols shatters the silence of the night. The firing sound is so rapid we nickname these guns paper cutters. The steady methodical pounding sounds of the BAR answer the paper cutters. Grenades explode next, then carbine fire is heard. Ten minutes of deathly silence follows. Then comes a furious German mortar barrage, and all is quiet. We wait for our phone to ring. Nothing happens for another hour. At 2:00 A.M. five men stumble through the blackout curtain into our aid station. They are lightly wounded. They are wide-eyed and dazed. Two have minor flesh wounds from grenade fragments; others, bruises and contusions from having fallen over brush and rocks in the dark. One sits speechless and just stares at the floor. The other curses a blue streak.

I am told that our patrol had stumbled directly into the German fox-holes. Hand-to-hand combat had ensued. Grenades were tossed back and forth at short range. It was a mad free-for-all. Three of our men lie dead in German positions. We cannot retrieve their bodies. Each patrol member gets a shot of Old General, a cup of coffee, and a seda-tive if he needs it. Soon they are composed. The minor wounds are dressed, and the men return to their company positions for some well-earned rest in their holes. We are probably also through working for the night. We sleep to the tune of incoming and outgoing artillery. We know the sound of our guns. We fire heavy artillery all night—twenty shells to Jerry's one—and the sound is music in our ears. Shells no longer disturb my sleep—only scabies, fleas, and cockroaches do.

Bright, sunny days are lovely. After breakfast I sit in an old rocking chair in my back yard, enjoying the green valley lying behind us. Liz-ards scurry through the grass and bask in the sun on small rocks; patches of blue and yellow field flowers are popping up here and there. I am so accustomed to the sounds of our tank destroyers (TD's) bang-ing off behind us that I would miss their sound should they ever cease firing. One of our Spitfires roars overhead, turns toward the Castel-forte—strafes the town in two passes—then disappears. My corporal is looking for a few stray onions and lettuce that may have survived the overgrowth of weeds. He is our chief cook and incorporates these choice vegetables with our five-in-one rations. We have set a small gasoline stove into the fireplace. It does not smoke. We have warm meals daily, powdered eggs, hash, canned potatoes, and beans. The fresh onions and lettuce, however, add that extra flavor. As the noon hour approaches, our mortars in front of us suddenly pop off with a sound barrage. I wish they had not, since it was all just so peaceful. Appar-ently, however, our OP (observation post) spotted a target. Perhaps a Kraut was sunning himself just as I was. In ten minutes the Germans answer with their calling card. A sudden rustle and bang—the mortar explodes before I have time to leave my chair. Shrapnel sings, and I make a mad dash for the station. M Company executive officer Lieu-tenant Peterson calls over to me and says, "Hey, Doc, better wear your armband, you almost got hurt."

Most of the afternoons are not too dull either. A British major and his sergeant pay us a visit. They have a routine that never varies. The sergeant carries a small portable mortar and six shells. He and the major walk into the open field approximately one hundred yards be-hind us, and at 3:00 P.M. daily have what they call their little shoot. They fire their mortar shells at three-minute intervals, then disman-tle the mortar and slowly walk away. I never learn what their objec-tive is. Following their shoot they brew and drink their tea in my aid station. I then engage the major in a game of chess. I never win a game. Following this he disappears, to revisit again the next day.

The only Germans I see captured the first two weeks on the front are the result of a daylight patrol. One of our privates stumbles into an empty house while on daylight patrol in no-man's land and enters a room, surprising a Jerry officer writing a letter. As he orders the officer out at gunpoint, fourteen other Jerries from an adjoining room follow. These prisoners march past our aid station on their way to battalion headquarters. They are an unimpressive lot. They look tired and unkempt and are without helmets. They were apparently sleeping when surprised. They do not look like the described supermen, but just like any other young kids put into uniform. The sight of these captives boosts everyone's morale.

On March 17, 1944, we are to be relieved for a short rest period. I do not cherish this thought. I have grown very fond of our house and consider sitting here practically a rest anyway. I feel it much more dangerous to return to the rear and be under artillery range than to sit here worrying only about airbursts and mortars. However, relief is ordered, and units of the new 85th Division take over. The moon is bright on the night of our relief, and Jerry keeps firing bright flares that light up the entire Garigliano Valley. No shells, however, fall close to us, and our return to the rear is uneventful. Sally of Berlin, with all her advance information, snafued tonight!

Once back in Casanova, our rest area, I soon wish I were back on the front. It is pleasant to know that you are safely out of artillery range, but routine inspections, dull physical examinations, and just giving shots takes the joy out of any rest. One big event occurs. I shall never forget it. This is a gala regimental officers' party held at the King's Palace in Caserta. Our headquarters company commandant is a Texan and an eligible bachelor. He has a pleasant and convincing personality and is gifted with humor and small talk, which appeals to all girls, both native and military. He is therefore the ideal contact man to supply females for our first big overseas party. Regimental order is that the invited girls are to be nurses only, from nearby military hospitals in Maddaloni. The latter is about thirty-five miles south of Casanova and close to Caserta, so that the girls won't have too much of a trip to the party. The preparations for our big dance are extensive and filled with thoughtfulness. For two days Captain Bellmont and I drive at least one hundred miles over dirt roads to Maddaloni and Caserta, where we comb all the hospitals, speak to the nurse supervisors, issue formal invitations, post notices on bulletin boards, and arrange for battalion vehicles to pick up the nurses at a designated time. We are told that all nurses will be duly notified of the coming occasion,

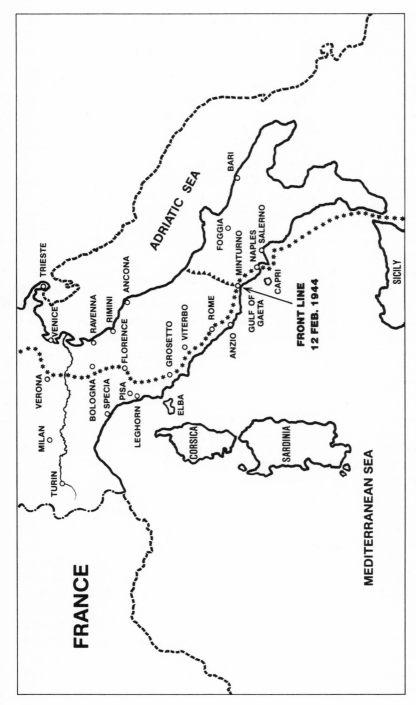

1 Route of the 3d Battalion, 349th Infantry Regiment: Arrival in Naples, February 12, 1944, and the Long Walk into the Alps

and we leave each installation with satisfied anticipation. Captain Bellmont buys flowers for table decorations and even fashions crude corsages. For several days before the dance each officer pulls dress blouse and pinks from his barracks bag, stretches and pulls them hoping to erase the wrinkles. More fortunate ones manage to borrow irons from nearby farmhouses and are able to actually press their clothes. Cases of native cognac and U.S.A. whiskey are procured by conniving and bargaining. A small orchestra is engaged. As the day of the dance approaches, the men shower under ice-cold water, polish buttons and bars for hours, shave off all beards, polish shoes to a high glow, and by nightfall, as a result of all these sacrifices, everyone looks spic and span, neater than they have looked for four months. This is the night of the big fling. Expectations run high. On to the dance in jeeps, weapon carriers, and two-and-a-half-ton trucks. I wonder what my girl will look like. It has been so long since I last danced, I have probably forgotten how. We shall probably be close to one hundred officers. This affair is really big!

The Palazzo Reale in Caserta is indeed a building fit for a king. It is a large, rectangular, three-story stone building over a block long. After detrucking, I can only stare at the rows and rows of windows. In the center, and at each end, stately columns mark the entrances. We walk through the center entrance and up a long marble stairway to a spacious ballroom. Tables have been arranged in cabaret style. A six-piece orchestra is playing U.S. music. A small vase with flowers adorns each table. The floor is waxed for dancing. Cognac can be had at the bar by the bottle, and set-ups can be purchased for the tables. Arriving at 8:00 P.M., we are apparently somewhat early. Only fifty officers are here so far, and the girls have not yet arrived. Men are sitting at the tables or congregated about the bar and standing in small groups exchanging front-line experiences. A sudden hush falls over the hall, and the first girls enter. Two nurses accompanied by a major walk to the regimental commander's table on the stage in the center of the hall. Fifty pairs of eyes scrutinize these two girls, then turn toward the door anticipating others. Six more girls appear. By 10:00 P.M. a total of eight gallant nurses have responded to our invitations, and the dance is in full swing. Eight girls for approximately one hundred officers makes a lovely dance. This will be a catastrophe; I can see it coming. The men are fast becoming drunk. Since you can't dance, you drink. It is absolutely asinine for one hundred to compete for eight girls. I gather enough courage to cut in on one couple but dance only fifteen seconds and am tagged. I do not even have time to look at the girl, let alone introduce myself. I take one crack at the dance floor, then join the rest of the men at the tables and pour down both cognac and whiskey.

The first casualty is a lieutenant, a medical officer of another battalion. He is being carried out by four men, as pall bearers would a coffin, only the corpse is singing opera and is no longer fully conscious of his surroundings. The inebriated doctor is usually very serious and an introvert, but the cognac stimulated him beyond all expectations. Others rapidly follow and are either carried out in the same manner or manage to stagger away or even crawl. The trucks in the courtyard are soon filled with inebriates. A constant battle has started in the men's room. Another officer, but this time from Regiment, imagines himself to be the heavyweight champion. He has taken up his position just inside the swinging doors of the washroom, and no matter who enters, a roundhouse swing on the jaw usually finds its mark. At least fifteen men are felled by this surprise attack. However, a captain from my battalion, a two-hundred-pounder, is only slightly jarred. With the captain's first counterblow, the offender, the regimental officer, collapses like an empty sack. He is then tossed head first down the long marble stairway. I look away because the results are gruesome. I do recall seeing the regimental officer several days later. His face was still a bruised mess, and his front teeth were missing. I remember nothing else of the dance. I do not recall how the girls fared. The trip back to Casanova is also a complete blank in my memory. As a result of the dance, however, I vow never to date American girls while in Italy. They apparently felt it too much of an effort to make an appearance for us at the palace in Caserta.

Ten days in the Casanova rest area is enough. After the big blowout in the palace of Caserta, I am happy to return to the front. I hear that I shall return to the same aid station I had left. That, too, is good news. The most happy news, however, is the announcement that our big brave regimental commander has been relieved of his command, and his permanent replacement will be Colonel Crawford. I now have confidence in our leadership at Regiment. The rumor is that the relieved colonel made tactical plans not in accord with division plans.*

Our trip back to the front is again uneventful. We follow a slightly different road than on our first trip, for we approach closer to Castelforte, the little Cassino. Only a few 88 bursts (88-mm shells) annoy

*A hint that this rumor was correct is suggested in John P. Delany's *The Blue Devils in Italy*, 1st ed. (Washington, D.C.: Infantry Journal Press, 1947), p. 51.

us, most landing at least one hundred yards off the highway. Arriving back on the front, we find that our old aid station has not changed. We feel right at home.

Our division continues its harassing fire. I am told that 1,500 artillery rounds, 400 TD rounds, and 700 mortar shells is an average shoot for the day. It is rumored that toward the end of spring a big offensive may start. The hills in front of us look formidable, and I frequently climb to our battalion's observation post to study the terrain to our north. Should we ever attack in total darkness, I would like to be familiar with at least the first few miles of the attack route. On the OP all sorts of enemy activity can be seen if you wait long enough. A barrage of mortar rounds pounds an innocent-looking knoll approximately five hundred yards ahead. Boards and branches fly in all directions. We have scored a direct hit on a German machine-gun position. German medics appear waving Red Cross flags and evacuate the wounded. On another day several tanks appear in the valley. One of our shells falls directly into the open turret, killing all occupants. Enemy movements increase daily. The enemy must be expecting an offensive.

Nightly patrol activity continues. Near midnight, when patrols usually clash, the sharp sounds of machine-gun fire, Browning automatic rifles, grenades, and machine pistols echo through the night. An occasional prisoner is captured. Our patrols pull some directly out of their holes while the victims are sleeping. Most of these are war-weary Poles recruited by the German army. They offer little resistance and seem to welcome capture. They speak freely in Polish, and we learn that elements of the German 94th and 71st Divisions oppose us. They state that any German officer captured by us is court-martialed in absentia, and that troops in general are encouraged to snipe whenever possible. As Poles, they are sent out in combat groups with one or two full-fledged, die-hard Germans in command. They are closely watched lest they desert at an opportune moment. Satellite troops under German command are thus apparently in common usage.

We, too, lose an occasional man as prisoner. On a dark night one of our men has simply vanished from his foxhole. We surmise that he fell asleep and an alert German patrol snatched him from his foxhole. We all hope that he reveals nothing when questioned by the enemy.

Our patrols often suffer tragic casualties. Second Lieutenant Liebenstein of K Company and his patrol of three men attack a German machine-gun nest on Mount Ceracoli. After fierce fighting in total darkness, Lieutenant Liebenstein drags a surprised and scared German from his foxhole. As the lieutenant retreats with his prisoner, he trips the wire of a German booby trap and is seriously wounded and unable to move back with his patrol. With the booby trap's explosion, German mortar and artillery fire crashes into the patrol's path of escape and makes any attempts to evacuate the lieutenant impossible. He orders his men to abandon him. Later in the night my medics and Captain Felts cautiously search no man's land for hours, but the lieutenant is nowhere to be found. Have the Germans carried him off dead or alive? The lieutenant will probably receive the DSC (Distinguished Service Cross), but I doubt if he will ever hear of it. He was only a young kid, small, thin, and blond, yet ordered his men to leave him dying to save themselves!

Easter 1944 is a novel one. Chaplain Oscar Reinboth of Seward, Nebraska, chaplain of the 2d Battalion, sends an Easter message to the Krauts in German. A loudspeaker had been hauled up the mountain by mule pack the night before and placed in position on the forward slope. No shots are fired for hours after his message. The day is cloudy but warm. I spend Easter morning sitting in my sandbagged backyard, fully enjoying the peace and quiet. I inhale the wonderful fragrance of nearby apple, peach, and cherry blossoms. Lemon trees, too, are beginning to bud.

On Easter afternoon shooting again begins, but not as many rounds appear to be fired as usual. The Germans are not firing any airbursts today, and GI Joe rides delapidated bicycles and mules over the road in front of our station.

Toward the end of April, spring has come to the Garigliano Valley in all its glory. The field behind me is covered with red poppies. I have never seen poppies in full bloom before, and they remind me of stories I read of Flanders and World War I. The fruit trees all blossom, and their odor contrasts strongly with that of the acrid powder smoke. Lilies in a tin can even adorn the tables in our aid station.

The Germans are now firing propaganda leaflets. The stories they contain are most amusing. They speak of soldiers selling apples on Wall Street and of fat Jewish capitalists dating our girls back home.

Letters from home arrive regularly and boost morale. Only one letter from home makes me furious. My mother speaks of threatened unemployment in the U.S.A. since war contracts are rumored to be on the decline. It sounds as though some folks at home are enjoying this endless killing and are afraid that it may come to a sudden end and some may lose their well-paying jobs. Now I wish that some of these people were over here with us.

On April 20, 1944, I renew an old friendship. Capt. Charlie Jones suddenly walks into my station. Jones is with the Collecting Company of the 85th Division and out on a reconnaissance tour. He speaks of relieving us shortly. His division has just moved up. The last time I saw Charlie was as an intern at Lankenau Hospital in 1942. Neither he nor I had any inkling that either one of us was in Italy—yet we would meet in this old farmhouse. Over a gallon of wine we exchange more pleasant memories.

On April 26, 1944, elements of the newly arrived 85th Division relieve us, and we move to the rear for the second time. Again, we quarter in a city of pyramidal tents and are on garrison routine. Since I am trying to keep up my log of events as accurately as possible, I must find out somehow how the other Allied fronts are doing since this might have a bearing on our activity in Italy. The Army paper *Stars and Stripes* gives some information. Visiting officers from division headquarters know a little or can at least transmit rumors. Regimental headquarters knows more than battalion, and I must inquire from whom I can. Some letters from home are also informative. I knew that the Allies had landed at Anzio on January 1, 1944. I now learn that the troops involved were British commandos and division troops, the American 1st Armored Division, 3d Infantry Division, units of the 82d Airborne Division, and a regimental combat team of the 45th Infantry Division. GI Joe knows nothing of all this. The troops at Anzio are still bogged down and have been waiting for over three months for us to take Rome from the south. At the present time two American divisions are in the vicinity of Cassino. To their right are troops under British command, and these consist of many nationalities, Algerians and Moroccans under French officers, Poles, Indians, New Zealanders, and Canadians. On our left or western flank are still British divisions. I learn less about our front than the others.

The Russians are already about four hundred miles west of Moscow and only about one hundred miles from the Lithuanian border and only about three hundred miles from eastern Poland. In the Pacific the Solomon and Marshall islands have been cleared. I can't find out what is happening in Burma.

On May 3, 1944, Lieut. Gen. Mark W. Clark, Fifth Army commander, visits our rear area for an inspired pep talk. We now know that the next few days will constitute a big buildup. General Clark's closing words sound ominous. "I promise you it will be soon."

On May 6, 1944, I am back on the front. Once again I sit in an old farmhouse in the middle of the Garigliano Valley, but approximately two miles south of my former position. The enemy cannot observe us, however, since the valley is now overgrown with lush vegetation. I must strain my neck to glimpse over the tall grass and bushes in order to see the mountains to our north. I am told that we are in reserve, and it is rumored that D day is not far off. The moon is full and the birds sing at midnight, confused by its brightness. Around our farmhouse is a small vineyard. Strolling over small paths and through neglected grottos, I stumble upon tanks, cannons, and half-tracks. They have all been so well hidden and camouflaged that I do not see them until I am practically upon them. The buildup of weapons has truly been tremendous during the past month. The entire valley is loaded with death-dealing armor, all hidden and silent, ready to spit fire and death on command, but now just waiting, waiting for the big day, the day on which everyone can prove his worth. General Clark spoke the truth. It will be soon.

I do nothing all day but just sit and wait. The battalion troops are dug into the meadow or quartered in other deserted farmhouses. They, too, only wait. Finally on May 11, 1944, the battalion commandant calls all officers to a conference. We meet in the kitchen of a battered house. The colonel announces that D day will be today. H hour will be 11:00 P.M. All weapons in the valley will open fire simultaneously, pound the enemy relentlessly for one hour, then troops will overrun the dazed enemy before he has a chance to recover from the constant shelling. The 351st Infantry Regiment will attack on our left, the 350th Infantry Regiment to our right, and our 1st and 2d Battalions will attack through the center. My battalion will be in division reserve, ready to attack wherever additional reinforcements will be needed. For the first twenty-four hours my battalion will be a spectator, then push into the fight where the opposition is strongest. The 85th Division will fight on our left flank, and the French colonial troops will be on our right flank. I learn nothing further. I write a brief V-mail letter home and attend religious services after supper. For supper I eat little. From 7:00 P.M. to 10:00 P.M. I play chess with one of my sergeants. I can't concentrate, and play blackjack for twenty dollars a card with officers from Headquarters Company. I either go into this fight loaded or broke. What's the difference? I win over two hundred dollars and now worry where to carry all that money. It is 10:55 P.M. Everyone is silent. For the first time in my life I am counting off minutes, then seconds.

Breakthrough of the Gustav Line

MAY 11, 1944–JUNE 13, 1944

11:00 P.M. — H hour of D day. Huge leaping sheets of bright flashes illuminate the entire Garigliano Valley and are followed by the thunderous roar of a thousand cannons. The foundations of our house rock from the blasts. The roar of the guns is so deafening that you can shout at the man standing next to you and still not be heard. Tons of steel fly through the air. The murderous roar of the guns is so loud I can't possibly tell if the Germans are shooting back. I venture outside the house and see sheets of flame spring from behind every bush. The hills to our north are spattered with phosphorus bursts that illuminate the entire horizon. I don't see how the Germans can stand much of this. For one entire hour the terrific barrage continues. Our attack troops jump off with the first muzzle roar. Their attack must be successful, for they could not possibly have better artillery support. I only hope that our artillery keeps shooting well ahead of them and will not be short, or we will be swamped with casualties. At twelve midnight the shooting slackens off, the troops calling only for fire as needed. From a distance I can just about tell which objective seems to be next, since all guns suddenly seem to aim their missiles on that particular target, the mountain to be taken looking like a volcano with craters bursting forth from all its sides. Being in division reserve, I don't know when we will be called upon to move out. I hope it will be daylight. At 4:00 A.M. I finally fall asleep, the explosions still rumbling on.

I am up at 7:00 A.M. We have spectator seats. Through field glasses I can clearly see French tanks rumbling into Castelforte to our right. Goums (North Africans in the French Expeditionary Force) on foot follow behind. A heap of rubble seems to hide a German self-propelled gun. A short flame burst from a tank's muzzle, and the heap of rubble is enveloped in a sheet of flames. The self-propelled gun has been pulverized. The foot troops rush by and surround the next objective. The fighting for Castelforte lasts all day.

We sit and wait. I do nothing. All the mountains in front of us are enveloped in a haze of smoke. Artillery fire never stops. I have no idea how our troops are progressing. By nightfall we still have not moved. At 9:00 P.M. we finally receive sudden orders to move out. Santa Maria Infante, a strong point in the German Gustav Line, has not fallen. The 351st Infantry is still battling to enter this rubbled village. The high ground to its north must be taken, for it is from there that the Germans are raining heavy artillery fire on all approaches to the town. Our first move is to Tufo, a small village in the mountains directly to our north. Twenty-four hours ago Tufo was still in no-man's land— now it is ours. The small dirt road leading to Tufo has already been cleared of mines, and we can go by jeep. As our jeeps bounce over the pockmarked mountain trail in total blackout, we are rocked by constant artillery blasts. Our large guns are all placed along the shoulders of the trail, and their sudden fire actually shakes my jeep from side to side. My helmet is jolted from my head. I can feel the heat waves from the guns' muzzles against my cheeks and am temporarily deaf and blinded by the guns' explosions.

In Tufo we are in a midnight traffic jam. The few undamaged houses are occupied by aid stations, headquarters, and supply personnel of the 351st Infantry. Our troops only increase the congestion in the village. The one and only road through Tufo is narrow, and one vehicle only can pass at a time. With troops also using the road, vehicles crawl at a snail's pace. Ammunition trucks, water jeeps, ambulances, mules, and foot troops fight each other all night for the right of way. The cursing doughboys walking in total darkness suffer sprains and bruises, and vehicles frequently run over their feet. My sergeants locate a small hotel in the center of town, and we move in, hanging our Red Cross flag on its door. It's not much of a hotel. The first and second stories have been shot away, but the basement and courtyard are undamaged. I treat casualties as they drift to us. Mostly sprained and broken ankles. I see only a few gunshot wounds, for our battalion has not yet begun to fight. Tomorrow morning we shall move out of Tufo, up the Minturno–Santa Maria Infante Road, bypass resisting Santa Maria, and take the high ground to the northwest of the town. For approximately one hour I sit in the open-air courtyard of my aid station, potted palms still standing on a beautiful flagstone patio. Shells whine overhead continuously, and gun flashes illuminate the sky. If our basement has withstood one year's pounding in no-man's land, it will probably hold up another night.

May 13, 1944. It is 9:00 A.M. The sun is already warm, and I can sense that this will be a very hot day. My battalion moves into the attack. We walk out of Tufo in a column of ducks, five yards' interval between men, one column on each side of the dirt road. My two medical jeeps follow the rear of the column. The order is to move along the road toward Santa Maria Infante, for which the 351st Infantry Regiment is still battling fiercely. The road runs east-west, and the Germans are on high mountains to the north and have a commanding view of the entire road. They must be watching our every move. This road is surely zeroed in, but for some strange reason the Germans are not shelling it. Continuous mortar, machine-gun and small-arms fire is heard coming from Santa Maria. Water and ammunition jeeps race over the road past our columns and shower us with clouds of dust. I see jeeps loaded with wounded speed to the rear. Many of the casualties seem to have head wounds, and their bandages are soaked with blood. I stare at them in amazement. Gangs of prisoners, hands raised, dirty and dusty, wounded and confused, are herded past us. The fight raging ahead of us must be very stubborn. At noon our column comes

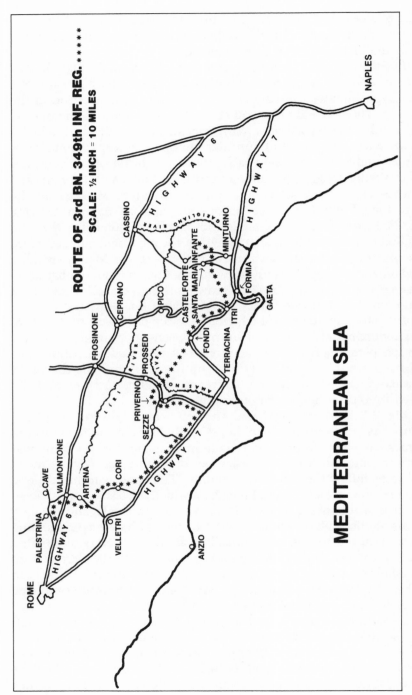

2 The Push to Rome from the Garigliano River

to a halt. A cemetery with only its church wall standing is on my left. To the right side of the road is an upward-sloping field. We are about three miles from Santa Maria Infante. My battalion is ordered to disperse into the field and await further orders. I hide my two jeeps behind the battered church wall along the left side of the road. Across the road from my jeeps is an eight-foot-deep gully about two yards wide. This will serve as temporary aid station.

Our first casualty occurs almost immediately. The field into which the men have dispersed is still loaded with mines. One man has already stepped on one, and his right foot is blown off at the ankle. I give him morphine and apply an emergency dressing, hail a passing jeep which momentarily stops, load him, and off he goes to the rear. Our gully is very narrow, and I must evacuate fast and cannot permit wounded to accumulate. I climb up the slope of the ditch into the field to find the battalion commander. I would like to have advance information of our next move. The entire situation does not make sense to me. Fierce fighting rages ahead of us, and we are dispersed in a mine field just sitting and waiting. The Germans can clearly see us and must be getting ready to pick us off at any moment. Walking toward the commander, I narrowly miss stepping on several mines myself; they are well buried and only the detonator is visible above the ground, resembling an aluminum canteen cap. My orders are brief and rather vague. I am to remain in my present ditch behind the church wall along the road. My location will be the battalion's rear aid station. Our troops will not proceed to Santa Maria but move across the road through the mined cemetery and into a valley, then up Mount Civita, from which the Germans are directing fire on the approaches to Santa Maria. An advance aid station under command of Captain Felts will follow the troops and set up at the base of Mount Civita. When this is accomplished, a messenger will be sent back to guide me and my handful of medics to the advance aid station.

One by one the doughboys cautiously slip through the mine field, and in two hours all have disappeared into the valley. At 4:00 P.M. I hear abundant small-arms fire and know that they have met resistance.

The road in front of me is now clogged with vehicles. Tanks have been called up to help the 351st Infantry smash into Santa Maria. The tanks are slowly rumbling over the road at twenty-yard intervals, and the supply jeeps weave back and forth between them. Foot troops can no longer use the road, it is so crowded with vehicles. At 5:00 P.M. all traffic on the road stops. It is overloaded with vehicles trying to push into Santa Maria. The Germans must have been waiting for this moment. An unmerciful barrage of 88s is poured in on us. The Germans' artillery, which has been silent all day, has now opened up with everything at its command. One shell falls directly into the open turret of a tank, and the vehicle explodes in flames. All occupants are killed. Tank after tank is hit and disabled; they are jammed too close in formation to dodge the incoming shells. A passing jeep receives a direct hit and disintegrates in a cloud of smoke and dust. Whining shrapnel fills the air, and chunks of hot metal land in my gully. We are swamped with casualties occurring directly in front of us. Wounded jump out of burning vehicles and run to us. Others crawl along the road to reach us. The direct hit which I myself expect at any moment fortunately never occurs. Shells explode on the field above us and on all sides. I am really in a hot spot and have no business here. Where in the hell is my guide? Why does he not return and lead us away from here? I can't sweat this murderous fire out much longer.

I have little time to bemoan my situation. We pull wounded after wounded into the gully, hastily put on a bandage to still the flow of blood, give them shots of morphine, load them onto one of our jeeps, and rush them to the rear, away from this crowded hell hole. We do not even have time to write out emergency medical tags, the tags put on all casualties listing the type of wound or illness and the emergency treatment rendered. I don't know where my jeep driver takes them. There must be some type of medical installation to the rear, for he makes one trip every thirty minutes. He is a courageous fellow, drives through constant fire, and never loses his head or nerve. Now the Krauts are firing airbursts over us, and these fragments, too, shower our ditch. One man already wounded and awaiting dressing is struck in the shoulder. I have no choice but to seek better shelter. My jeeps closely hugging the battered church wall in front of us have been joined by a tank also seeking refuge. During each barrage of airbursts we crawl under the tank, and when it is over we rush back into our gully and treat newly arrived wounded. The entire situation is a nightmare. Perhaps my guide has stepped on a mine and lies dead in the valley?

It is almost two hours until sundown. I cannot wait for news from my battalion any longer. A jeep stops at my station and drops off several wounded. I ask the driver if he knows of any infantry command post up the road. He states he thinks there is one about a mile below Santa Maria. If this is true, this command post may have radio contact with my battalion. By radio I might then learn of its location. Not wanting to lose my vehicles, I choose to walk toward Santa Maria rather than drive. At a moment when I think the shelling has somewhat slackened, I depart. I walk rapidly, neck retracted and with strained ears anticipating the next barrage. I scurry anxiously past burning tanks and overturned trucks. I have walked less than one-half mile when the first barrage of 88s arrives. I am certain that I shall be hit. With each burst I automatically fall to the ground, then scramble back to my feet and run twice as fast. For some stupid reason I think that the field off the road to my left is safer than the road itself since fewer shells are bursting there. With one giant leap I jump off the road's shoulder and into the sloping meadow. A sudden hiss rushes past my ears. I expect to be blown to pieces. I have no time to fall but instead am knocked over by the blast and showered with dirt. I lie breathlessly. Within seconds I realize that I can move both legs and arms. I have no pain. I frankly expected death; however, I am not even scratched.

Bracing my hands to get up, I almost set off a mine buried directly in front of me. In my stupidity and gripped with panic, I have jumped into a mine field! I must get back on the highway. I muster all the strength I have left and, side-stepping dangerously exposed mines like a football player does would-be tacklers, leap back onto the road. I continue my mad dash along the road until I have reached the ruins of a house, supposedly a command post. Wet with perspiration, I stumble panting through the doorway and to my utter disappointment learn that this rubble heap is occupied only by a wire-laying crew. I have followed a false lead and have almost been killed. Now I must get back to the cemetery and my men. I can't possibly run through all that fire again. The jeep of the wire crew is ready to leave for the rear. I jump into the back seat. The driver has traveled this road all day. He is magnificent. At fifty miles per hour and kicking up a tremendous cloud of dust, he zig-zags past burning debris and shell craters. Incoming shells pockmark the road behind us. In less than two minutes I am back behind the church wall of the cemetery.

The irony of it all is that while I was gone, my guide arrived. He is not very helpful. The poor fellow is shell shocked, shakes all over, sobs, and is in a severe state of anxiety. To get back to us he had dodged mortars and airbursts and had stepped on a dud mine — its cap fluttering two feet into the air but the mine not going off. He is incoherent and at this moment a very unreliable guide. I insist that he must pull himself together and show us the way. Finally, he regains some composure and agrees to make the effort.

We cross the road, snake through the mined cemetery and into the valley. Our jeeps can't follow since we are going cross-country. My drivers remain behind and we attempt to hand-carry our medical chests. After the first five hundred yards we find that this is impossible. The chests are too heavy and cumbersome and the going is too slow. We empty the chests and throw them away. We stuff most of their contents into our aid kits and musette bags; we fashion bags out of our blankets and fill them with medical dressings. Trying to follow the trail of our troops is not difficult at all. I could do so without a guide. All I need follow are the discarded gas masks, blankets, empty mortar shell casings, and machine-gun cartridge boxes. We proceed cautiously and walk over the same path the troops before us have made. By doing this, we hope to avoid mines. We skip from cover to cover, running fifty yards at a time, then resting, but at the same time surveying the trail ahead of us for our next dash. Shells are still hitting the Santa Maria Infante road, but these are now way over our heads. Only airbursts annoy us. We hit the ground frequently as they explode directly above us. I treat wounded here and there. They are lying on the trail. Our forward group with the troops did not have time to care for them. Lieutenant Thompson lies under a bush with a shell fragment in his abdomen. He is in great pain and so happy to see me. I dress his wound and administer morphine. I lay him on his blanket and cover him with my own. I mark the spot where he is lying and shall send litter bearers to him as soon as I have reached our forward station. We follow this procedure with each litter case we meet along the trail. The ambulatory wounded tag along with us.

We reach our forward station at dusk. It is really not a station, just a location. We are at the base of a hill. Its reverse slope is steep and we dig in. Our troops are to climb high Mount Civita during the night and surprise the enemy at dawn. Our boys have fought all day yet they shall climb all night. We medics are busy, too. It takes until midnight to bandage all wounded and send back for the litter cases left along the trail. After the wounded have been collected and grouped together in one spot, the liaison man from Collecting Company contacts his outfit, and they are evacuated by litter crews to the nearest accessible trail over which ambulances can travel. At 1:00 A.M. I dig my slit trench and practically fall into it from sheer exhaustion. My first day of actual fighting lies behind me. I shall never forget it. I have not really slept for the past forty-three hours. Another session like yesterday, and I doubt if I shall last. The shells are still roaring overhead onto the Santa Maria road as I try to shut all the events of the past two days out of my mind.

At sunrise on May 15, 1944, we move approximately one-quarter of a mile around the mountain base to a deserted farmhouse. Our troops are on top of huge Mount Civita. The twenty-eight 88-mm guns that have been shooting up the road to Santa Maria are captured. German wounded stagger down the mountain to us. Some lay on the slopes uncared-for all night; nevertheless, they are still insolent and won't talk. Most of them are still too confused to actually realize that they have been captured. Our day is relatively quiet and the flow of casualties not too heavy, since we have taken the enemy by surprise during the night, and most of the casualties have been suffered by the Germans. The flies and fleas in our house give us more trouble than anything else. That evening we watch German planes drop flares and bombs on finally captured Santa Maria. Tomorrow morning we shall set out again, this time to climb the Monti Aurunci Ridge, the tallest mountains of which are over fifteen hundred meters high. During the night two mules on which to carry our medical supplies are brought to our aid station.

May 15, 1944. We leave our farmhouse at noon and follow our battalion of troops walking single file, the direction northwest, to the base of the Aurunci mountain ridge. These mountains run parallel to the western coast of Italy from Minturno to Itri and begin their upward slope from the coast approximately two to three miles inland. We are to walk along the ridge, our mission to reach Itri as quickly as possible and to cut the Itri–Pico road. This would cut the Germans' supply line to Gaeta and Formia in the low country to our left. The U.S. 85th Division is fighting here, trying to push up Highway 7, the Via Appia, and the lower highway to Rome.

The climb up the Monti Aurunci Ridge is tremendous. We follow a goat trail and at times must clamber on all fours. The path is straight up. One of our mules carrying cartons of plasma and litters with it falls down the slope when halfway up. We release the other animal, for the footing is too difficult. Our only solution is to hand-carry all our plasma, litters, and dressings. With supplies distributed among nineteen men, we finally manage to carry a fairly large quantity by hand. It makes climbing awkward, but we have no choice to do anything else. The higher we climb, the barer the mountains become. On these high slopes we see all the deserted Jerry foxholes — dug into rocks and all over four feet deep. In their hurry to retreat they have left their packs, mess gear, helmets, letters, guns, and first-aid kits behind. We would like to gather some of these articles together as souvenirs, but we are already so loaded down with equipment that we must pass it all up. Near the top of the ridge there is no vegetation. The terrain is all rock. There is no cover except under the overhanging ledges of large boulders and in the crevices formed by the soil's erosion. Our welcome near the top of the ridge is not a pleasant one. German artillery and mortar positions down in the valley to our left spot our column silhouetted against the skyline. We receive constant airbursts and mortar barrages. For cover I scurry under the overhanging edges of the boulders. For protection against airbursts you need cover directly above you. Fortunately, all our wounded remain ambulatory and can tag along with us. We cannot evacuate them along the trail over which we have come — the road back is much too hazardous.

Approximately every mile we descend into a deep ravine; most of our casualties occur on either entering or leaving these deep gorges. The Germans know that climbing up or down the sides of these gullies takes time and that our column must practically come to a halt. Most of the Kraut mortars are therefore directed into the ravines. Unfortunately, many Italian civilians who have fled the lowlands have also sought refuge here. Consequently, each ravine is a nightmare. Shrapnel strikes both civilians and doughboys. The opposing sides of the ravine give each exploding shell an echo, which adds to the fright of all the civilians. Women and children scream and the soldiers curse. The call for "Medic" is heard constantly. We hurriedly set up an aid station at the bottom of each ravine, usually in the thatch-roofed huts used by goatherders. We cannot look for cover but must take our chances. A small spring or stream often flows along the bottom of the ravine, and we desperately need water to cleanse the wounds and replenish our canteens. It has not rained for three weeks, and thirst adds to the misery of the wounded. We do not have time to give the wounded much attention. We often start the plasma infusions and must leave the man before the plasma has run in. To keep up with the troops and not get lost in the darkness is our big problem. The walking wounded will find their way down into the valley at dawn and will inform the rear-echelon troops of the litter cases left in the ravines. I have never heard of any men being forgotten.

Upon clambering out of one ravine and back onto the ridge, ten men are suddenly felled by one shell. It is too dark to see them, and I can only hear their moans. I or one of my medical technicians crawl to them and whenever possible pull them into caves. Throwing a blanket over myself and the wounded, I turn on a flashlight and treat the wound as best I can. I can't apply splints, for I have none. I usually use the man's rolled blanket instead, and this leaves him shivering in the cold all night. I hate to leave these men behind, but I am forced to move on. Here again, a lightly wounded comrade will remain with them and seek aid in the morning.

We continue our push. We walk all night and at the same time watch the 85th Division raise hell down in the valley to our left. Tank fights rage along the Via Appia. By the flash of the guns and exploding shells, we can tell how far we are ahead of them and above them. Soon we are so far out in front and so confused by the terrain that we must radio back to our supporting artillery to throw phosphorus shells onto our objective. This done, we plod on until daybreak. To rest and sleep is not even taken under consideration. The enemy is on the run, and we must follow. All night and all day we continue our trek over the mountains. The only occasions for rest are the one or two hours it often takes for the battalion commander to receive new orders once an objective is reached. Then we simply fall to the ground and sleep. Artillery and mortar fire harass us continuously. Our artillery cannot counterfire since we are too far ahead, and the doughboys must therefore engage the German artillery and mortar positions with bazookas, portable mortars, and grenades. Many die as heroes, wiping out positions single-handed, in order to let our column advance. At times we are completely stalled for hours, pinned down by mortar fire. Finally, mule pack artillery is called upon to support us. When the German guns are thus silenced, we move on. At dusk on May 19, we approach the outskirts of Itri. It has taken us six days to slug our way ten air miles along the Aurunci Mountain ridges.

May 19, 1944. It is shortly before midnight. We are trying to enter Itri from the south and are staying off all the main highways leading into the town, since German tanks are still lurking behind curves in the road waiting to shoot up any approaching vehicles. To enter by way of the surrounding hills, we are forced to scramble through olive groves. There is no moon, and the night is pitch black. Walking through the groves, men slip off the six-foot-high terraces. Our column frequently comes to a halt, for we do not know which way we are going. Our battalion scouts, our lead company, and battalion commander have advanced forward so rapidly that our main body of troops is now far behind and lost. By frequent radio calls we try to locate them and ask them to send a guide back for us. While we wait, men fall asleep on their feet. They are exhausted after their six-day chase over the mountains. We hope to get a good night's sleep in Itri.

After a two-hour wait in the olive grove, the guide from our advanced group finally finds us and leads our column to an old farm on the Itri-Pico road approximately one-quarter mile from the town of Itri itself. The colonel is raging mad; he has been waiting here for two hours; we should have followed him closer; now we are at least three hours behind the running enemy. There will be no sleep tonight. We cannot even wait for rations or water. The Germans are on the run and we must race after them — straight up Via Appia or Highway 7 to Fondi. We are reminded to quit beefing. We have no right to be tired. We will get rations tomorrow; tonight we must chase the fleeing Krauts. Aching backs, blistered feet, hunger, and thirst must be ignored. After all, there's a war on, so says the colonel. He orders the battalion onto the highway, one column to walk on each side of the road. Our march shall be through Itri, then up the main highway north in the direction of Rome. I, K, L, and M companies will rotate every six hours as lead company; the medics will bring up the rear. One-half of the medical detachment will follow the troops on foot; the other half will set up in the northern outskirts of Itri to receive any casualties that might occur on the march. I am told to set up in Itri. Having received orders, we move out, first to pass through Itri itself. I follow the foot troops in my jeep, which has finally caught up with us after ten days. I remain approximately one hundred yards behind the column, eyeing each house we pass as a potential station in which to seek cover at any moment should our troops suddenly be shelled. The battalion's march through Itri occurs without casualties. As my jeep crosses what looks like the town square, several mortar rounds crash in on us. I am stunned. I thought the Germans had fled the town. However, they must still be in the hills around Itri. They must be shelling every time they hear vehicles. They probably have no idea that they have been bypassed. As dark as it is tonight, I don't see how anyone can tell where you are going or what ground has been taken. By morning we shall probably have confused Germans behind us, in front of us, and on all sides.

One shell explodes on the street, and shrapnel bounces off the jeep. Instinctively I leap from the vehicle and jump into what appears to be a shallow ditch. Instead, it is a dry moat eight feet deep. In my plunge downward I scrape both my hands raw on the cement walls, lose my helmet, and sprain my right ankle. One of my men falls on top of me. After coming to our senses, we climb out of the moat. In the darkness we spot a shot-up church and seek refuge in its basement, hanging our Red Cross flag on its door so that our location is readily seen. The basement is filled with Italian civilians crying and praying. There is no light, and I can't see much. Off one corner of the basement is a small room that apparently belonged to the priest. It has no windows. Here we can light a candle and treat casualties. Fortunately, we have none. The boys on the highway must be doing all right. It is 3:00 A.M., and we might be able to sleep three hours until daybreak. Completely exhausted, I lie down on a narrow, red plush sofa with broken springs. After several hours I awaken. My face is swollen and itches. I have been bitten by bedbugs, which are all over the couch, are crawling up the walls, and are now in my clothing. I am a remarkable sight as we leave the church at 6:00 A.M. to catch up with our walking troops. My jaw is swollen, my left eye is shut, my hands are bandaged from the scrapes the night before, and my right ankle is sprained. Italy is a hell of a place. When not plagued by the Krauts, we are victims of vermin.

We leave the battered Itri on Highway 7 and head north. Our troops have walked five miles during the night, but by jeep we catch up to them in less than fifteen minutes. They are a tired, rough-looking bunch. The column is momentarily halted and strung out for over a mile. The men sit on the sides of the road—some sleep—others eat C rations. Most have over a week's growth of beard. None have washed for the past nine days. Their feet are blistered. The morale in spite of everything is good. "On to Rome, then home," is the slogan running through everyone's mind. It's that thought of getting back home that keeps the men going.

Soon the column is back on its feet, and the march continues. I have a very peculiar sensation as I string along at the rear. Who is on our flanks? We are walking up the main Italian highway to Rome and meet no resistance! That is most unlike the Germans. The low hills on either side of us must be swarming with Jerries. If they want to, they can pick us off like ducks in a shooting gallery. We are never attacked by any large groups of the enemy, but constantly harassed by small die-hard groups of Krauts. These snipe at our column with rifle grenades and mortars. What disturbs me most is that I can never tell where the sniper fire is coming from. Shells are shot at close range, and you have no time to think. I duck automatically at the sound of everything. I am fully aware of the fact that once you hear the shell, the danger is long past. The ducking reflex, however, is hard to eliminate, and I always feel foolish afterward.

Our tanks cannot keep up with us. Theoretically they should follow our column. The Krauts, however, have blown huge craters into the road at regular intervals, and these must first be repaired before the tanks can support us. The craters are usually mined, as well as the road shoulders and the paths off the road surrounding them. Each crater is therefore truly a hazard, for both the foot troops and the tanks. The lead scouts are the most frequent casualties, for they have no time to wait for the mine-sweeping crews but must take chances. If the center of the crater is not mined, then the ground around it is. At each crater the same question arises—where are the mines this time? The shoe-mine casualties are heavy and demoralizing. A man's foot is usually blown loose at the ankle, leaving the mangled foot dangling on shredded tendons; dirt and rocks imbed themselves into the splintered stump. Additional puncture wounds of both legs and groin make the agony worse. I have no time to clean the wounds. All I can do is administer morphine for the pain and apply a thick padded dressing; splints are useless, since the foot cannot be saved anyway—it has lost its blood supply. These wounds bleed remarkably little. It is because they are so contused. Only very occasionally am I forced to stop hemorrhage. When I do so, I simply incorporate the clamp in the dressing. The men are left along the side of the road with walking casualties and are evacuated by ambulances, which follow the road repair crews and tanks. The latter try to follow us for support as rapidly as possible. Their guns are more effective against sniper nests than those of the foot troops.

Along the Via Appia, German thoroughness in defense is very noticeable and impressive. Approximately every twenty yards along the entire road are six-foot-deep foxholes clearly marked with a pole and sign reading "Deckung," or cover. Such pre-prepared holes must have been a blessing to Germans caught on the road by strafing Allied planes. Their abandoned and demolished "Volkswagens" are so well camouflaged with paint and shrubbery that you do not spot them until nearly upon them. Even the fatigues of the dead Germans lying on the sides of the road are camouflaged, and the corpses are usually spotted not because they are visible but because of their odor.

We approach the outskirts of Fondi at 3:00 P.M. The men are tired, dusty, and thirsty. Their feet are blistered and their nerves on edge. Fondi is supposedly another Nazi stronghold, a key defense town in the so-called Hitler Line. At this moment Fondi looks deserted. High mountains loom to the north of it. Our troops cautiously approach. If the Germans have left the town, they can only be in the high mountains ahead of us and are probably at this very moment looking right down our throats, just waiting to let us have everything they have left. I hear only sporadic rifle fire from our lead companies. One of the first buildings I pass on entering Fondi is a bakery shop just ten feet off the highway to my right. This shop is built of solid field stone, has two floors above it and a large brick building directly in front of it. A small cobble-stoned alley leads to its side entrance. I immediately pick this bakery as my aid station, until our troops have passed through Fondi and seized the first hills to the north.

My choice is timely and good. Bedlam breaks out on the highway the moment I enter the bakery. German 88s and mortars plaster the street and houses at its edge. Our tanks have moved up and are sitting in the center of the town, catching all the heavy stuff. Infantry seeks only momentary shelter in the houses and keeps edging forward from door to door, trying to move through the town and into the hills. If only our planes could support us and bomb those hills! Planes, however, never seem to be around when you need them most. My jeep drivers are marvelous. They zig-zag between tanks and shell bursts, pick the wounded off the road, and bring them to the bakery. Time and time again they make record round trips under heavy fire. They rely on speed, have some slight faith in the large red crosses painted on the hoods, mumble many prayers, and bank on lots of luck.

Casualties are heavy. The fight for Fondi lasts a good three hours. The floor of the bakery is soon covered with wounded. We work rapidly. Most wounds are caused by mortar and artillery fragments, and compound fractures are numerous. For the first time the ambulance can pull right up to the station and evacuate the casualties as soon as they are dressed and splinted, and this prevents us from becoming overcrowded. The bakery also has spring water, and we can actually wash some of the dirt out of the wounds prior to dressing. For the first time in two weeks I enjoy myself. I can see what I am doing, apply adequate dressings, give men water to drink, and stay with them for a little while. Most of the serious casualties even receive a unit of plasma to combat shock. While on the move we seldom had time to give plasma, and this little station is like heaven. Head wounds are many and serious. Most occur in tank crews when tanks take a direct hit. Many die on arrival—their heads are covered with blood, and on examination their skulls feel like shattered egg shells. The crunching and slipping sensation the broken skull plates impart to the hand and the deep coma of the patient tells even the unexperienced aid man that death is imminent. Our morgue in the backyard is soon full.

By 7:00 P.M. the heavy fire has ceased, and enemy shelling is only sporadic. It looks as though by nightfall Fondi will be in our hands. We won't be able to spend the night here, however, since we are already alerted to keep moving and ascend Mount Passignano. That's the infantry. You almost kill yourself to take a town, then can't enjoy it for even a few hours. Most of the men are too tired at this stage to care about anything. They'll keep moving, and if they can't walk, they'll crawl.

We wait in Fondi until it is totally dark. I wouldn't mind remaining here for the night. The Germans who lived in this bakery lived in style. They left behind empty cases of gin, wine, and food. Even a portable icebox has been abandoned. Their helmets, gas masks, and stacks of letters received from home have been left lying scattered over the floor in their hurry to depart. I read a few of their letters in which the families are thankful for the gifts sent them from Italy. Both the Krauts and their families, however, are apparently just as homesick as we are.

In the backyard is a small goldfish pond fed by a spring. Just before nightfall I take a complete bath at its edge—the first washing in nine days. I am told it is the nineteenth of May.

At 11:00 P.M. Fondi is completely in our hands, and the battalion moves out. It is probably best not to remain for the night anyway, since Jerry will probably bomb it, hoping that we have remained in town. The mountains to the north are safer, and the enemy snipers and mortar crews can be more easily surrounded in the dark. Dead tired, we walk through shot-up Fondi and into the hills. An occasional German shell still screams into the town and explodes off the highway, reminding us that the German rear guard will remain alert during the night. In total darkness we stagger over mountain mule trails until well beyond midnight, finally establishing our aid station together with battalion headquarters in a stone hut on the slope of a heavily wooded hill. The night is too dark to see anything. The doughboys are in the forest around us. Carbine, BAR, and rifle fire is answered by German "paper cutters" all night long. One of my aid men brings in a German wounded. A bullet has entered his chest below his left shoulder blade and has emerged by way of a large hole below his left nipple. He is smoking a cigarette. As he exhales, smoke pours out of the holes in his chest. He is not bleeding, but grunts with each breath and coughs frequently. He is perfectly happy with the first-aid dressing I apply and asks for nothing else. He considered his wound a very casual one. In about twelve hours he will probably be in shock. Other minor gunshot wounds come to us the rest of the night. Both the wounded and we get very little sleep, since our stone shack is also filled with whimpering Italian civilians. Babies and children cry incessantly. Whenever gunfire breaks out on the outside, the women scream. Millions of fleas add to our discomfort, and we dig and scratch the whole night through.

At 7:00 A.M. on May 21 we are on the move again. I have had approximately one hour of sleep. The orders are to take some mountain approximately three thousand yards to our north. It is a formidable hill mass — several mountains merge, meeting at the top to form a sort of a huge pyramid, its slopes consisting of many deep draws and crevices. On the highest peak stands what resembles an old deserted and broken-down mansion or castle. I believe the mountain is called Cima Del Monte; I am not sure. I have climbed so many mountains lately, all with so many different names, so that I am somewhat confused.

We assemble at the base of what I think is Cima Del Monte. The peaks are our objective. We are told we shall probably meet stiff resistance. Somewhere on our right flank are the French Goums, and we are told to stick a band of adhesive tape on the rear of our helmets just in case the battle should rage through the night and the Goums and we should run together in the darkness. The French colonials have been ordered not to practice their knifework on their allies. The latter they identify by tape on their helmets. All this is just another pleasant thought added to the already existing suspense.

On the map I see no houses — only mule trails and goatherders' huts. It looks as though we shall again have open-air aid stations. I am very much concerned over the evacuation of the wounded. The grades are practically vertical in spots. Before we begin our ascent, I arrange with the liaison man from the Collecting Company to set up litter-bearer stations of four men each, every one thousand yards. It will take one squad of four stretcher bearers at least several hours to traverse that distance.

Our hike in single file up the most passable draw is slow from the beginning. Rocks, boulders, brush, and pot holes hinder our ascent. Often we halt for a half hour for the lead company to check its bearings. By noon we are halfway up to the top. At 4:00 P.M. we have covered three-fourths of the distance. The lead company is only several hundred yards from the top. As expected, hell and fire suddenly descend upon us. The Krauts pour 88-mm shells into our draw, and mortar fire onto all the approaching slopes. The lead company is met with a barrage of machine-pistol fire and is soon engaged in hand-to-hand combat. We have no cover to speak of. We hide under boulders and in crevices. Casualties are heavy. Moans, groans, and curses are heard everywhere. We are always on the bottom, and the Krauts always on top. The terrain is constantly in the enemy's favor. I always feel as though I am being led to slaughter. Most of the boys are.

We treat the wounded where they lie and hastily apply bandages. All we need do is stem the flow of blood, then direct litter bearers to the spot. We can spend only a few moments on each man. The constant hail of shrapnel sends us all sprawling every few minutes; we pull wounded under the ledges of boulders so that they are protected, and move on.

At nightfall we are still engaged in bitter fighting. I can faintly make out two goat huts approximately two hundred yards to my right, but farther down the hill. I realize, however, that it will be dark too soon for me to reach them. Consequently, I give up all hope of seeking shelter for the night and choose to remain with the troops of Headquarters Company. Near midnight we dig our foxholes into the stony ground. After two hours I have a hole just deep enough in which to barely curl up with my head below ground level. Having lost my blankets during the day's fighting, I shiver through the night. The past day has been hot, perhaps 85 degrees, but the temperature now must be about 40. We are fairly high in the hills, and the temperature changes are amazing. The shooting stops around midnight. All the troops are dug in. They have not reached the top. All three rifle companies are near the ridge, and the heavy weapons company below them in the center. We are just below the latter. In the morning the Krauts will have either pulled out or will have reorganized for a new fight. We shall see. Heavy artillery lulls us to sleep—cold, fitful, hungry, and very tired. I am thankful to still be alive.

The warm rays of the morning sun are most welcomed. I stretch my aching back and kinked joints and finally stop shivering. We have all dug our holes in very exposed positions. We are three-fourths of the way up Cima Del Monte. I neither see nor hear the enemy. I eat my last package of C rations for breakfast but have no water with which to wash down my dry biscuits and cheese. My next move is to find the hole of the headquarters commandant and learn the orders for the day. I know that it will be the same old order—take this mountain, then another and another; only the time of the move will be different.

About mid-morning I have located the spot of the battalion command post. I learn that my senior medical officer, Captain Felts, has spent the night in one of the goat huts farther down the slope and that most of the casualties drifted to these huts during the night. Now that it is daylight, the slopes are more thoroughly combed by litter squads, and all the stray wounded are collected; the dead are tagged and carried off by Special Service personnel. By noon we are all fairly well reorganized. We are ordered to continue our ascent, to take this mountain, then move on to Mount Rotundo, then Mount Alto. Our eventual objective is to continue slugging to the northwest and to cut the road running between Priverno and Prossedi. This secondary road connects Route 7 and Route 6, or the southern and middle highways to Rome. Both are constantly strafed by our fighters, and cutting the road between the two will force the Germans into the Sacco River Valley, where, because of difficult terrain, their retreat will be slowed and their panzers caught in a pincer maneuver.

Strangely enough, not a shot is fired all morning. The Germans must have pulled out. Our column moves slowly up the hill toward a wide saddle. The entire aid station moves along at the rear of the column. As the lead company crosses the saddle at the top, the Krauts let us have it with everything they have left. The saddle is zeroed in with 88s, and shells explode at minute intervals. Men have only several seconds to cross the saddle before the next barrage pours in. Many are hit, and our advance is slowed appreciably. Now mortar fire is again poured onto the slopes and on those waiting to cross. Casualties are so heavy we must remain behind and care for those that have fallen. My sergeants and I once again scramble halfway down the mountain to the goat huts and establish our station. At least we will have an enclosure in which to work. The straw roof protects us only from the sun but not from shells or shrapnel. However, we have no choice. In our hustle down the slope we fall frequently. Captain Felts, almost forty years old, shows signs of overexertion. On reaching the hut he very reluctantly asks me to check his heart; he thinks its rhythm is abnormal and his chest feels full. My examination reveals that his heart is fibrillating and he is on the verge of heart failure. I write out his emergency medical tag with great remorse. He has been a fine and brave companion and excellent medical officer, but a man over thirty-five is already too old for rugged mountain warfare. Now I am in full command of the medical support of this battalion and at a time when the situation looks mighty critical.

I choose to follow the troops with two of my sergeants. Until this mountain is taken, the hut will continue to be our aid station. Most of the heavy casualties are in the saddle, and I crawl back up the mountain to its immediate vicinity. Bedlam exists here. The only place where I can treat the boys is on a rock ledge; it has a roof of overhanging stone and is almost a small cave measuring about three by six feet; here I am safe from a direct overhead hit and am only twenty-five yards from the saddle. One of my sergeants together with company aid men drag the wounded to me. Sergeants Marceau and Torres do a magnificent job. Marceau remains with me, and Torres spots and runs to the fallen. Wounded after wounded are pulled into the cave, a dressing applied, and if able to walk or crawl, told to make their way down to the hut and away from this hot spot. Litter cases are placed close to the cliff's edge and await the stretcher bearers. Some lie and wait all day. Whenever a litter squad returns, they replenish me with plasma. The waiting litter cases receive as much plasma as we have time to give. Their bayoneted rifles serve as poles on which we hang the bottles of precious fluid. On two occasions plasma bottles are shattered by flying shrapnel, and we start all over with new infusions. Metal whirs through the air and bounces off the rocks. The casualties in the saddle increase. The troops finally decide to abandon this route and try for the ridges again. Here they run into small-arms fire and grenades. The stories of wounded coming to me off the ridge are fantastic. Men are shooting each other at a distance of five yards; grenades are tossed back and forth; some never fire a shot but simply rush upon the Krauts with bayonet; some of our men are fooled by false surrenders but never live to tell the tale. A German surrenders waving a white cloth in one hand and, when approached to be disarmed, shoots his would-be captor with a pistol hidden in his other hand.

At sundown the mountain is finally ours. The price has been high. The saddle, however, is still zeroed in, for the Germans apparently realize that the trail leading through it is the only one over which our supply mules can travel to replenish our boys who have forged ahead. Just as I have treated my last casualty, a long mule train led by Italian mule skinners appears directly below me, headed for the saddle. I sense a catastrophe in the making and decide to remain on the rock ledge until the mules have passed. The first five mules cross without incident, then the 88-mm barrage resumes. The sight is pitiful. This is slaughter. Mules are hit and, if not fallen, gallop wildly off. Rations fly off the animals' backs in all directions. The entire mule train is destroyed. The Italian mule skinners are hysterical and make no effort to collect any stray animals. They cry and shout and run off weeping in all directions. To treat them is impossible. None of them will hold still long enough to be bandaged. They scramble off the mountain, leaving a trail of blood behind them.

It is dark before I know it. I have no idea where my troops are at this moment. Will they dig in for the night in front of us, or will they keep moving? I shall never find them in the darkness. I have only one choice—find the goat hut aid station below me and remain there for the night. I spend a good hour trying to find it in the darkness. It is loaded with wounded. The litter bearers are far behind in their job. The terrain is too rugged. It takes two hours to carry a man down the slopes in total darkness. Several squads lose their bearing and wander aimlessly all night. We have many battle fatigue cases too. Some men cry and shake; all these receive a large dose of sodium amytal and pass out like a light. Wounded are brought to us from the ridges all night long. The vermin and fleas in this hut rob even the tired casualties of their sleep. None of us gets any rest. At daybreak we barely finish dressing all the wounds. Will this day be as miserable as the last? I don't see how it possibly can.

My first objective on this morning of May 23 is to make contact with my battalion. There is no shelling on the top of the mountain. The saddle is quiet, too. We break up our station and climb upward to the ridge. Not knowing where to go, we decide to follow communications wire. These wires have been laid by our advancing column, and they must lead somewhere. On our way to the top, I pass many dead. We tag those not already tagged by the aid men. I stumble across Lieutenant Pierson, killed by a bullet wound. I briefly recall how we rode in the same rail car from San Antonio to Camp Patrick Henry. He was a soft-spoken, kindhearted young fellow, a schoolteacher by profession. A bullet is lodged in his head. He valiantly led his platoon in the attack. He is now a dead hero. As I tag the dead men, I recall the brief periods of friendship I had with each one of them. Many I treated repeatedly for minor ailments now lie still and cold before me. How insignificant were those callouses and aching backs compared to the mortal wounds that have now felled them! It's a strange thing, but I seem to recall most vividly only the minor encounters I had with each dead man while he was alive. As I stumble upon one corpse after another, war seems more futile than ever.

My attention is diverted from the dead by one of my sergeants, who asks me to observe a long column of troops approaching us from the rear on our right flank. The column moves very rapidly down one slope and up another. In about thirty minutes it should reach us. Are these bypassed Germans? We hide behind boulders until we can get a close look at them. I finally recognize their long column as French colonial troops, or Goums. They are the boys who are expert at knife work. At they reach our position, they come to a halt. For the first time I have a chance to get a close view of these fellows I have heard so much about. They are a fascinating lot; French officers are in command. The native warriors wear dirty gray robes, and their long hair is braided in pigtails. They sing, chatter, and howl. Many carry chickens under their arms, and some herd goats before them. All are armed with large machete knives. They bivouac for their evening meal by building a large bonfire directly on the skyline, kill one of the goats, and roast it over the open flames. The Krauts must be able to see them for miles away, but the Goums are completely unconcerned. They plan to bypass our troops after dark and carry on their silent warfare during the night. I suggest to my sergeant that we find our battalion as soon as possible before we tangle with these boys in the dark. They may not remember us. We are told that they receive fifty cents per enemy ear. I would like to keep mine.

A valley lies before us. We descend into it along a trail on the forward slope, following the communications wires. Along the trail we come across two Italian mule skinners with head wounds. Both have compound skull fractures and are sobbing hysterically. We apply skull bandages but give no sedation. After reassuring them that litter bearers are only a short distance behind us, we move on. The next casualty is a communications man. He is dead. He has apparently been struck by a stray mortar round, laying the wire that we are following. He has a gaping wound in his left thigh and has died from a rapid massive hemorrhage from his left femoral artery. All we do with this poor fellow is tag him.

By 8:00 P.M. it is dark, and we have made contact with the rear men in our battalion. We are at the base of either Mount Alto or Rotundo, I don't know which. We wander aimlessly around in the dark for many hours; first along one trail, then another. The men are tired, and several drop in their tracks from sheer exhaustion. Many have diarrhea, and I have no pills left to give them. Sprained ankles are numerous. We tape them in total darkness. Men curse under the burden of heavy packs. At 1:00 A.M. the leaders of our column apparently have decided that we are lost. We shall rest along the trail for the night. In the morning we shall correct our bearings. We can't even hear the work of the

Goums on our right flank. The men simply lie down on the trail and sleep. Only a few have kept their blankets, but even those without them are oblivious to the cold, night air—they are too exhausted to notice.

I make my way to the head of the column and to battalion head-quarters. It is located in another sheepherder's hut, and the medics are welcome to two of the three rooms. While the battalion sleeps, we are kept busy treating sore feet, aching backs, and all the other minor complaints we have been forced to ignore the past days of constant fighting and walking. The medically ill, those with severe diarrhea, and the combat fatigue cases are examined, sedated, and tagged to be evacuated in the morning. All the men look rough indeed. By candlelight they look worse than by daylight. Their eyes are red from lack of sleep. They have not shaved or washed for twelve days and look like bums. By 3:00 A.M. we have filled one of the rooms with non-battle casualties. Not until then do I have time to eat my K rations.

In three more hours it will be daylight. I fall asleep sitting on the floor in the corner of the room, completely ignoring the fleas and roaches as well as the mice that scurry between the snoring bodies.

On the morning of May 24, 1944, we have good news. Our ration train of mules brings food, water, and mail. It also bears the rumor that the beachhead forces at Anzio have kicked off the day before and are forging their way inland. If we keep moving across the hills, we shall meet them in several days. The retreating Germans will soon be trapped. Our morale gets a big boost. On to Rome. As I look at the map my enthusiasm lessens. Thus far we have covered only one-third the distance. Unless we meet less resistance or a miracle happens, it looks as though we have twenty-four more days of mountain warfare ahead of us.

Our objective today will be the mountain village of Pisterza, high on a cliff. Beyond it lies the Amaseno Valley and River and then our goal, the Priverno-Prossedi road. Our trail to Pisterza is over more mountains. One ridge always seems higher than the next. Resistance is light. Snipers with light mortars harass us occasionally. We cannot search them out—they have too much cover and good camouflage. By afternoon we approach Pisterza. The Germans are expecting us, for they are shooting airbursts over the hills of the town. They must not have direct observation, however, since only a few bursts explode directly above us.

Pisterza is deserted. Not a soul is in the town, but the church bell is ringing. Only the clergy apparently have stayed behind to welcome us. Most of the houses are locked, and the population has sought refuge in the hills. Our lead scouts report that from the northern edge of the town they can see the Amaseno Valley and the Priverno-Prossedi road. The valley is filled with German trucks, half-tracks, self-propelled guns, and tanks. A whole German panzer division is regrouping below us, but all we have are mortars, machine guns, rifles, and bazookas. The men are disgusted. For once we look down Jerry's throat, but because of the terrain our artillery is too far behind to support us and shoot up such a beautiful target. Some of the men must actually be restrained from clambering down the hills and attacking the tanks with only their bazookas.

We are held up in Pisterza for the rest of the day. I understand the situation as follows: We can either move through the German tanks at night or wait until they voluntarily withdraw as our flanks catch up with us. I seek out a good, solid stone house in the village, crawl into a bed, and sleep for a good three hours, only to be awakened by shouting returning civilians. I drink plenty of vino, examine a few sick babies, and am served an absolutely delicious fried-egg supper as a reward for my services.

On the morning of May 25, we proceed cautiously forward down into the Amaseno River Valley. The lead company meets scattered resistance, mostly small-arms fire. We cross the Amaseno River without incident. The riverbed is practically dry, and we only get our feet wet. I stop momentarily to take a bath, which is interrupted only once by an airburst. I don't think that the Germans fully realize that a whole battalion is crossing through their lines. The brush is heavy, and cover is good. As we reach the Priverno-Prossedi road, we encounter a roadblock. The point in the road we are forced to cross is covered by a Jerry half-track with machine guns firing upon us from the left, and another machine gun is firing upon us from the right, so that we are subjected to cross fire. One man dashes across the road every few minutes. Just before it is my turn I say a little prayer, then run like hell. The entire battalion crosses without a single casualty and disappears into the brush. Ahead of us is another mountain with rather bald slopes. Toward evening we are on it. Mortars fall in on us, and there is little cover. Darkness saves us from taking a beating. We are ordered to dig in and wait. In two hours I have a good slit trench about four feet deep. Casualties are brought to me, and I treat them directly from my hole. The night is amazing. The Germans are locked in the Sacco River Valley on our right. They can't get to Highway 6 nor Highway 7, since we have cut the road connecting the two. The French command the high ground to their right, and we the high ground to their left. The 85th Division is clearing the lowlands along the coast and Via Appia on our far left. We and the French are bringing up heavy artillery over the good roads now in our hands. Shells are poured into the trapped Germans trying to escape out of the valley. Below us the land glows from phosphorus bursts. Machine-gun tracers fill the sky. Heavy artillery slams into the valley and makes it a living hell for the enemy.

We witness murder the entire day. We have spectator seats. The rumor is that we have trapped two German panzer divisions, which are now being annihilated by Allied artillery and planes. We cannot move forward, since the French on our right flank have pinched us out and the Anzio forces are cutting inland. We shall sit tight all day to prevent Germans from escaping the trap.

On May 28 the valley below us is quiet. The entire Priverno-Prossedi road has been cut, the Amaseno River Line cleared, and the Eighth Army is finishing off the apparently trapped Germans. During the night of May 29 we move off the hill. We hear that trucks with hot food are awaiting us in the valley somewhere below. Again the battalion loses its way, and we wander aimlessly all night. One GI shouts in despair, "Put a shell through me and get me out of this misery." At sunrise we reach the valley somewhere near the Priverno-Prossedi road. Our rear kitchen trucks arrived during the night and a hot breakfast is ready. It's a good breakfast although a strange one. We have hot pancakes, and each man gets a bottle of beer. Mail is distributed. It all seems too good to be true. Right now the war seems to be practically over. That's what I think. I am ordered to go on a quartering party in the vicinity of Anzio. Before leaving, however, I manage to take a fast bath from water in a nearby well.

By noon on May 29 I am on my way along the Via Appia, or Highway 7. I ride in a small convoy of jeeps. Each company has sent an officer as representative. We are headed for a new assembly area, and each of us will choose a camping site for our men; the latter will be brought up by truck later. We drive along Highway 7 for approximately eighteen miles. For the first time in months I see flat beachland. Burned German tanks, self-propelled guns, and many trucks lie capsized along the road; the decaying enemy dead have not yet been removed, and their stench is sickening. Approximately seventeen miles inland from Anzio we turn right and drive over a secondary road to the outskirts of Cori. Along this road and in old German dugouts rest men of the 3d Infantry Division, the men who held the beachhead since January 22. I visit II Corps Headquarters located in a field tent. Here we are assigned a meadow on which to bivouac. We stake out ground on which to camp, then send back guides for the troops. These arrive during the night. We camp here in pup tents for two nights, catch up on much-needed sleep, and write letters home.

I do some thinking. I have been with combat infantry for only eighteen days, but during this time I have learned much. I was never taught military strategy but I have already come to certain conclusions:

It seems that an enemy stronghold, be it a city, town, small village, or just a mountain, is never assaulted head on. It appears that if at all possible, it is first bypassed and then an attempt is made to cut whatever escape route the enemy might have to his rear. If during this procedure high ground overlooking the objective can be seized, then all the better; from this vantage point the artillery observer attached to the battalion can direct division artillery to pour heavy shells onto the objective to soften it up. Shells are cheaper than the lives of men. Not until the Germans realize that their positions are now untenable and start to retreat do our troops attempt a frontal assault, and by this time this usually amounts to what news dispatches call mop-up operations.

Many a mop-up operation, however, can be a horrendous small-arms firefight. Many of the enemy dug into forward posts might not have gotten word that their main body is retreating. Communication wires to their positions were probably cut by our artillery shells. Such small groups of enemy usually fight to the last man and, by inflicting many casualties, are called fanatics. I don't think they are fanatics. They simply are ignorant of the overall situation. If they had been told to run for their lives, they probably would have. Since they had no order to evacuate, however, they did their duty, tried to hold fast, and were killed doing so.

Movement toward an objective held by the enemy is usually made at night. Night attacks take advantage of the element of surprise. To awaken in the morning and realize that your flanks have been overrun and your exit cut off can be demoralizing. However, night movements toward an objective can also be a nightmare for our troops, especially over unreconnoitered mountain trails. Frequently there were no trails at all. To date I still have not figured out how the head of our column has repeatedly managed to find its way without getting lost.

Another axiom in seizing an objective seems to be this: never take the easiest and hence obvious route such as a main highway or a secondary road. The Germans expect you to come this way, and therefore such routes are heavily mined and defended. The route to take instead is the most illogical one to the enemy and the most difficult one for us. This means mountain climbing, and that is after all what we practiced for months.

When everything goes well and we see Germans retreating ahead of us, why do we frequently stop and dig in? I can only assume we are too far out in front and must wait for the outfits on our flanks to catch up. Our battalion is fighting along only a tiny sector that, however, is part of a long line of fighting troops running across Italy from east to west, and this line must be kept straight. I can think of no other explanation. When we fight for several days and nights without any rest, we are probably catching up.

Who knows what is going on? The most important man, the fighting combat infantry man, knows the least. He only knows that he is heading north, is supposed to take the next hundred yards ahead of him, and then the next and the next and the next. The mountains he is to eventually occupy he knows only by number and not by name. I suppose that the reason for his not knowing more is that should he be captured he won't be able to give the enemy any valuable information. Giving objectives numbers or code names apparently also permits the radio operators to talk more freely over the air.

A company commander probably knows only his company's objective, the battalion commander only his battalion's objective, and the regimental commander only his regiment's objective. Division knows much more of the overall picture, corps knows still more, and Fifth Army has all the brains. Without ever having seen the terrain, be it good or bad, Fifth Army does all the thinking and planning, but GI Joe, who knows the least, does all the fighting and dying.

I as a medical officer am never oriented in advance of our division's overall plans. Thus far I have had to pump either our battalion commander or our headquarters commandant for information as to where our division was going and who was on our flanks. I am told only of our battalion's next immediate objective, and nothing more. To keep better oriented, I intend from now on to listen very closely to all conversations between the officers of Headquarters Company, to save all the small campaign maps issued before each push, and to pump all wounded prisoners for information. Whenever a lull in action permits I intend to scribble notes and then hide them in my aid kit. Once back in a rear area the notes will be transferred to the bottom of my barracks bag for future reference and orientation.

On June 1 and still in the vicinity of Cori and in an assembly area four miles southwest of Valmontone, we are attached to the 3d Division. Our orders are to fight our way to the north, our objective being to cut Highway 6, the large central highway to Rome. We are to cross the highway just north of Valmontone and prevent the Germans on our right, still holding Valmontone, Cave, and Palestrina, from retreating along Highway 6 to Rome. After cutting the highway we are to proceed across country for Palestrina. The 3d Infantry Division, which had such a tough time in Anzio, will be on our fight flank, and the 85th Division will be on our left flank. We move into the attack at

sundown. We walk for miles over a narrow dirt roadbed. Our tank destroyers, heavy artillery, and heavy tanks shoot from behind small hills
and from the fields along our path. It is too dark to scrutinize the terrain or to see exactly where you are going. Harassing artillery loops
in an occasional shell, and only two men are wounded by shrapnel
throughout the entire night. They have leg and arm wounds and are
not seriously hurt. They are left in the ditch in which they were felled
and will walk to the rear at daylight.

By morning of June 2 we still have not contacted the enemy. We
continue our chase without resting. We follow small dirt roads well
marked by 3d Division troops, who passed over them before us. One
of these signs reads, "Purple Heart Alley—Proceed with Caution." The
terrain now consists of fields dotted by small hills. Behind each hill
could be retreating Germans. To get to the hills we must always cross
an open field first. After noon our lead company makes enemy contact. Mortar, machine-gun, and pistol fire break out suddenly. The battalion rapidly deploys to surround the enemy-held hills. There are no
buildings in which to put an aid station, and mortar fragments keep
us hugging the ground. The last farmhouse I recall passing was at least
a mile to the rear. It's too late to retreat to there now; casualties are
occurring all around us. I spot a dense grove of trees to my right and
practically crawl to its edge. This looks like a wonderful spot—a small
forest in which we are completely hidden from view. The Germans
must have just left here, however, since their foxholes littered with
parts of their equipment are everywhere. I jump into one of the ready-
made holes and order my sergeants to direct the litter bearers to this
spot. In several minutes, however, I realize my horrible mistake. Some
of our tanks have also chosen this woods as cover, and they are drawing heavy enemy counterfire. German shells burst against the trees,
and fragments ricochet all over the place. While I am closely hugging
the edge of my hole during a barrage, a shell fragment passes through
my pants leg without as much as scratching me. This woods is a living hell. Every few seconds during treatment of a casualty I am forced
to jump back into my hole, and the poor fellow lying wounded is left
exposed for additional injury. Both doctor and patient are becoming
more nervous after each barrage. I decide to make this patch of woods
a litter-bearer station only. My only thought is to get the hell out of
here. As the ambulance draws up to collect three litter cases that have
accumulated, we rapidly load, also jump into the vehicle, and race
over the bumpy meadow a mile to the rear into the farmhouse passed
an hour ago.

Back at the farmhouse, we spend a very busy afternoon. We set up
our aid station in the wine cellar. Our jeeps bring in casualties every

few minutes. Many die on arrival from crushed skulls resulting from grenades thrown at close range. Gunshot wounds are numerous. Abdominal wounds are frequent for the first time, all because of the close-range fighting raging ahead of us. We have good rear medical support. Ambulances can travel over the narrow dirt roads, and the wounded do not pile up. We give an abundance of plasma. Many German wounded arrive together with ours. They all wear armbands identifying the Hermann Goering Division. After bandaging the head wound of one Jerry prisoner and giving him a shot of my whiskey, I try my hand at a little interrogating. I ask him how many men are left in his regiment and receive the answer, "Ein deutscher Soldat veraet nichts" (A German soldier reveals nothing). Since that is what I would have expected any captured American to say, I feel ashamed of ever having pumped him for information. He is a good soldier even though an enemy.

After dark the fighting slackens off enough for my aid station to move up. The Germans always seem to retreat at night, giving us no chance to rest but only to chase after them. On our way forward we still encounter casualties not yet evacuated from the afternoon's fighting. I stumble upon many a familiar face shot through the head. Most are dead. A few are still barely breathing. Treating those with still a faint flicker of life in them in total darkness is a distressing job. Tagging the dead in the dark, with a blanket thrown over you and the corpse, thus permitting the use of a flashlight, is most time-consuming. By midnight we arrive at a railroad bed and small shot-up station. The building is full of holes; these we patch with shelter halves so that we can light candles. Two rooms of the station are crowded with waiting wounded. We work all night dressing them. Mortar shells fall all around us at sporadic intervals. I treat many Germans. After dressing them, I inquire if they would like to have anything else to make them more comfortable. The most frequent wish is for a small piece of candy. What trivial wishes at serious times!

I leave the railroad station at daybreak on June 3. I follow the battalion over more fields and around more hills. My battalion is at least a mile ahead of me. We are again moving very fast, since the Germans have retreated during the night. My only casualties along the trail are abandoned wounded Jerries. They lie in their holes with compound fractures and are suffering from shock. We treat them just as though they belonged to us. Early in the afternoon we reach high ground overlooking Highway 6. Resistance is light. We have apparently cut across country along a trail where we were not expected. We have bypassed Germans on both sides. At the point of crossing Highway 6 are a group of German foxholes and dugouts, and I rest here for several minutes, checking my map and getting my bearings. The abandoned dugouts are filled with maps, canteens, radios and shovels. From several dead nearby, I salvage a few swastika decorations, mess gear equipment, and a collapsible shovel. The latter I carry with me for the next year.

We cross Highway 6 without meeting resistance and push on to Palestrina. The terrain consists mostly of fields and rolling hills. Somewhere to our right, a tank battle must be raging. I had been told of screaming meemies, but never heard them. They screech before landing and explode with a deafening slam. They are morale busters. Hustling through the fields, I am happy not to be in a tank outfit.

At nightfall we dig our foxholes into a small hill. We have orders to rest for the night. We are in a vineyard on the reverse slope. On our march we have avoided the enemy all day and covered a good distance. A night's rest after an all-day hike is welcome. During the night Jerry planes are very active. They are dropping flares, antipersonnel bombs, and do a good bit of strafing. I imagine that they are concentrating on Highway 6; we, however, off the highway and in the hills, are safe from their attack. We send out advance patrols to scout ahead for the enemy. They return reporting that a large number of German troops are dug in approximately one mile ahead of us. At dawn we shall attack them.

On the morning of June 4, 1944, we probe cautiously ahead. We must enter a small valley beyond which lies a secondary road leading to Rome. After approximately only thirty minutes we contact the enemy. It's the Hermann Goering Division again. They greet us with a heavy mortar barrage. The suddenness of the barrage results in many casualties. My aid station is again in the open air, near a large birdbath in the middle of the vineyard.

We treat casualties during lulls between barrages. One German runs frantically up the trail toward us. He is completely naked; not one stitch of clothes is on his body. On examining him, I find he has grenade fragments in his lung, abdomen, and legs. I can't imagine how he can even stand up, let alone having run at least a half-mile to reach us. He may have been taking a bath when surprised by our troops, was probably considered dead, but when consciousness returned, apparently headed in our direction. Another Jerry arrives, both buttocks peppered with shell fragments; he refuses to sit or lie down. After a heavy dose of morphine he finally consents to lie on a litter on his stomach. As we lag behind treating more wounded Jerries than our own, our battalion has moved at least a mile forward. We are asked to follow more quickly, since more casualties have occurred up front. Dodging mortars, we dash a half-mile forward and establish an aid station in a small cemetery. We are on the forward slope, but the cemetery has a solid four-foot wall and directly behind the wall is a tool shed. The stone walls of the shed are over two feet thick, and we are safe. We remain here all afternoon, treating one casualty after another. The litter bearers bring in one German who is practically eviscerated. On pulling back his blanket, I see several feet of gut spilled out over his abdomen and laying between his legs; every time he coughs, more bowel spills out; to make matters worse the bowel is perforated in numerous places and fecal material pours out of the holes. He states he was hit eight hours ago. Amazingly enough he is not even in shock. To put a dressing on his abdomen is impossible without first replacing the bowel; on his way to the rear without a dressing he will probably spill all his viscera. Our hands are dirty and nothing is sterile. Under intravenous morphine anesthesia I tie off all his perforated loops of bowel with black silk string and stuff all gut back into the abdomen. I partially close his wound with large stay sutures of silkworm gut. I can't approximate the wound edges entirely since the morphine anesthesia fails to give enough muscle relaxation. When finished I can at least put a tight binder around his abdomen so that evacuation is possible. He receives two units of plasma and smokes several cigarettes. Not once has he complained. On his emergency medical tag I make the notation that he is an emergency and has complete intestinal obstruction and needs immediate surgery. I would love to know if he is living today.

By nightfall we receive sudden orders to stop our advance and pull back. The French on our right have pinched us out again, and the Hermann Goering Division will be slowly annihilated by them. The Germans realize this and many surrender. They are all very confused, for we seem to be everywhere, and even their command does not seem to know what orders to issue next. They state that most of their divisions have been decimated. Many of the enemy are very young; some appear no older than sixteen. Some state that they have been in line for only four days. The young enlisted men talk freely. Captured officers, however, are always silent.

We reorganize during the night and slowly retrace our steps to the rear. I don't know where we are going. By morning, June 5, we are on a secondary road. After several hours we are walking along Highway 6. Soon we meet trucks parked in a field ready to roll us into Rome. A road sign reads "Roma — 10 km."

This war is more confusing all the time. So we shall ride into Rome on trucks! I always thought that capturing a city would be the toughest battle of them all. I can no longer figure things out. Before boarding the trucks, the troops are warned to beware of snipers. It would be a pity to be shot after surviving all the past days. My jeep follows

88th Division soldiers mop up in captured Santa Maria Infante, while others pursue the enemy in the mountains to the north. *Below:* Town Square in Itri. Courtesy U.S. Army Signal Corps.

88th Division soldiers in the Amaseno River Valley, west of Highway 6, on a road toward Rome during a lull in the resistance; other units were moving north along Highway 7. *Below:* Approaching the outskirts of Rome, a battle-weary dogface carries his mortar in a confiscated baby carriage. Courtesy U.S. Army Signal Corps.

"Other elements of the 88th Division had entered Rome." Courtesy U.S. Army Signal Corps.

Photo of Klaus Huebner taken in 1944.

German-held stronghold of Volterra, from which the Germans had observation of fifteen miles. Courtesy U.S. Army Signal Corps.

Rest area in an olive grove in the vicinity of Villamagna. *Below:* Snaking through orchards and fields on the way to the Arno River. Courtesy Eugene Engelen, Park Ridge, Ill.

the convoy of slowly moving trucks. The outskirts of Rome are in shambles. German vehicles lie overturned all along the highway, many charred—some still smoldering. The rumble of artillery fire can be heard north of Rome. My battalion is apparently not the first in Rome. While we were clearing out the hills, other elements of our division entered the day before—hence our present journey in trucks. Rome itself is undamaged. The welcome is tremendous. The streets are jammed with civilians cheering our convoy. Our vehicles barely have room to pass, and we ride at a snail's pace. Civilians mill about our vehicles throwing flowers and shaking our hands. People shout and clap their hands. Their exuberant welcome appears very sincere. For the first time in six months we see splendid buildings, well-paved streets, clean-looking children, and beautiful girls wearing lipstick, silk stockings, and, for a change, also shoes. Many people weep as they shout their welcome. Children jump into my jeep and hitch a ride. Our trip through Rome is fantastic and seems like a dream.

We stop on the southern banks of the Tiber River, detruck, and deploy across the Milvio bridges and into the gardens and estates overlooking the Tiber River. In the Pincio Gardens our artillery has set up its guns and is pumping shells after the fleeing Krauts, concentrating on peppering Highway 2, leading north from Rome. My battalion is resting in some millionaire's garden. It is lovely estate with a large swimming pool. We are not permitted to enter the home. We do, however, shed all of our clothes and jump into the water. An occasional German artillery shell aimed at the Tiber River bridges makes this an unusual swimming party. Late in the afternoon we are ordered to move out. We must chase the Krauts fleeing to the north. Rome would have been a beautiful spot in which to spend the night. As we doggedly walk up Highway 2, I look back at Rome with a longing in my heart. I would give six months' pay to sleep in a hotel bed and between sheets. Even women enter my thoughts. It is all wishful thinking —very pleasant though. The 3d Division men are the lucky dogs to garrison Rome while we take up the pursuit.

Our hike is through fields closely paralleling Highway 2. Our pace is rapid, and we suffer no casualties. We walk all night, through wheat fields and meadows. The men of M Company curse under the heavy burden of mortar plates, machine-gun belts, and mortar shells. I guess these are the sort of forced marches we trained for in the States. One needs stamina to keep up.

On the morning of June 6 we finally rest for several hours in a small patch of woods. Civilians tell us that the Germans are only six hours ahead. Our tanks and tank destroyers follow us closely and do all the shooting. We continue our trek over small hills and through fields.

For occasional brief stretches we walk along the highway where knocked-out German tanks and vehicles remain a familiar sight. Signs along the road are all in German such as "Licht Aus" (lights out). Snipers shoot at our column from our flanks on numerous occasions. We send out patrols, which quickly annihilate them. At times we are pinned down by machine-pistol fire until the sniper is shot—then move on. At nightfall we dig our holes into a low hill and rest for the night. The only wounded are Germans, which are brought to me by aid men of the lead company. Most are men who were wounded and left behind in the fields. For the first time I see wounded enemy of the 1st Parachute Division. One nineteen-year-old, wounded in both legs, has nothing in his possession but both pockets are full of candy. I also treat another eviscerated Jerry, but this time with terrain more favorable for rapid evacuation I attempt no surgery. Scattered machine-gun and sniper fire echoes through the night but no longer disturbs my sleep.

We are on the march again on the morning of June 7. We pass through several small villages and are cheered by the townsfolk. It takes about twenty minutes to pass through a town, but during this time we feast briefly on vino, bread, eggs, and ham. We finally stop on the northern edge of one village, and I am assigned a stone house in which to set up my station. We are told that our halt is indefinite. We have lost enemy contact. Mechanized troops are taking up the pursuit—the Krauts are running too fast for foot troops to keep pace. Ahead of us is a small river. The troops rest on its banks, and all go swimming. Kitchen trucks catch up with us and we have hot meals. On the highway to our left, tanks and artillery roll forward. I am told we are in Mazzano Romano. We have now had one hundred straight days of frontline duty with thirty-one days of active combat and have moved 109 air miles since May 11. The rumor is that we are being relieved and are going to the rear to a rest camp. Rome here we come! The biggest news is almost unbelievable. We hear that our troops invaded Normandy yesterday, June 6, 1944.

Albano, Rome, Tarquinia

JUNE 13, 1944–JULY 5, 1944

On June 13, 1944, we leave Mazzano Romano by trucks and jeeps and move back to Albano, a small town twelve miles south of Rome. We shall now be in Army reserve. We must pass through Rome to get to Albano. We drive back over Highway 2 and are impressed by the havoc wrought by our planes during the past few days. The road's shoulders are strewn with wrecked tanks, trucks, ambulances, and dead horses. The Germans used beautiful animals to pull some of their supply vehicles. They must be of a Danish breed, for they are large, broad, and sturdy, have long manes, braided tails, and even though now dead still look clean and well groomed. Out of purely sentimental reasons, I feel sorrier for the dead horses than the fallen enemy.

We pass through Rome. It is wonderful to see a big city again. The sidewalks are crowded with jay walkers. Ladies in fashionable dress ride through town on bicycles; apparently they are out shopping. Very few automobiles are on the streets, and those that are have been converted to charcoal burners; large stacks curve skyward from the exhaust pipes and puff dark clouds of smoke. We feast our tired eyes on the clean buildings, the well-kept parks, and last but not least on the many girls in gay-colored dresses. Our ride through Rome is much too rapid!

I am not very happy in our camp in Albano. We live in pyramidal tents set up in an olive grove directly along a well-traveled road. We are showered with the dust kicked up by every passing vehicle. I believe Italian roads are the dustiest in the world. It has not rained for five weeks, and the dust is as fine as flour and clings just as tenaciously. One passing vehicle can make you look as though you have just crawled through a grain mill.

We return to Army camp life; everything is once again strictly GI. Chow lines, sick call, inspections, lectures, and all other precombat activities are resumed. Our general has always been a stickler for basic routine and absolute discipline. Many men dislike him for that reason, but most of us owe our lives to his harping on fundamentals. In combat strict adherence to the latter principles has always paid off.

Approximately two hundred new faces confront me on my first battalion health inspection. To me that means that we have lost approximately one-fourth of our battalion in our first campaign, and we still have a long road ahead of us!

Lake Albano is not far away. On the first Sunday I have free, I drive to the lake for an afternoon of swimming and relaxation. Troops are assigned a special area of the beach; under such circumstances it is impossible to make social contacts with civilians.

One fine day I finally receive a twelve-hour pass to Rome and am permitted to take my jeep and driver. I feel lost not knowing where to go, whom to see, or what to do. I spend the day just like any other tourist—enter Rome via the Porta San Sebastiano, visit the Forum Romanum, the Coliseum, tour the Janiculus with its public grounds, walk around the various piazzas, and look at innumerable fountains and churches the names of which I shall never remember, unless I return some day and have more time. My jeep driver is not at all interested in all the ruins. He says that to him the Forum Romanum looks like an old quarry. After driving through most of Rome for two hours, I arrange for him to meet me in three hours in front of the Fontana di Trevi, so that he may roam about at will while I continue my sightseeing on foot. I know that he will have a much better time than I. He hints so on our way back to Albano. He agrees that I probably saw and learned a lot of things while he actually felt them. Privates always have a better time than officers anyway.

My social life begins on the night of our first battalion officers' party. Battalion headquarters has requisitioned a small villa nearby. Captain Bellmont once again has made all the arrangements. Invited have been Red Cross girls, both American and Italian. I have little hope that this party will be a success, for I still vividly remember the fiasco at the Kings Palace in Caserta. I hear that spiked punch will be served and that we shall have victrola music.

I arrive groomed and polished at the villa at 5:00 P.M. on the afternoon of our cocktail party and buffet supper. American Red Cross girls are well represented, and they are immediately surrounded by our officers. The Italian Red Cross ladies are not in uniform and to me are more attractive in civilian dress. In the spring I vowed never to date an American girl again as long as the war would last, and I intend to stick to this agreement I made with myself. All told, we are about twenty-five officers and fifteen girls, and it is shaping up to be a good party. Hors d'oeuvres are passed around—strictly GI food but dressed up and disguised a little to make it taste better. At the bar are cognac, wine, punch, and whiskey. For the first two hours I do nothing but eat and drink a little and make an estimate of the situation. A regimental supply officer is dancing with a petite Italian blonde; since he is a southerner and a livewire socially, I know that sooner or later he will circulate and will relinquish his lovely lady for at least several minutes. At that moment I shall make my play. The major, however, sticks doggedly to his date. When at last the rye runs low, the major is called upon to replenish it. The girl is left standing alone for only a few seconds, and I am at her side. I ask her to dance, and she agrees with what I sense is genuine sincerity. Her name is Maria. She is as light as a feather and a wonderful dancer. She is so easy to talk to and so full of enthusiasm that conversation is no effort at all. Each record ends much too soon. I could dance with Maria all night, and tell her so. She glowingly thanks me for the compliment and promises to do her utmost to give more of her dances to me than to anyone else. When not dancing with her, I admire her from the sidelines. Maria

is about five feet two and about one hundred and twelve pounds. She
has very light blonde hair and sparkling blue eyes. Her fair skin re-
quires no makeup except a light touch of lipstick. Her light-blue dress
matches her eyes. She is small and slender, yet still very feminine.
From her features I would judge her to be in her late twenties, but
her manners make me believe that she is in her early thirties; she
has too much poise, acts to sensibly, and speaks too knowingly to be
much younger. I speak very little Italian, but Maria speaks some English and good German, so that we get along famously. I am somewhat
disappointed to hear that she is married. She quickly points out, however, that social customs in Italy permit a bachelor to date a married
woman. She lives in Rome but her husband is behind enemy lines
in La Specia. I do not inquire whether he is a Fascist or Partisan. As
I dance with her, I forget all about war, politics, and the Army. I shall
always recognize her perfume—a blend of lilacs and lilies of the valley, which sends my senses reeling. I have never held a woman such
as Maria in my arms and enjoyed it so much. The night is over much
too soon. She senses my desire to be with her as long as possible and
cleverly arranges for me to accompany her home. All the Italian girls
have been brought from Rome by truck and are to return in the same
manner. Before the trucks depart she tells me that at an opportune
moment when the major is not looking she will quickly and unno-
ticed jump into truck number two and keep quiet while other couples
board it. At the very moment the truck departs I jump in also. I am
taking Maria home while the major is still looking for her. I have no
qualms of conscience, however. After all, I think I am doing his wife
in the U.S.A. a big favor.

Even the eighteen-mile ride to Rome in a bouncing two-and-a-half-
ton truck is rather romantic. At least, I feel that way. Maria is good
company any time. She sits close to me, which is enough. I expect
no more. We drop her off at her home in downtown Rome at 4:00 A.M.
I make a date with her for six days hence. I shall then have a week's
pass to the Hotel Excelsior, the Fifth Army's Officers Rest Center. She
is to meet me in front of the hotel. For the first time since being in
Italy I don't regret being here.

The week following the meeting with Maria passes more slowly
than any other, or so it seems anyway. On the morning I finally leave
for Rome on my week's pass I am more exuberant than I have been
for a long time. I have definite plans, have a beautiful date to look
forward to, and a whole week of rest and leisure ahead of me. I feel
carefree and have no worry in the world.

I check into the Hotel Excelsior at 10:00 A.M. What a place! Bell-
hops jump to help you. I am taken to a spacious double room with

bath, shower, bidet, and balcony overlooking the main drag. Just the thought of sleeping between sheets, and clean ones at that, is like an incredible dream come true. All this, however, is real. I call for room service and have three martinis. Then I take a leisurely tub bath, the first in a year. I have never enjoyed a bath more. I then dress to meet Maria.

Maria is in front of the hotel at exactly twelve noon as prearranged. She looks more beautiful than ever. I certainly am a lucky guy! She knows the Hotel Excelsior well; it is the best in Rome. She is quick to add, however, that she has not visited the hotel since our officers have taken it over. I soon realize why she said this, for having been here would be detrimental to her reputation as a lady. The lobby is filled with women. All look beautiful and are dressed only in the tightest of costumes, which accentuate their figures to the greatest advantage. Most of the girls are whores who have gained entrance to the hotel in the company of an officer but never left the hotel after the officer's pass was up. As long as they do not leave the hotel no one bothers them. Once outside, they must find a man to take them back inside. Very few ever leave. To eat, they must be accompanied to the dining room by an officer. Their meal ticket is, therefore, the man with whom they sleep. Since a new crop of officers arrives weekly, they are busy sleepers and constant eaters. But such is war, and who cares? Everyone has a great time. There's a rumor that soon a new drug will be on the market that will cure gonorrhea in twenty-four hours.

I have several rum cokes with Maria at the downstairs bar. I see that she is somewhat shocked at the company the officers are keeping but is broad-minded enough to realize that in times of war such associations are inevitable. We then have a leisurely lunch in the dining room, where a string ensemble plays Latin and Viennese music. In the afternoon we go window shopping, then return to the hotel for the tea dance. I enjoy every minute I am with her. Slowly I learn more about her. She is apparently well-to-do and socially quite active. She speaks of having important political appointments, during which times she cannot see me; she apparently has household servants who manage some of her affairs. Last but not least, she also has a sixteen-year-old son. Maria fascinates me more all the time. Who is this girl that agrees to be squired about by a lowly first lieutenant like myself? Being a medical officer has probably helped me somewhat in making an impression. However, I don't think that Maria is that way. I believe she does things only because she likes to do them.

That evening we have dinner, then dance at the hotel. She insists that she must be home by 11:00 P.M. She is very emphatic about the time. She prefers to walk rather than take a taxi home. Rome is of course blacked out at night. We have a wonderful time walking down the middle of the dark, deserted streets. She is ever so cheerful and regrets that I must take her home so early, but such is her custom and that is that. I really don't mind. Her home is in a large apartment house in an old but very fashionable part of the city. I bid her goodnight at the entrance and try to find my way back alone. Of course I get lost and don't get back to the hotel until well after midnight. These streets are really dark, and the thought of hoodlums jumping me is constantly on my mind. Life at the hotel at 1:00 A.M. is still a merry-go-round. Most of the boys are well intoxicated, and the girls look sleepier than ever. I have a few more martinis at the bar, then retire to my room. As I step out of the shower the door opens and a nice-looking young girl steps in; she has had a few drinks but is not dead drunk. She wants to sleep here for the night. Believe it or not, it's all too sudden for me, and the nice memories of Maria are still too fresh in my mind. I tell her something of being a "dottore," have many bambinos at home, am very tired, and shove her out of the door. I sleep alone, very soundly, and am most proud of myself at having resisted temptation.

Breakfast the next morning is most amusing. Officers eating alone have spent a quiet night. Those with ladies have been active. These ladies accompanying the officers are the sleepers. You can plan your objective for the night by remembering faces.

With Maria the week passes quickly. The days simply fly by. I accompany her on shopping trips. One afternoon we see "This Is The Army," starring Irving Berlin. I sneak her past the guard with the explanation that she is a member of a USO troupe. The musical is in the opera house. We have box seats and sip cognac.

One afternoon we devote strictly to sightseeing. Maria is very wise. She suggests that I give her my money and that she will pay all the bills. At the end of the day she will return the unused amount. She feels that the Italians cheat all the GIs and that she will pay the Italian prices and no more. Thus she pays the driver of the horse and buggy we hire on our sightseeing tour. We ride through parks and along the Tiber River. I am led through the Vatican and the Catacombs. Everything is explained to me. We buy fruit, ice, candy, and a corsage for her. She suggests that we eat supper at an old famous Italian restaurant off the beaten path and never frequented by GIs. It is at the edge of a park. It is an old building with high-ceilinged rooms and columns. The waiters are in full dress. She is immediately recognized by the headwaiter, and we are ushered to a table for two under a roof of potted palms. Two violins play for us throughout the entire dinner. We have steak and a very good wine. It is probably mule steak, but what's the difference—the company makes up for it. Mule or no mule, it has been an excellent dinner. By 11:00 P.M., however, Maria is safely at home.

On another afternoon I have lunch with Maria at the Fifth Army officer's lounge. This is in an old wine cellar, dark and cozy. The cellar is cool and the candles burn with a soft flame. We take all afternoon to eat and listen to music. The wine has put me into a very mellow mood. The orchestra softly plays "Lilli Marlene" and other top tunes of the day. We talk of everything and anything. There just does not seem to be enough time to say all you would like to say. That wine cellar I shall always remember too! Maria speaks the same thought. We spend the evening at the hotel taking in a floor show. Not having eaten supper, I ask her to come up to my room and we shall order sandwiches. To my surprise, she agrees. We have anchovies, tunafish, and cognac. At 10:30 P.M. I take her home. Once again we have had a most pleasant time. I am too fond of Maria by this time to demand anything that both of us might later regret.

On my last day in Rome, Maria invites me to her home. She states that it will be for afternoon tea. I make my appearance promptly at 3:00 P.M. The elevator is not working, and I walk to the second-floor apartment. A butler answers the door. He ushers me into the living room. He states that madame will be with me shortly; she is at present in a business conference. As I wait, a maid serves me vermouth and cookies. All this is really not bad, but just a little too fancy for me. I feel somewhat uneasy. I have not been treated like this for many years. Soon Maria appears, radiant as ever. We have tea and cake; later, some cognac. We then sit on the balcony until well after dark. At last I bid her good-bye. My guess is that I shall never see her again. I really don't expect to get out of Italy alive, for from what I have seen so far, the law of averages is against me. She does not object to my kissing her. She has an indescribable softness to her lips and body. I only linger a few moments, then leave. To stay here longer would lead to ruin. I return to the hotel for my last night and get royally drunk.

Upon returning to Albano, I find my battalion alerted to move to Tarquinia, sixty miles to the north of Rome. On June 23 we complete our move. Tarquinia is near the coastal city of Civitavecchia. We are still in Army reserve, only have been moved further to the north, should we be suddenly needed up front. We again sleep in pyramidal tents, and camp life continues. The troops engage in hikes, tactical problems, and listen to more lectures. At night, movies are shown in the recreation tent. The weather is very hot and dry. At noon the temperature is often 100 degrees. On two occasions I drive to Civitavecchia, fifteen miles away, for a swim in the Mediterranean. The beaches are still mined, and we cautiously walk through the sand to the water's edge. I always remain only long enough for a good swim; lolling around on the mined beach is taboo and still much too dangerous.

One afternoon I contract the most common illness prevalent at this time, diarrhea. I begin to feel terrible and for a while think that it is only due to the heat. When I finally take my own temperature, however, and find it to be 105 degrees, I decide that it is time to evacuate myself. I sign my own medical ticket and leave for the division clearing station. I am fed sulfadiazine pills and, as bad luck will have it, am completely well in two days.

On June 28 we are gathered together for a division ceremony. We parade before General Mark Clark and are commended but at the same time given another pep talk. Medals are awarded. We sense a new push on the agenda, probably in the very near future at that. Our stay in Tarquinia is highlighted by a regimental party. When Colonel Crawford plans a party, it must be successful. His supply officers have worked day and night to requisition and obtain food and drink for this affair. Champagne, wine, caviar, whiskey, cognac, turkey, fresh vegetables, figurines carved out of ice, and gallons of sherbet adorn the table in the town hall of the village. A GI orchestra plays. This is a gala affair and has been planned well. Red Cross girls and nurses have been invited and are actually here. I have a blind date with an Air Corps nurse but do not enjoy myself. Ever since Caserta, nurses are still on my blacklist. Our battalion supply officer, Lieutenant Jenkins, has a surprise for me. His date is an Italian Red Cross girl from Rome. He drove sixty miles to get her. She has asked one of her girlfriends along, who of all people turns out to be Maria.

Seeing Maria again, and quite so unexpectedly, is wonderful. I quickly ditch my date and have no trouble finding another escort for her. Maria and I dance all night, and when the party breaks up at 2:00 A.M. it is much too soon. Most of us are fairly drunk. Lieutenant Jenkins and I will drive our dates back to Rome in his jeep. In the confusion of saying good-bye to everybody and waiting for service at the check room, I lose track of Lieutenant Jenkins and the girls. I comb the alleys outside for his jeep. I am not sober and never do locate my party. I later learned that they too looked for me, but finally gave up and drove off to Rome. For me it has been a sad farewell. When would I see Maria again? I walk back to my tent quarters very depressed. I cannot put Maria out of my mind for hours and thus get little sleep. I am very disappointed for not having been able to accompany her back to Rome. She did not deserve such an unsatisfactory farewell.

What is so mysterious about Maria? Since she has a sixteen-year-old son, she must be about thirty-six years old yet looks much younger. Why were her son and husband in La Specia? Why did she have so many political appointments? Where did she learn her good German? Was her husband a Fascist, and is he still with the Germans hoping that the Fascists will someday regain control? Whenever the subject of her husband or politics came up, she cleverly changed the subject.

Whenever we discussed my bachelor status and I expressed interest to marry as soon as the war is over, she would avoid eye contact as though to say, "Don't consider me; I'm not available."

I also wonder what Maria saw in me. I was not a macho figure. As intern on the obstetrical ward I once overheard one woman say to the other, "Dr. Huebner delivered me. I like him, he is a cute little fellow." This one remark made a lasting impression upon me and had some influence on my behavior from then on. I had to overcome the stigma of being described "little" by overachieving in something that would attract attention and compensate. I was only five feet, seven inches tall and weighed only about one hundred and twenty-five pounds. I have the good fortune to look Nordic, with blue eyes and hair about as blond as hair can get. I was sinewy because of my fondness for athletics. Perhaps I reminded Maria of her son, heaven forbid. Even though I was twenty-seven years old, I looked no older than twenty-one. This has always been one of my misfortunes. Even now the officers in my battalion have given me the nickname of "Little Doc."

I must have interested Maria in other ways than her comparing me with her son. She drove fifty miles over war-torn roads in an open jeep just to see me for a few hours. I think I fascinated her, and she felt helpless to do something about it. By this time in my life I had learned to attract a woman's attention by trying to get her to talk mostly about herself. I always pretended to be an intent listener. Most girls had considered me good company just because I listened. I would also discuss events in which I had learned she was interested. Once, a girl described me to her brother as one of the most fascinating fellows she had ever met when in reality I never spoke more than a few words all night because she did all the talking. I was perfectly happy to let Maria talk, and while she did so, I could adore her.

If Maria thought just for a fleeting moment that I considered her a mother figure in turn, she would have been really mistaken. I was much too attracted to her. Sex, however, was never discussed, although I would have gone to bed with Maria with the greatest of pleasure had an opportunity presented itself. However, she would have had to make the first move because I would not have had the nerve to suggest this to her. I was too afraid that she might say no, and then it would be all over. Maria kept me hoping, and that was fascinating.

After several hours of conversation any man can tell if a woman is attracted to him sexually, and I know that from her responses Maria was, but was too sensible to lose her head and have a guilty conscience once her husband returns. She was tempted, and probably found it adventurous to resist.

I must be in love with Maria for her to so occupy my mind. Whether she is in love with me I don't know. Since Maria is married, however, there is no future in continuing to see her. A more intense relationship can only result in unhappiness and disappointment because of unsurmountable obstacles. Having definitely decided never to see Maria again for the good of both of us, I have put my mind at ease and go to sleep. However, I shall never forget Maria.

I can sense another campaign coming up. Again, to keep my log up to date, I inquire about for answers. Some fellows speak Italian and have seen makeshift local newspapers. All I can find out about our Italian front is that on the western coast we are in Pisa on the Ligurian Sea and near the middle we pass almost through Florence and in the east the Eighth Army is in the city of Ancona on the Adriatic Sea. In southern France the Allies must have moved fast. I am told that the city of Nice is in our possession, and we are on the outskirts of Geneva in Switzerland. If this is so, a line drawn between these cities is a straight line north to south. In western Europe the Allied forces are apparently close to the Dutch border, in the center Luxembourg has been passed, and General Patton is only about seventy-five miles from Strasbourg on the Rhine River. As far as the Russians are concerned, I learn that they are about to enter East Prussia and are in front of Warsaw, Poland. How far they are from Hungary nobody can tell me. All I learn about the Pacific is that the island of Guam is back in our hands.

On July 5, 1944, our rest period ends. Infantry is needed two hundred miles north of Rome. Another push begins.

Push to the Arno River

JULY 5, 1944–JULY 28, 1944

We leave Tarquinia by trucks and jeeps and drive most of the night. We drive approximately one hundred and fifty miles, first along the Highway 1 through Grosseto, then inland on secondary roads to Pomerance. The last few miles are over oxcart trails to just south of Volterra and close to the Cecina River. Here we assemble in a valley just behind a small ridge. Volterra lies about six miles to the north. We are to support the 1st Armored Division and drive toward the Arno River to just west of Florence. Tanks are having trouble. They are approaching the Tuscan Hills from flat land, and the Krauts have all the advantage. The Germans are dug into ancient strongholds and have clear observation for at least fifteen miles all around. Only infantry can dislodge the enemy; tanks alone can't do it.

Several miles to the south of our assembly area is the town of Larderello with its electric plant. This plant utilizes natural steam escaping from the ground. I am told that a shell has hit one of the large pipes, and from a distance of a few miles I have trouble distinguishing the hissing noise the steam makes from that of incoming and outgoing artillery shells.

On July 6, while still in the assembly area in an open meadow, I am promoted to captain. Captain Bellmont lends me a set of captain's bars, and Colonel Yeager pins these to my collar. Shortly thereafter an incoming artillery shell hits the site of I Company's command post, killing Lieutenant Foss and wounding five other officers. Lieutenant William Konze miraculously escapes injury because he has gone to the aid station for some aspirin for a headache. That night we sleep in foxholes.

We enter combat at 3:00 A.M. on July 8. The battle plan sounds simple. Volterra is a central stronghold lying between Cecina on the coast and Siena inland. Volterra must fall, for it is strategic. The 88th Division is to first bypass and later take Volterra and then drive to the Arno River. I learn that the 349th Infantry is to bypass Volterra on the right. The 350th Infantry will at the same time try to bypass Volterra on the left. As part of the 349th Infantry, my 3d Battalion's mission after passing to the right of Volterra is get behind the enemy and occupy a hill designated simply as 44, located about one and a half miles north of Volterra. The British and French on our right flank will try to push on to Florence and Siena, while other Fifth Army units on our left flank will drive up the coast for Leghorn and Pisa.

At 3:00 A.M. it is dark. We move out in single file. As the sun rises I can see the terrain and shudder. Bald hills and bare fields lie ahead of us, and the Krauts are apparently sitting in heavily fortified farmhouses waiting for us to approach. It is a hot, dry, clear day, and visibility is at least fifteen miles. In the distance tanks look like small black bugs trying to crawl slowly forward. Their tracks kick up clouds of dust, and every incoming shell creates a geyser of more dust and smoke. We first make our way toward Volterra by heading for the small village of Mazzola three miles away in which perhaps a half-dozen houses are still standing. Heavy artillery fire is encountered as we approach. The Germans seem to have saved lots of ammunition for this

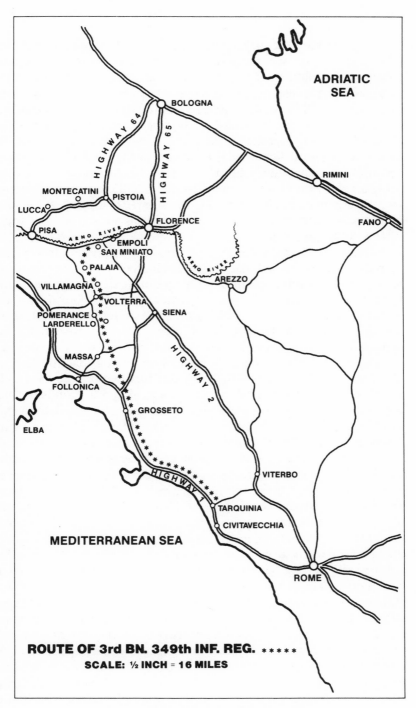

ADRIATIC
SEA

HIGHWAY 64

HIGHWAY 65

BOLOGNA

RIMINI

FANO

MONTECATINI
LUCCA
PISTOIA

PISA
ARNO RIVER
FLORENCE

EMPOLI
SAN MINIATO

PALAIA

ARNO RIVER

VILLAMAGNA

AREZZO

VOLTERRA

POMERANCE
LARDERELLO

SIENA

HIGHWAY 2

MASSA

FOLLONICA

GROSSETO

ELBA

VITERBO

HIGHWAY 1

TARQUINIA

CIVITAVECCHIA

MEDITERRANEAN SEA

ROME

ROUTE OF 3rd BN. 349th INF. REG. ✶✶✶✶✶
SCALE: ½ INCH = 16 MILES

3 The Push from Rome to the Arno River.

day. The Germans are making full use of their accurate 88s, but their 20-mm guns seem still more accurate. The loud cracks of landing artillery shells make my heart pound. After each crack I look about, still cowered, for casualties that might have occurred. Each time I also feel grateful still to be alive. At first, all the casualties are caused by shrapnel. We treat the wounded on the reverse side of the open slopes, then collect them together at the foot of each incline to be evacuated to a better location. Once the little village of Mazzola has been taken, I plan to set up an aid station in one of its shot-up houses and there bring all the wounded together. Throughout the entire morning we work in sweat and dust and blood. The sun beats unmercifully down upon us. My throat feels dry, and the odor of smoke and hot metal lingers in my nostrils.

As planned, my aid station in Mazzola is a farmhouse. It is mostly all rubble on top but still has a usable cellar below. The covering rubble is excellent protection from more incoming shells. The main road leading into Volterra and which we must cross next lies only about one and a half miles north of Mazzola. The men of our battalion are already approaching it. From the wounded coming in we can tell that combat is at close range. The wounded confirm this by saying that the Germans were hiding in haystacks and firing machine pistols. Many machine-gun nests and a few lone fortified houses have to be silenced before the men can advance. Several heroic groups of three to four rifle men are assigned to such tasks and accomplish their missions by using bazookas and hand grenades. These fellows have guts, more than I could ever muster up. Their casualty rate is very high.

Whenever a variety of weapons are used, the number of casualties passing through our aid station is high and the wounds vary in character. This is the case today. Direct hits with 20-mm shells are no problem because the victim is dead. Most men felled with penetrating head wounds from machine-gun bullets are also dead. Shrapnel from 88s and "Nebelwerfers" or screaming meemies is disabling, but many victims will survive if their wounds are in the extremities. The survival rate of large penetrating wounds of the abdomen depends on the amount of invisible internal hemorrhage and how fast the patient reaches an evacuation hospital, where blood can be given and emergency surgery performed. Today an ambulance will not dare to evacuate anybody until it is dark. Frustrating to me is that we can only put on emergency dressings and give plasma and morphine and decide whom to evacuate first, since we must treat on the run and keep moving. I abhor several types of wounds. One chap has a shrapnel wound that destroys the sinus beneath his right cheek, and half of his eye is hanging loose. This is a tough case to bandage in a hurry.

Another chap has his lower jaw missing, and you can see his entire bloody gullet and vocal cords; he has no chin to hold a bandage. I see two cases of dirty wounds, the bones splintered just above the ankles and flesh torn away caused by mines. Such wounds lead to eventual amputation because they will never heal, since the blood supply here even in a well person is rather poor. One case shot in his low back can't move his legs at all. He will probably be a cripple the rest of his life. I shall never know, since once I have seen a casualty with a serious wound, I will never see it again; I do not have the opportunities for follow-up. I am grateful that I do not have any burn cases today.

Our artillery, I am told, is of tremendous help. The observer with our battalion has often radioed back to his unit to plaster with shells targets only about one hundred and fifty yards from our positions. Most shells fall dead center. Our artillery also marks our objective with smoke shells, or else we would probably never recognize it.

After most of our battalion had crossed the road to Volterra, we also move forward. Crossing the road, I see a smoldering tank that still draws heavy fire and is hazardous to be around. A dead German lies in my path on the shoulder of the road. The Germans apparently had no time to retrieve his body because of our artillery. I simply cannot get used to the sickening stench of warm sewage emitted from decaying flesh and guts.

From the road the path to Hill 44 is over fields flanked by knolls, many of which are still occupied by stubborn Krauts covering the retreat of their main body of troops. It is now 6:00 P.M. It has taken us fifteen hours to advance five miles, and the going was bloody. I am very proud of our wounded. Their faces were usually grim and covered with dirt and sweat. They were all very stoic. They moaned and groaned because of their wounds but none were hysterical or whimpered. The litter bearers told me that most lay quiet until found, and there was never any frantic cry for help. We had been well disciplined. I am also proud of myself. So far I have managed to stay calm and do my job well. I always experienced momentary fright when an exploding mortar or artillery shell was a near miss but managed to hide this feeling from my men. This was also self-drilled in discipline.

Shortly after setting out toward Hill 44, our lead company sends word back that the fields are full of mines. We are all dead tired, dirty, and hungry, and this is horrible news. Casualties again occur in large numbers. Men felled by mines are trapped, and further pounded by artillery. From a position just behind a small knoll, I and my technicians are repeatedly forced to slip into the mined fields and treat the wounded. After several missions and for some peculiar reason, I suddenly become completely indifferent to either life or death. Survival now is only a lucky break. The wounded must be treated, shelling is very heavy, and cover is simply not available. Automatically and without realizing it, I must have done things that later were called heroic. The official citation for the Bronze Star medal I thus unknowingly earn states:

> On 8 July 1944, north of Volterra, Italy, Capt. Klaus H. Huebner, 3rd Battalion surgeon, 349th Infantry, displayed great personal heroism and exemplary devotion to duty in hostile fire while administering aid to the wounded and supervising their evacuation. When the 3rd Battalion suffered heavy casualties during an attack on German positions, Capt. Huebner made his way across open terrain in full view of the enemy while a concentration of artillery and mortar shells burst around him, increasing the toll and imperiling every move. Constantly exposing himself to the murderous fire, with utter disregard for his own safety, he attended the casualties, dressing their wounds and directing their removal. As the advance continued, foot mines were encountered and new casualties were sustained, among them two men whose feet were blown off. This courageous Officer, fully aware of the great risk to his life in moving through the minefield, unhesitatingly made his way to the side of the injured soldiers and, stopping the flow of otherwise fatal hemorrhages, saved their lives. By evening Capt. Huebner had worked continuously for fifty five hours, walking many miles but despite exhaustion, he steadfastly refused to stop for rest, heroically devoting his full attention through the night to the wounded of another battalion, administering aid and laying adequate plans for their evacuation to the rear. By his selfless heroism in the face of murderous German fire, risking his life to give immediate aid to casualties who were falling about him as he worked, Capt. Huebner saved many lives which otherwise would have been lost. His unselfish devotion to the wounded has won the admiration of the entire command. . . .

> Joseph B. Crawford,
> Colonel, 349th Infantry,
> Commanding.

By nightfall July 9 we are one-half mile from the base of Hill 44, which was our battalion objective. We occupy a farmhouse that has just been taken. All casualties found thus far are gathered together and taken to its basement. By 11:00 P.M. we have treated all the wounded, and our battalion has long bypassed Volterra. We follow the troops walking north, over more hills and meadows. At 3:00 A.M. we are in a valley at the base of Hill 44. We establish our aid station in a barn. After two shots of liquor, I curl up for my first chance to sleep in fifty-five hours.

From July 10 to July 12 we move only approximately three or four miles. I suppose we are waiting for our flanks to catch up. We are slowed down by snaking through many mine fields, which again are covered by 88s and mortars. In a pig stable on one deserted farm I encounter two Germans who have been lying here for three days. Both are medics and both have one foot missing; their stumps are not even covered. They had been forced to lag behind their troops and while trying to catch up have stepped on some of their own mines. I soon find that practically all the surrounding terrain is mined, and before the day is over we have twenty more shoe-mine casualties.

On July 12 the terrain becomes just a little more mountainous. We walk through forests without much opposition. That afternoon I rest in a farmhouse in which the civilians have remained behind. The farmer's wife has a six-month old baby with stomach cramps and diarrhea and a high fever. I reassure her that the child does not have appendicitis and will get well on paregoric, sulfadiazine, and forced fluids. In the meantime one of my technicians assists the farmer with a cow giving birth to a calf. For our services rendered, the lady fries for each of us four delicious eggs.

On the afternoon of July 13 we approach Villamagna. We scurry over knolls and through orchards. Villamagna lies on another ridge. We walk up toward the village through an olive grove along a path about three feet wide. The Krauts are waiting for us. As the lead company approaches the town, it is slowed down by rifle, machine-gun, and mortar fire. To make matters worse we soon learn that the path into town is also heavily infested with shoe mines. As the first mines detonate, the men jump off the path into the olive groves, and these unfortunately are also mined. We bandage leg stump after leg stump. Shrapnel bounces off the trees. I expect to lose one of my feet at every move. We are still on the path bandaging stumps as darkness falls. Thus far, only three-fourths of the village is in our hands. I must get to it before it gets completely dark, so that I can find an aid station in which to work, since most of the casualties need plasma. Using a large stick, I probe the ground before each step and thus gradually inch my way forward. Reaching Villamagna, I enter the first building I see. It is a small grocery store. The windows are broken, chairs and counters overturned. I hear moans in the darkness. Many untreated casualties are lying on the floor. Most of these are again shoe-mine casualties that have crawled into the building for protection. I worm my way through the debris and with the aid of a flashlight apply pressure dressings and administer morphine. Mortars are pounding the street outside. The Krauts have pulled out, know that we are in the town, and keep harassing us. At 1:00 A.M. on July 14, Villamagna is finally in our hands. I cautiously leave the store and step outside. I locate battalion headquarters a few houses down the street and set up my aid station next door to it. Litter bearers collect casualties from all the buildings and bring them to the station. We work throughout the night, splinting, bandaging, and administering narcotics. Villamagna has been a tough objective to seize, being a strongpoint in the German defenses along "Bloody Ridge."

The next morning we assemble on the lawn of a large mansion in the northern edge of the town. It is a beautiful home of over twenty spacious rooms, with marble stairways, stately columns, terrazzo floors, balconies, and large windows. The latter are all broken, the furniture is overturned, closets and drawers ransacked, and their contents strewn over the floors. Paintings and pictures torn from the walls lie on the floor. Large mirrors and statues are broken. Unfortunately, this beautiful mansion being occupied by Germans has been subjected to attack by our troops. Now we are sitting here awaiting further orders. One more day of rest is welcome, and I have no objections.

In the afternoon of July 15 we move out, with the town of Palaia as our objective. We should reach it within forty-eight hours. We walk over hills the entire afternoon, that whole night, and until the sundown the next day. After dark on the evening of July 15 we approach a road leading to Palaia, which is about six miles away. We establish our aid station in a barn along the road and rest here for the night.

On the morning of July 17 we move out to attack the enemy. Throughout the morning snipers in trees give us plenty of trouble. Several men in our column are picked off one by one. Patrols are sent out to find the snipers. They are killed as soon as they are spotted. When we are approximately four miles from Palaia, enemy fire becomes heavy and steady. Artillery has zeroed in on the road over which we are walking. The Krauts have spotted our column, are aiming to get us, and will apparently defend Palaia. The shout toward the rear of the column of "Medics needed up front" is heard frequently. As casualties increase, I look about for an aid station. I take refuge in the first house I see. It is located in the bend of the road about ten feet off its right shoulder. It is a two-story farmhouse, cow stable downstairs, living quarters upstairs. A six-foot bank is in front of it. This bank is good protection against incoming artillery. It has thus far saved this stable from total destruction. The upstairs living quarters have already been shot away. We can't close the doors to the downstairs stable since these, too, are unfortunately shattered. At least we have overhead protection and a good stone-and-dirt wall in front of us. On the road about thirty yards ahead of us is a large mined shell crater, which slows down our troops. The Krauts have anticipated this and continuously pound it with artillery. Consequently, casualties are heavy. However, we, being only thirty yards away, rush forth quickly and retrieve them. All have shrapnel wounds. I am working on a poor fellow with half of his face blown off; he is bleeding profusely from an open sinus and broken nose; I have just completed packing his nose and the hole in his cheek and still have one artery clamp hanging on a persistent bleeder when a terrific explosion throws me across the room. My patient instinctively rolls over on his face and loses all the packing I just finished inserting. An 88-mm shell has exploded directly in front of the open doors. The blast has keeled all of us over, but luckily all the shrapnel has bounced off the walls without striking anybody. I repack the poor fellow, who at this stage is just about dead from loss of blood. This place is not a good spot. One of my sergeants reports a combination spring and wine cellar in the back of this stable. Here the walls are four feet thick. To get to it we must step outside and run around to the rear of the house. We do so, one man at a time, and then only between shelling. The wine cellar is not very big but very safe. It only has about five feet of head room and is about eight by eight feet square. We have just about enough room to give casualties plasma. The wounded are lying between wine barrels. We are lucky in having moved, for the stable receives several more direct hits. When the flow of casualties ceases, we move out. I sure hate to leave all this wine behind.

We head for the next farmhouse, which according to my map is approximately one mile away. One by one, at three-minute intervals, we cautiously leave our cellar, step onto the road, and dash toward our objective. We must all pass through the mined crater ahead of us, which is still zeroed in. Between shells we scamper through it on the double. We really race the next thousand yards and reach our objective without casualties. This house, too, is just off the road and surrounded by many olive trees, which catch most of the exploding shells. Thus we are harassed by only tree bursts and are relatively safe from direct hits. We remain here for two hours treating more casualties, which are constantly occurring just on the outskirts of the town.

At 7:00 P.M. our troops have cleared out Palaia. Casualties suffered in the town have been treated by aid men and are lying in houses awaiting my arrival. By the time I enter Palaia the fighting has stopped. Only an occasional mortar round slams into the village. I set up my aid station in an abandoned doctor's office. His bandages and instruments come in handy. Palaia, however, will not be safe for tonight. I am sure that the Germans will send over planes tonight and bomb us. No civilians are in the town, and this is a bad sign. Our orders are to remain here for the night. Before I do so, I shall look for a building more solid than the one I am in. Soon I find one, just made to order. It is two doors away in an ordinary-looking dwelling that has been converted into a spacious cave. I have never seen anything like it. From the living room a trap door leads to a dugout clay cellar eight by twelve feet. From its floor another trap door descends into a cave at least thirty by twenty feet. This cave is thus at least twenty feet underground. The Germans must have just left here, for their radios, switchboards, maps, wine, cognac, and other equipment have all been hastily abandoned. The lower cave has a rear exit leading to a river-bed. This has been an ideal spot for German headquarters. No one would suspect a cave within a house. Its inconspicuous rear exit must have been most convenient. Our night here is very safe. We are tempted to drink the wine and cognac, but suspicion that it might be poisoned stops us from doing so.

The next morning our path is through orchards and vineyards. I pick apples and grapes off the trees and gorge myself with fresh fruit. Resistance is light. Palaia must have been the Germans' last deter-mined stand. Our next fight will probably be at the Arno River.

Snaking our way through orchards and fields, we pass the small town of Buccinano, which is one mile south of San Miniato and the Arno River, and dig in but send reconnoitering patrols toward San Miniato. Florence, under the attack by the British and French, is only fifteen miles to the east. On July 24 the battalion moves toward San Miniato along a ridge overlooking the Arno River. Combat is sporadic but very fierce when it does occur. The Krauts battle fanatically for every farmhouse. Often our boys, having taken the first floor of a house, battle the enemy trapped on the second floor. Grenades are pitched in and out of windows and up and down stairs. All houses are booby trapped and must be entered with the greatest of caution. To clear some of the houses of the enemy, our troops call for very close artil-lery support. Not infrequently they ask for shells to destroy a house fifty yards away from the one in which they themselves have sought refuge. That's putting an awful lot of faith in your own artillery.

All heavy fighting ceases by July 26. Twenty-three days of active combat are behind us. We have cleared out all the Krauts from the southern banks of the Arno. I am in a lone farmhouse. From its top floor I can see the river. Word spreads quickly to the surrounding homes that a doctor has arrived. All the sick babies from a five-mile radius are brought to me. Most have either diarrhea, tonsillitis, swol-len glands, or skin infections. None are diagnostic problems. They respond well to treatment. My reward is food. I indulge in noodle soup, baked chicken, fried rabbit, pork chops, steak, fruit, and aged Tuscan wines. After living on crackers, cheese, and cold hash for three weeks, this, brother, is a real feast.

On July 28, we are relieved by the 91st Division. The night of relief is a memorable one. I sit in front of the fireplace at battalion headquarters and philosophize with the colonel. With the help of good Tuscan wine, the conversation is very stimulating. Near midnight I ask the colonel just what the disposition of the troops is at this moment. He states that all of our men except a small skeleton crew here at headquarters have completed their move to the rear two hours ago and that relief troops won't come up until dawn. He does not think that many Germans are still around nor will they recross the river to see if we are still here. The thought that I am sitting here in this farmhouse drinking wine with the colonel at midnight with neither troops in front nor behind us is somewhat uncomfortable. We finish our wine at 1:00 A.M., climb into our jeeps, and in bright moonlight rattle toward the rear.

Return to Rome for Relaxation

JULY 28, 1944–SEPTEMBER 17, 1944

Our rest area is in another olive grove in the vicinity of Villamagna. Pyramidal tents are once again our living quarters. The battalion's battle casualties are replaced. Approximately two hundred and fifty new faces appear. I now realize that we have already lost and replaced one half of the battalion since starting our push up the Italian peninsula. Thus far, my chances of having remained alive have been about fifty-fifty.

The troops continue their training. The new men must learn from the veterans. Night after night, in total blackout, we cross a dry riverbed in imaginary boats. We are simulating crossing the Arno River. All these dry runs are becoming mighty monotonous but are probably necessary.

Movies are shown in a meadow at night, and several USO shows visit our area. I see "Gas Light" with Ingrid Bergman. Replacements talk about a singer named Frank Sinatra who is setting the musical world on fire, but none of us here have ever heard him. It is rumored that he might tour Italy in the near future.

The arrival of the officers' liquor ration is always a big event. One night, while playing poker in a tent, six officers and I finish one quart each. Our little party ends in toasts, speeches, songs, and boisterous laughter that can be heard a mile away. At 3:00 A.M. a hazy figure in shorts enters the tent to protest the noise. I announce the newcomer by shouting, "Look at the head on that one," and as my eyes gradually begin to focus realize too late that our protesting guest is none other than the battalion commander himself. The next morning I am ordered to report to his tent, where I receive a stern lecture about conduct unbecoming an officer and am threatened with demotion because of inebriation and so forth. Unfortunately, I am never demoted or replaced. No matter what I do, it is apparently my fate to remain with the infantry.

A Medical Administrative Corps officer joins my aid station complement. This is an improvement. He is not a doctor but a first lieutenant trained in medical administrative duties. He relieves me of the burden of lecturing to my boys, taking them on hikes, and leading them on those monotonous night problems. The MAC officer's addition to a medical detachment of a battalion is an innovation. Now instead of two physicians in each battalion there will be only one, plus an MAC. This arrangement makes more front-line physicians available to more outfits and divisions.

At this time we also hear the very encouraging news that the Yanks are only fifty-five miles from Paris.

I am offered another five-day pass to Rome, this time to accompany enlisted men on leave. My only duties are to see that they get to Rome safely and that all return. I shall not be quartered at the Hotel Excelsior but at the officers' quarters of the Forum Mussolini. The latter has been converted to a recreation hotel for enlisted men and is very well managed and supervised, a far cry from the tempest raging at the Hotel Excelsior. I have nothing to lose by accepting the pass, and leave for Rome.

Even though quartered at the Forum Mussolini, I manage to spend most of my time at the Hotel Excelsior. Temptation is too great. I gain entrance to the hotel by borrowing another officer's pass. I spend most of my hours at the bar, talking to friends who are also on leave. One afternoon, however, I see the stage show "Over Twenty-One." I spend another entire day touring the outskirts of Rome. I even muster up enough ambition to climb the old Military Tower. Nero supposedly watched Rome burn from this vantage point. I spend all the nights at the Forum Mussolini except the last one. Parts of this night I remember, other parts are a complete blank.

My adventure starts in the late afternoon in the Hotel Excelsior. I am sitting at the bar drinking rum and Coca-Cola. Supper is announced and all guests leave for the dining room. In the recreation room across from the bar remains a lone girl, sitting on a Ping-Pong table. As I catch her eye, she beckons with a smile and asks me to play a game with her. After an entire afternoon's session at the bar I have difficulty focusing on the ball, but after the strenuous exercise expended during three fast games, I sober up completely. Not until then do I wake up to the fact that this young lady might like to play more than just Ping-Pong. She speaks very little English, only just enough to make herself barely understood. Having completed our game, I invite her to the bar for a drink. In the course of conversation she digs into her purse and produces a recent Italian health certificate, giving her name, address, age, and date of most recent blood test for syphilis, which by the way, is negative. From the caduceus on my collar I suppose she deduced that I am a physician and just wants to prove to me that she is clean and healthy. Her certificate of course is no guarantee, but it is a rather strong hint that she apparently has no plans for this evening unless I am it. We do not eat supper but remain at the bar until 8:00 P.M., then go upstairs for dancing and the floor show.

Lillie is a knockout. She is very popular and knows many of the officers. However, she won't leave my side and clings to me tenaciously. Lillie isn't a day over eighteen, although she insists that she is twenty-one; her certificate substantiates her claim, but I am sure it is a fake. Lillie simply loves a good time. With long blond hair, and sexy, she is a cuddly creature. She is about five feet two, and all her curves are in the right places. She drinks only half the amount I do, but has just as wonderful a time. What if Lillie wants to make a night of it? I must take some action. Shortly before midnight I bump into a good friend, also a physician, from clearing station of our division. I inform him that I have no place to stay for the night except the Forum Mussolini at the other end of town. He offers to share his room with me. He explains that he and his roommate plus girl friends will occupy the beds, but that there is plenty of room on the floor. The beds all have double mattresses and it will be a simple matter to take one apart and put it on the floor. After all, we have slept in far less luxury than that in the past few months. I accept his suggestion and promise him that should I stay for the night I shall sleep on the room's adjoining balcony so as not to disturb his activities. At 1:00 A.M. the orchestra plays "Auld Lang Syne," and Lillie asks, "Where do we sleep tonight, baby?" Her question poses no problem, and I answer, "On an open balcony, but I'm sure you'll be comfortable."

Arm in arm we climb two flights of stairs to the room. My friends and their dates have not yet arrived. My first move is to tear one of the beds apart. Not being sober, I find it a difficult job that involves a good bit of fumbling effort. I can't lift the heavy mattress but drag it instead out onto the balcony. I also swipe a sheet. Things are beginning to look cozy. The August air is warm, the sky clear, and the chances of rain remote. I look back into the room to see what Lillie is doing. She is sitting stark naked on a vanity bench applying makeup. She says, "Hello, baby," and walks out onto the balcony inspecting the situation. Spotting an officer two balconies below us, she cheerfully calls out, "Hello, Major." I assume she knows him. Lillie is unabashed. First she wants to dance in the nude, then engage in a little playful wrestling. She finally pulls me down onto the mattress. Her response is immediate and intense. She seems to live for moments like this. She is unrestrained and almost animal-like, with no inhibitions whatsoever. I am now sorry that I drank so much. I would like to have a clearer memory of this evening.

Just before I fall asleep, I vaguely hear my roommates inside, bouncing and frolicking, then sudden complete silence. I awaken sometime during the night, rather cool, for Lillie has wrapped herself in the entire sheet. Since I don't intend to shiver the rest of the night, I nudge Lillie to arise. Somewhat drowsy, we carry the mattress inside. Activity on the beds has subsided, the occupants are fast asleep. Our move under cover, however, has fully awakened Lillie. She is livelier than ever and inexhaustible. Her vitality knows no bounds.

At 7:00 A.M. I awaken. The room's other five occupants are sound asleep. I quickly dress and wake up Lillie to say good-bye. I must be at the Forum Mussolini at 8:00 A.M. and take my charge of enlisted men back to Villamagna. Lillie awakens only momentarily. Sleepy-eyed, she wishes me luck and says, "Hurry back to Rome baby, I love you." I reach into my wallet, pull out forty dollars in military currency, and press it into her palm. She looks at the money and gives it back to me. "No money, baby, I love you," she says, with a few honest-to-goodness tears in her eyes. I leave confused, not knowing what to think of Lillie.

Arriving at the Forum Mussolini, I shower and shave, then eat a hearty breakfast. As a prophylactic measure I immediately dose myself with sulfadiazine and swallow pills for a whole week.

My trip back to the division rest area is uneventful. The only discouraging news I receive is that our division commander, General Sloan, has been replaced because of a chronic skin ailment. You hate to change horses in midstream, especially if you have finally learned to have full confidence in your leader.

On August 31 we break camp and move a short distance to the vicinity of Scandicci, near Florence. We are still in reserve but at the same time are backing up the 442nd Japanese-American Regimental Combat Team. These boys are good and really need no backing up. However, Army orders say you need reserves, and so it shall be.

For seventeen more days we do nothing but loaf. We are in a fruit orchard and sleep in pup tents or out in the open on cots surrounded by mosquito netting. The weather is beautiful, warm and dry during the day, and pleasantly cool at night. This is perfect combat weather, yet our Fifth Army lines are not moving. We let good fighting days slip by, all because of Allied plans to invade southern France. Every farmer, every civilian, and every GI seems to know that southern France is to be invaded. I would hate to take part in this invasion, it is such an ill-kept secret. The Germans must be laughing out loud. We can't move forward since our Fifth Army has been stripped of three veteran divisions, the 3d, the 36th, and the 45th, all three to be part of the invasion force. Only three veteran divisions remain in Italy, the 34th, 85th, and 88th. New outfits to replace those we have lost are the 91st Division, the Brazilian Expeditionary Force, and the 442d Regimental Combat Team.

For days on end while sitting in this fruit orchard I play poker, see outdoor movies and stage shows, drink whiskey, eat grapes and figs, and generally fight boredom.

My greatest disappointment is the replacement of our battalion commander, Colonel Yeager. He is promoted to another regiment. I'll take my hat off to Colonel Yeager anytime, a gentleman, a fearless fighter, a man I respect and would follow anywhere. Our new colonel, Colonel Hess, will have the impossible task of proving himself as good a man as Yeager.

Colonel Hess is very polite to me. His first greeting is, "Hi, Doc; you're a good man to know."

I know why the colonel is polite to me. He thinks no different than all the other men. Someday in the near future he might need my services. Not only that, but I can also be his adviser in the very important matter of the morale of his troops. The sick and wounded always beef first to their doctor. Once hurt, they express their sincere opinions. The insult of being wounded suddenly makes them very talkative, and in a semiconscious state of shock they often express opinions they never dared mention before. I always know more of the battalion morale than the battalion commander.

Medically, I do absolutely nothing except treat a few cases of gonorrhea. Someone has hidden a girl in a pup tent; she does a twenty-four-hour business and spreads the disease around a good bit. Her nickname is "Queen of Florence." We get rid of her, and my business falls off too.

On September 16, 1944, we are alerted. The rainy season has started. This is a hell of a time for a new push. Maybe it won't last long. I am glad I can't look into the future. On September 17 we break camp to move into new assault positions. We shall finally fight our way across the Arno River, something we have practiced for weeks. But lo and behold, nobody has told us that the British, very slowly and methodically, have captured Florence with several bridges intact. We cross the Arno in jeeps and trucks, a hell of a note after months of practicing crossing that damn stream. Not until now am I told that during the past two weeks our 1st Battalion has scouted several small villages to the north of Florence and met with no resistance.

The Apennine Campaign and the Gothic Line

SEPTEMBER 17, 1944–NOVEMBER 8, 1944

The night of September 17 is dark, the moon obscured by dark clouds. We enter Florence on a highway that reminds me of East River Drive in Philadelphia. The road is lined with old trees, their broad tops forming an arched roof. We cross the Arno River in a few seconds, riding over on a British-built Bailey bridge (a temporary bridge built by the Corps of Engineers). Our convoy drives with lights on. From this I assume that the enemy must be a good distance to the north. Florence itself is not badly damaged. The only houses within the city that are demolished are those at important crossroads or road junctions. Their debris forms road blocks, which our engineers clear rapidly. Once we are through Florence, blackout regulations are enforced. We drive in darkness along a paved single-lane highway for approximately six hours. Now and then I doze off, only to be jolted awake by terrific explosions. I am convinced that a bomb has been dropped on the road. No bombs, however, have fallen; our Long Toms (long-range, large-millimeter cannon) are shooting from positions near the highway. Their eardrum-bursting roar and blinding flash scare me half to death each time they fire. If I only knew that they were about to shoot, I could prepare myself for the shock. However, it is too dark to see their position, and every shell is a sudden scare and surprise. After each explosion my driver throws the jeep into a short burst of speed as though trying to escape from the unknown. No matter how steady my nerves, those big shells, whether going out or coming in, continue to give me the creeps.

Sometime after midnight and still on the highway, our trucks come to a halt. My staff sergeant, who has preceded us by going on the quartering party last night, is here to meet us. He states that our assembly area is at the base of Mount Altuzzo and that no farmhouses are available. He leads us off the highway over small trails to a chicken shed located in a ravine behind a small knoll. He informs me that the terrain ahead of us consists of nothing but mountains. I try to find my

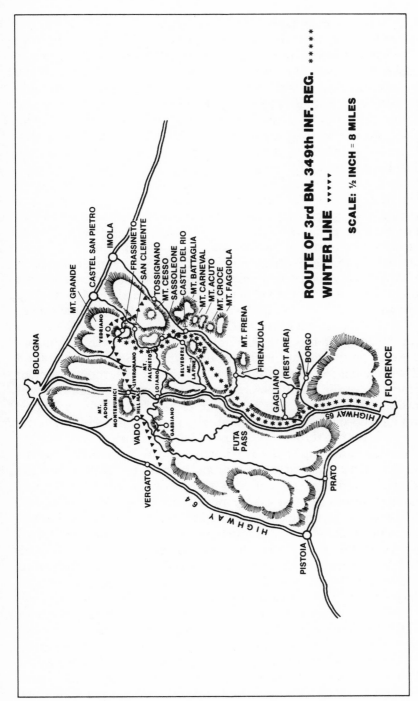

4 The Apennine Campaign: The Breakthrough of the Gothic Line and the Shifting Winter Line

position on the map. From what I can gather, we are just off to the right of Highway 65 about fifteen miles north of Florence. Highway 65 is the main road from Florence to Bologna. It cuts through the formidable Apennines, or little alps. Futa Pass lies about ten miles ahead of us and Radicosa Pass about twenty miles. The Germans will probably defend every foot of this rugged country. The Apennines make up the Gothic Line, the last line of defense before the Po Valley. The mountains on my map show elevations of 879 meters, 903 meters, 922 meters, 968 meters, and up. In my future I see nothing but mountains, mud, rain, and Krauts.

Our chicken-shed aid station is so full of fleas that I choose to sleep in a straw-padded hole on the outside. I can't see anything of the terrain except rocks and brush. Tank destroyers and artillery shoot all night supporting the 85th Division, which is fighting to conquer just one more of the numerous mountains ahead of us.

At dawn I am awakened by a drizzling rain. We are ordered to pack up immediately and move a half-turn around the base of our present knoll, since the enemy ahead of us has not been dislodged during the night and can now observe us. By noon we are out of the enemy's sight. The troops dig in, then have a C ration lunch.

In the early afternoon of September 19 I venture forth on a reconnaissance party together with five line officers. Since my battalion will follow the 85th Division's attack in the late afternoon, some of us must scout the terrain beforehand. Our reconnaissance party will move as far as the present front line of the 85th Division troops, through whose lines we shall eventually pass and press on, with the hope of breaking through the Gothic Line defenses.

We walk slowly up Highway 65, which at this point snakes uphill through a dense pine forest; twisting and turning, it runs close to cliffs and under overhanging boulders. It is unpaved, and the thin, slippery mud flows downhill like a slowly moving stream of lava. Dead horses, dead Germans, and dead GIs lie half-buried in the mud. Enemy barbed-wire defenses are scattered throughout the forest off the road. I shall always remember this forest. It is a dead one, half of the trees are felled, and those still standing are bare and splintered. This forest, raked for days by heavy artillery, is truly a cemetery of trees. Our artillery has assumed precarious positions along this road; guns are perched on shell-pocked shoulders at a dangerous angle and threaten to slide down the cliffs with each recoil. I can't imagine how these heavy guns were ever brought into position past and over so many obstacles. Felled trees blocking the road frequently slow our walk, and we are often forced off the road and into the remains of the forest. Here we stumble past Jerry dugouts littered with gas masks, letters, pictures, shovels, and helmets. Barbed wire stretched at intervals and booby traps usually force us to take to the road again. Once on top of the mountain, we encounter the company command posts of elements of the 85th Division. Deep shell holes serve as dugouts. In one large crater are eleven disarmed enemy, waiting to be led to the rear. One of their number is wounded. I treat the hole in his hip and speak to him in German, which he understands poorly. He states that he was shot by one of the men in this group; he tried to surrender but the others objected to his idea. He is a Pole, the others are Germans.

From atop the mountain and from behind rocks we study our maps and the terrain ahead of us. We try to visually memorize every land feature over which we shall push during the next few days. I cannot see very much—fog and rain obscure the details of each mountain. At 3:00 P.M. we retrace our path and return to our waiting troops. These are ready to move out, having only waited for our return.

Once again our battalion moves out in a column of ducks. Our path is up the mountain and through the forest, the highway being too muddy and also blocked by stalled or sliding trucks. We reach the ridge about an hour before dusk. I no longer see any men of the 85th Division. They apparently advanced, for machine-pistol and small-arms fire can be heard ahead of us. We move over the ridge and down a slope and are soon back on Highway 65, but this time are walking downhill on the other side of the mountain. We pass over many dead horses and Germans. Their stench is sickening. By nightfall we are just off the highway in a narrow ravine in which is nestled a lone farmhouse. The troops are ordered to dig in. The battalion command post will take over the top story of the house, and the aid station the ground floor. The ground floor turns out to be a tool shed. It is now dark and raining heavily. By the glow of our shielded flashlights, we clean the shed of its tools and debris. Everything we touch, we toss outside. I am finally settled and ready to rest for the night. I grope for my blanket pack and, once having found it, find that it has acquired a foul odor. I investigate and find that I had laid it into a pile of Kraut feces. In disgust I throw the blanket outside. Sergeant Fertig while groping for his equipment puts his hand into another pile. He mutters curses and now hates all Krauts more than ever.

We spend an uneventful night in this dark, damp, and crowded shed. A heavy rain falls throughout the night and at dawn still shows no signs of diminishing. We are apparently still reserve troops, for our field kitchens serve us a hot breakfast. We loaf all day, watching the downpour turn the ground into still deeper mud.

At nightfall we are ordered to proceed forward. We are still following elements of the 85th Division. As soon as they stall, we are to move through them. They apparently moved well during the past eighteen hours, and our march tonight will be a forced one, for we must stay close behind them.

The night is pitch black. It is still raining hard. I haven't the slightest idea where we are going. All I know is that the direction is north. We slog over hills, down ravines, along and across creekbeds, sliding, falling, stumbling, and cursing. I strain my eyes to keep track of the man ahead of me. Men falling out lose the column within seconds and are left alone. Those ailing and exhausted simply crawl into the first barn or haystack they see, and fall asleep. Along the higher ridges wind whips up the steady rain and chills you to the bone. The rain has soaked through my coat and all my clothing. I feel miserable. As the column momentarily comes to a halt, I sit down on the trail in a puddle of water six inches deep. I no longer care what happens or what I do. I have never felt lower in my life.

At one point in our march we cross over a creek on a wooden bridge. Two men ahead of me, apparently assuming the bridge has a railing, walk to one side to reach it, find none, and fall eight feet into the creek bed. In trying to climb down the creek's bank to reach them, I fall also but remain unhurt. Both of the fallen GIs have head lacerations. I dress their wounds by throwing a blanket over them and myself and turning on my flashlight. Treating casualties in this manner is time consuming and always causes me to lose contact with the rear of our column. Treatment of the casualties completed and not knowing the trail, we just sit on the bridge and wait. Some supply personnel must sooner or later pass over the trail. After approximately thirty minutes we hear the sound of approaching mules. As one of the animals crosses the bridge, I grab its tail and hang on to it for the next two hours. When the mule train finally halts, I find that it has caught up to the rear of my battalion. Our troops are momentarily halted near a farmhouse. I look for the nearest barn, take off my wet coat and gear, and lie down in the warm straw next to a munching cow. It is 5:00 A.M. September 21. We rest until dawn.

There is no visible sunrise. The sky is gray, the air damp and foggy. At 10:00 A.M. we continue our march over one large mountain and around another. From atop the latter we look down upon the Firenzuola–Castel del Rio road. We are to descend this mountain, cross the road, and take the mountains on the other side. According to my map we are at a point about two miles east of Firenzuola. We are apparently bypassing the German stronghold Firenzuola on our right flank. Perhaps the 85th Division will now drift off to the right and fight for this city. We have had no enemy contact these past two days, and we are just about due for some action. Instinctively, I sense trouble ahead. Descending the mountain toward the road, I come upon several abandoned dead of the 85th Division. Their mortars lie in a pool of blood beside them. Suddenly we see six Germans pushing a cart up the road toward Firenzuola. They are apparently unaware of our presence and must be lost. Anxiously we watch their every move, and our men must be restrained from shooting them, for this would reveal our positions. These stray Germans will be captured anyway by troops farther up the road. As the small enemy group approaches a group of houses, a machine gun rattles from the top floor. One German falls dead, the others surrender to the 85th.

Once down on the road I feel very uneasy. It is a narrow road with many sharp turns and cut through rock. I feel trapped and helpless. I have the feeling as though a hundred enemy eyes were watching my every move, just waiting for the correct moment to open fire. I am only too happy to dodge into the first farmhouse I see and establish a temporary aid station.

After a few hours' rest we are off again. We proceed along the road for about one-quarter mile, then leave it to climb another mountain to our north. The easiest way up is to follow a draw. Halfway up we finally receive what we have all been expecting, a heavy artillery barrage. For this draw to be so accurately zeroed in, the Germans must have been watching our every move for at least several hours. They have saved their ammunition and have waited until we are in such a location where each shell will take the greatest number of lives. They are seldom wrong in their calculations. Their artillery and accuracy remains superb, much to our dismay. Shrapnel flies all over the place, ricochets off boulders and sprays the entire draw. I sweat out each shell with a prayer. With each whine I dive to the ground, then rapidly rise to treat a casualty's wound before the next shell comes in. The troops waste little time in leaving this ravine. They scatter rapidly and move forward on the double. Soon the ravine is empty except for about two dozen casualties, still lying here and there and awaiting treatment. It takes me about two hours to administer to all of them. Shells keep pouring in at regular three-minute intervals and greatly hinder my progress. Once the last man is dressed, I and the three medics with me dash up and out of the ravine and to the north. I see no sign of our troops. We step onto a trail that runs horseshoe fashion along the mountain slope, a vast valley lying below us. I surmise that our troops have taken this same trail; I doubt if they descended into the valley. We calmly walk along this trail for several miles. It is deathly quiet and almost dark. The Lord only knows where we are. It is very eerie, and I am very anxious. At any moment we could possibly be either shot or captured. After rounding a sharp turn in the trail, we are suddenly in a small village of perhaps six houses. Only a handful of our advance troops are already here. This time by pure mistake the medics are ahead of the column instead of behind it. The battalion apparently is taking a different trail to this village, and we have used the obvious one that could have meant disaster, but luck was with us. With only a few of our fighting men in the village, I have my pick of houses for an aid station. I choose the one most solidly built. An Italian woman serves us fresh-baked bread and noodle soup, a delicious feast. The battalion moves into the village an hour later, and we are all reunited for the night.

At dawn the next morning we move forward. We have acquired a guest during the night, a Jerry POW, who is now lugging our rations and plasma. He has a slight flesh wound on his right arm but otherwise is quite well, except for his morale, which is very low. I listen to his sad tale of capture. He was a member of a German patrol. His company is somewhere on the next mountain. The patrol was sent out to scout for us. He became separated from it. Stalking through the night, he suddenly heard machine-pistol fire a few feet away from him. He became startled and shouted to whom he thought was his comrade, "You crazy fool, quit shooting unless you have something to shoot at." His comrade, however, turned out to be one of our own guards, who was examining a captured German machine pistol that accidently fired. Our man quickly pounced on the Kraut, thus making him an unhappy prisoner of war.

I speak to the colonel and tell him that this prisoner insists that a company of Germans is near us and that if we continue on our present trail we shall bypass them. The colonel pays little attention. We cross over one ridge, descend into a valley, and enter a small village, where we rest for one hour. During this time I treat several medical cases, some with high fever. We then proceed up another mountain, leaving the sick in the village to be evacuated later. After three hours of steep climbing we are at the top and are looking down on the valley and the village below us. One of our officers who has been scrutinizing the valley through field glasses suddenly shouts an alarm. He has spotted what appears to be a platoon of enemy walking toward the village we just have left behind. This group of Krauts must be the bypassed Germans our prisoner has been talking about. If they reach the village, our abandoned wounded will be their prisoners. Our men hastily set up several machine guns and mortars and fire on the enemy, pinning them down and halting their advance. At the same time a patrol is hurriedly dispatched, its mission to scurry back down into the valley, encircle the enemy, and as the covering fire lifts, move in for the capture. Within an hour this mission is accomplished. We capture thirty confused Krauts. One of their number is a wounded sergeant with a compound fracture of the femur. He is carried to us on a litter by the prisoners. It takes the prisoners a good two hours to climb up to us. They arrive tired and dejected. Their commanding officer is very disgusted. A month ago he was still on the Russian front, finally obtained a one week's furlough, returned to Germany where he was married, was promoted from lieutenant to captain, then sent to Italy. His company was sent out to delay our advance, became lost in the mountains, and now is captured without a good fight. He had no idea that we were already in this vicinity. He has goofed his first assignment and considers his military career at an end.

The rest of the night we spend on this mountain. We sleep in the cellar of a farmhouse and lock the prisoners of war in the adjacent barn. Here I treat their wounded sergeant. I cleanse his wound, apply a pressure dressing, reduce his fracture, splint his leg, and give him plasma. While my sergeant and I work, the prisoners are commenting on our technique and good equipment and clean uniforms; they appear most satisfied with the treatment given their wounded comrade. They are unaware that I understand every word. Having completed treating the sergeant, I turn to them as a group and in German bid them a good night and a happy future. They stare in amazement as I close the barn door.

September 23, 1944, is warm and sunny. At 4:00 A.M. we set out climbing more mountains, our next objective for the day being Mount La Fine. This is another formidable hill mass, one of the highest before the Po Valley. The terrain is again to our disadvantage. To reach Mount La Fine we must first pass through a dense oak forest, then over a flat meadow two miles wide, then up sheer cliffs to the top of bald La Fine. A large white cross stands on its bare summit. The Germans will undoubtedly defend La Fine to the bitter end. This mountain is strategic and will be taken only at the cost of many lives.

The oak forest is infested with Italian collaborators armed with German machine pistols. They are hidden in trees, behind rocks, and in hastily built dugouts. They snipe continuously and are hindering our advance. While the battalion halts, L Company is dispatched into the forest with orders to kill all and take no prisoners. In two hours the forest is silent.

The next hazard is the crossing of the two-mile-wide meadow at the foot of Mount La Fine. Our heavy artillery is blasting La Fine continuously. I am positive that the meadow is heavily mined and zeroed in. At ten-yard intervals the men of my battalion leave the oak forest and commence their treacherous walk across the flat, open plain. Looking through field glasses, I can barely see a road running around the base of La Fine. This road is dotted with occasional houses, and one by one these suddenly blow up in a cloud of dust and smoke, hit either by our tanks or artillery. I feel as though I am embarking on my death march as I follow the troops across the meadow. La Fine ahead of us is probably crawling with Germans looking down upon us from a height of about 993 meters, watching our every move. We are completely at their mercy—they can shoot at will at perfect targets. Even though our artillery gives us constant covering fire, we are very exposed on our flanks. The first mile is uneventful except for the anxiety that accompanies all uncertainty. Will I survive the assault on La Fine? I am scared to death yet can't afford to show it. The chaplain and I walk together. It is definitely comforting to have him at my side. I know he is a better Christian than I am. God will surely spare him, and if He does I, walking with him, will probably be spared also. I have suddenly become a superstitious foxhole Christian.

Midway across the field we are suddenly caught in machine-gun cross fire. I suspect Italian collaborators that our troops have missed. Bullets whistle by and kick up small puffs of dust as they strike the ground. The suddenness of the attack makes us all instinctively hit the dirt. Since we have no cover, however, we are better and quieter targets lying flat than when up and moving. I shout to my medics to rise and run. At top speed we race the last mile across the meadow, losing helmets and dropping equipment. We reach the base of Mount La Fine panting, sweating, dusty, and thirsty. None of my medics have been hit. We could have lost many had we permitted ourselves to be pinned down.

Once at the foot of La Fine, we begin our crawl up its slopes. The battalion chooses the first accessible draw. I leave a small complement of medics behind as rear aid station in one of the shattered farmhouses at the foot of the mountain and follow the troops. What I do not understand is why we are getting so much fire. The draw we are ascending is hell. The shells we are receiving are coming from our rear. Either our own guns are firing upon us, or bypassed German artillery is shooting us up. The numerous airbursts make me suspect the latter. We have one casualty approximately every five minutes, and he is rapidly evacuated to the rear aid station at the foot of La Fine.

Our struggle up Mount La Fine takes a good five hours. Approximately three hundred yards from the top the rear of the column digs in. I am just in the process of digging my hole when a new enemy artillery barrage comes thundering in. This is all heavy stuff, too, at least 240 mm. The exploding shells blast large craters into the surrounding rocks. Shrapnel bounces all over the place. I rush to a rock ledge one hundred yards away, where the colonel is speaking over a field radio. He confirms my suspicions that the German fire is coming from our rear. He has just been informed that our flanks have not kept up with us, that we are way out in front, and that enemy artillery has spotted us on La Fine and is trying to knock us off. If we can hold out another hour until dark, we might have a chance to remain on La Fine. That one hour is the longest I have ever spent. One shell explodes and five casualties occur at one time. We rush to them where they lie, but before we can complete treatment, another shell drops in. We hit the ground, get up and bandage, hit the ground again, get up and give morphine, hit the ground again, get up and apply a splint. Soon I imagine that every incoming shell has my number on it. I duck and wince with each loud bang or whistle. We treat at least thirty casualties during that long hour, and each one is a complicated problem with respect to both treatment and our self-preservation.

After dark the shelling is only sporadic. We all dig in. Every soldier digs tonight. Those that have never paid much attention to digging holes are now digging hard, fast, and deep. We can all sense that we shall really catch hell at sunrise.

The chaplain and I dig ourselves a common hole. We dig three hours. We start at the base of an overhanging rock, dig six feet down, then burrow horizontally both to the north and south. We imagine ourselves relatively safe at the base of this inverted T-shaped hole. Approximately ten feet down the slope from our hole we dig a series of others in which to put casualties for evacuation after hurried treatment. Never before have I had such an exposed and unsatisfactory aid station.

The first night is like a nightmare. The sporadic shelling from the rear is now a lesser problem. The big problem is counterattacks met by the troops on the summit of La Fine. Hand-to-hand combat rages all night. The rattle of machine guns, the spurts of machine pistols, and the pounding of automatic rifles sound very close, and sometimes I imagine that combat is taking place only several feet from my hole so loud and distinct are the explosions, the shouting, and the clamor.

I do not sleep the entire night. Between treatment of casualties in total darkness I continue improving our hole, making it deeper and wider.

There is no visible sunrise. Luckily, September 24 is very foggy. Visibility is ten yards. German artillery does not have direct observation. We walk about on the slopes of La Fine. At the sound of any shell every man jumps into the nearest hole. All hits scored by the enemy are pure luck. Some casualties are really unjustified, such as direct hits on foxholes, of which there are several.

We spend two nights and three days on La Fine. On the second day the fire from our rear stops. The responsible German guns have either moved out or have been destroyed. Enemy counterattacks on top of La Fine, however, increase. German guns to the north are now pounding the summit day and night. Many brave GIs lose their lives on top of La Fine. Stories told by wounded coming down to us for treatment are real thrillers. Men are captured and recaptured. During hand-to-hand combat some are pushed off cliffs, plunging to their deaths in the valley below. Patrols get lost and are reported missing. Ground captured by us is pounded by enemy artillery until it is evacuated or every man is killed. Grenade battles rage at close range. Attacks and counterattacks are waged for three nights.

A steady drizzle adds to our misery on La Fine. We subsist on K rations only. Sleeping is difficult. Every night the chaplain awakens me several times, admonishing me for snoring. He is concerned that a lost German patrol might wander past our hole and drop a grenade. Once awake, I see shadows and many imaginary enemies. I worry about the progress on top of La Fine. If our men fail to ward off one counterattack, we will be overrun also. All these thoughts give me insomnia.

After three days on La Fine, enemy counterattacks cease. The colonel informs us that our flanks have caught up with us and our line of advance is again straight. The enemy is slowly retreating. Since the northern slopes of La Fine are too steep, we cannot go forward to advance but must climb back down the way we came and pass around the base of La Fine in order to move northward. We do so in the afternoon of September 25.

Three days of rain have made the slopes of La Fine very slippery, and it takes us just as long to descend as it did to ascend. The base of La Fine is now already a rear area. In our rear aid station we are served stewed rabbit and hot coffee. We also receive mail.

After four hours of rest we walk around the base of Mount La Fine, then head north. We follow mule trails over more mountains. Jerry knows we are coming; he keeps shelling our long column. Most shells explode against tree trunks, scattering the shrapnel in an unpredictable manner. Occasionally our column is forced to halt because of some obstacle ahead. I detest sweating out these long column rests. They are nerve-racking. Your chances of being hit while resting are greater than when moving. We trudge on all day and all night. On the morning of September 26 we run into troops of the 1st and 2d Battalions. The paths toward our separate objectives apparently cross. We are directed to dig into the reverse slope of a mountain and get a few hours sleep. A small stream runs in the valley about five hundred feet below us. I climb down to it, wash, and shave. The chaplain reminds me of snipers, but even those no longer worry me. Nothing upsets me any more; I am too tired. I feel somewhat better after a clean shave and climb back up to our troops. For several hours I watch enemy artillery pound a mountain approximately a thousand yards to our left. I haven't the slightest idea what the shooting is all about. Trees crash to the ground, and soon the slopes are bare and splintered.

At dusk we move forward again. I know nothing. No one has informed me what our objective is. No one seems to know anything. Why in the hell do we always have to move out at night when you can't see a damn thing? It seems to me that we could move ahead twice as fast in daylight. We slug over more mountain trails for about four hours. At 10:00 P.M. we are ordered to halt on the trail. We must wait for supplies. A mule train with rations is several hours behind us. We set up an aid station in a leaking wet sheepherder's shelter and treat sore feet, diarrheas, and sore throats. At 1:00 A.M. the mules arrive to replenish our K rations; we receive mail, but it is too dark to read it. At 3:00 A.M. we push forward again. I can't see where we are going; all I know is that it is uphill over bushes, rocks and around trees. At dawn we are on that ridge we have been trying to reach all night. Just at daylight a ridge is a hell of a place to be. Walking along the skyline is just meat for Jerry. Why we are not knocked off the ridge I'll never know. Either the Krauts have moved or their observers are asleep. After walking along the skyline for about a mile, we cross a small saddle in the ridge and step onto a dirt road. A large stone house stands just ahead. Its cellar is underground, and only the first and second floors are vulnerable targets. Small-arms fire can be heard just ahead, and we pick this house as our aid station. We will undoubtedly soon have casualties. We medics move into the building while Headquarters Company digs in behind the house and the rifle companies move ahead along the shoulders of the road and through the mountains and ridges overlooking Castel del Rio.

We aren't in the house longer than five minutes when we are shelled by self-propelled guns. We rapidly evacuate the first floor and race down the stairs into the cellar. The cellar is filled with civilians and many nuns. This house is either a church or a church home. As shells explode against the outside walls of the first floor above us and debris crashes down, the civilians and nuns mumble continuous prayers in monotonous low tones. We are indeed in strange surroundings. The usually boisterous and cursing soldier now mixed among praying nuns and civilians stands silent; he is suddenly awe-inspired by the implicit faith these folks have in the power of prayer. Many casualties are brought into the basement for treatment. The praying congregation continues to pray; it pays little attention to us, and we disregard it as we methodically do our job.

By mid-afternoon enemy fire ceases. Our troops are already several miles ahead of us—several ridges forward. Our next move is to catch up to them. How to find them is the big problem. I have had this experience so many times now that I am getting sick of it. While we lag behind treating casualties, the troops move on, and soon we are lost. Sometimes Headquarters Company has enough foresight to mark the trail it has chosen; sometimes it forgets to do so; then we depend on litter squads walking with the troops; eventually these retrace their steps with a casualty, find us, and on their return trip lead us to our battalion. Sometimes even the litter squads get lost; on these occasions we just wander around, look for communications wire here and there, follow the path of discarded equipment and shell cases, or walk in the general direction given us by a casual walking wounded who encounters us. When we are lost at night, we often walk around in circles for hours and finally give up and just lie down on the trail and sleep.

This afternoon Headquarters Company has marked the trail with pieces of gauze tied to bushes at regular intervals. The only trouble is, I can't see the gauze until I am about ten feet away from it. I can't believe that troops can have taken such a horrible trail; sometimes we walk along a ridge, then along a reverse slope, then along a foot-path of some sorts, then over no path at all but over rocks, brush, and bushes. It begins to rain, and for several hours we slip and slide, always straining our eyes for that lousy piece of gauze. Near sundown we step onto a dirt trail about four feet wide. We must be approaching a village. The path leads downhill. Visibility through the rain and dusk is about fifty yards. We no longer find gauze markers; I suppose Headquarters Company thought it common sense to just follow this good path. I feel rather uncomfortable. For all I know, we might be walking right into the enemy's hands. As medical officer I am supposed to be unarmed. At noon today, however, I acquired a pistol from a wounded officer. Just grasping it gives me more confidence; I don't even know if it's loaded, nor would I know how to unlock and shoot it, never having fired a revolver of this type before. Sergeant Torres is carrying an M-1 rifle—shame on him—he, too, has lost faith in his Red Cross arm band.

Shortly, we see a group of three farmhouses ahead of us. We cautiously walk on. I hear no voices nor see any signs of life. As I walk around a sharp bend in the road, I suddenly see the barrel of a large gun protruding from the bushes and covering our path. As the barrel rises slowly I am on the verge of diarrhea. Suddenly a GI voice shouts "Halt." Sergeant Torres answers, "Lower your barrel and go back to sleep." For a brief moment I have visions of being a Kraut prisoner, but the barrel of the gun is that of one of our own tank destroyers. The crew informs us that we are only about thirty minutes behind our battalion, which is heading toward Sassoleone.

The trail leads us down and onto a dirt highway running through a valley. A road sign pointing southeast reads "Castel del Rio." We, however, head north, cross a bridge, then follow the left-hand fork in the road, which leads up another mountain. At this moment a heavy mortar barrage falls onto the bridge we have just crossed. The enemy fire seems to be coming from our rear and right flank. Are we too far ahead again or are we lost? The Krauts must know that we are around and are shooting the roads at regular intervals. They can't have direct observation, for it is now almost dark and the heavy rain has reduced visibility to only a few yards. We slog up the mountain trail, our pace increased by the shelling behind us. After fifteen minutes we catch up to the rear of our battalion.

Our troops are a sorry sight to behold. They are digging holes just off the mountain road into the reverse slope. Every man is soaked to the skin. The mud is a foot deep. The men look as though they have just crawled out of a muddy river or filthy sewer. At this point it would take very little to aggravate them. I sense that they would now kill not only for self-preservation alone but also out of sheer hate for the miserable enemy responsible for their being here. I take one look at the situation and decide to retrace my steps and establish an aid station down by the road fork we have just passed. I'll take my chances with an occasional shelling rather than spend all night in a mud hole. I recall seeing an old house down by the road fork. If it is still vacant, I'll move in.

We medics proceed with our plan. The house is still empty. Its first floor is still sound. We step over a dead mule lying in the back doorway, then black out the doors and windows with blankets, set up our litters on the floor, and finally relax. The roof leaks a little, but this is heaven compared to outside. We have no casualties. Rain is so heavy that even the Krauts have stopped shooting.

On the morning of September 28 we move out to rejoin our battalion. It is extremely foggy and cold. The pouring rain has changed to a constant drizzle. We slog through the mud back up the razorback mountain trail to the spot where we left our battalion. However, we can't find it. It has apparently advanced during the night. This time, however, we shall have no trouble finding it. The troops have left a well-marked path, foot tracks twelve inches deep. The Krauts can't see us, but nevertheless mortars fall onto the road every few minutes. This forces us off the trail and onto the reverse slope just below it. We slip and slide but are safe from the enemy fire pounding the forward slopes. After three hours we see our battalion command post. It is located near the top of the mountain in one of three houses clustered together in a group.

We medics are assigned to a barn. First we chase out the cows, then the chickens; of the latter we catch three and stew them in a large rusty kettle. The next day all of us have severe diarrhea. We remain for three days and four nights, and it takes just about that long for all our clothes to dry out. The troops of course are not as fortunate as we are; they are still living in holes, and the rain refuses to let up; GI Joe remains cold and wet. He is disgusted and curses. He hates Italy. He is going to stay for a while, however. He is issued long winter underwear, and that alone is enough to convince him.

Late in the afternoon of October 2, we receive orders to move on. One of the battalions of the 351st Regiment is far ahead of us and is having trouble on Mount Bernadini. Our mission is to help it. To reach it, we must first backtrack to the vicinity of Castel del Rio and from there take a new road fork. All roads leading to and from Castel del Rio are heavily pounded by Kraut artillery. Hoping to avoid heavy fire, we make our move at night. We hike over sodden roads and reach the rear guard of the 351st Regiment just before dawn. The front troops are bogged down by stubborn Jerry resistance. The only house we can find for an aid station is one already occupied by the 3d Battalion medics of the 351st Regiment. It is located on a slope just below the road winding around the mountain. There is no room for us in the house, but only in the lean-to behind it. We are here only a few minutes when a Kraut shell explodes above us and the roof caves in, severely shaking up six of my medics. I still have diarrhea from the chicken stew I consumed three days ago. Since the shelling and mines make it unsafe to walk about on the slopes digging catholes, my comfort station is the road just above us, which at this point hugs a steep bank and gives me adequate cover. Every fifteen minutes I dash from our wrecked shed to my chosen point in the road, squat down in a foot of mud, and let loose. More than once I am forced to move several feet because of tanks rumbling past. I swallow sulfadiazine pills by the dozen but my ailment lasts all morning. To the tankers passing by, seeing a captain with an armband and bare ass squatting in the mud must have been an admirable sight. I have learned my lesson and make a vow; no more native food. I'll stick to C and K rations no matter how monotonous.

At 11:00 A.M., after bitter fighting, our troops have taken several ridges to the north. My advance aid station group has already moved forward, and word is sent back to me that it is located in a large barn that has a solid underground cellar. About fifty casualties have piled up, and my presence is sorely needed. I shall have to make a two-thousand-yard forward move, all uphill, then over a rough meadow. I can see the barn against the skyline and all the shell holes around it. Two dead cows, their bellies bloated and their legs held stiff in the air, lie nearby. We scamper uphill and over the meadow toward the barn. We never stop running in spite of a brief mortar barrage, which splatters the field, and reach the barn safely even though breathless and shaky.

We are in a good spot. Our troops are only one thousand yards ahead. The barn is made of field stone, and its cellar is actually eight feet underground. Even a direct hit would have to come vertically down through the roof to harm us. The cellar is filled with bins of potatoes. My men are already peeling them for supper tonight.

The wounded receive my immediate attention. Most have small-arms wounds in their legs, arms, and chests. Shoe-mine casualties are again numerous. Among these is one of my litter bearers and one company aid man. Another one of my aid men is brought in dead, shot straight through the head. Several months ago I tried to get this poor fellow reclassified because of a glass eye. However, since he had 20/20 vision in his good eye, my request was denied. His buddy tells me he was shot while dressing a mine casualty. The Red Cross armband did not help this boy. He is the first medic I have seen killed thus far by an aimed bullet.

By nightfall we run out of splints and plasma. We wait until it is really dark—then evacuate all the wounded. Our supplies are replenished by morning, the ambulance bringing supplies on each return trip. We remain in this cellar for two days. On October 6, our third night, our troops take the small town of Pezzola and some high ground to the north. Again, there are many casualties that the company aid men and litter bearers have taken to a church about three thousand yards to our northwest. To reach this church, I must take the dirt road on my left below us, walk along it for about a mile, then take a path across a field and cemetery. As my column of twelve medics hurries over the road, tanks rumble past us. I hate to be crowded by tanks, since they always draw fire. Furthermore, their motors make so much noise, I can't hear the warning whistle of the incoming shells. We walk a mile in less than ten minutes, then branch off to the left and onto the path leading to the church. I see neither footprints nor tracks of vehicles. This path could very readily be mined. If it is, it's too late. I just keep walking, taking each step with definite unpleasant uncertainty.

The church near Pezzola is in shambles. Its basement, however, is still in good shape, and leading from it the Krauts have dug a huge cave at least twenty-five by fifty feet. We are again most fortunate in finding such a good place with such excellent cover. I won't mind staying here for a while and only hope that the Krauts haven't planted a time bomb somewhere within this rubble.

Several Germans are among our congregation of wounded awaiting us. The most seriously wounded is a German who insists that he is a walking case and not badly hurt. He has a hole in his back big enough for me to see parts of his lung expanding with each breath. He states that his company has had a rough night. When only four men were left, something hit him in the back and he fell. He shouted all night but no one came to his rescue. By morning he saw our medics using this church, so he decided to walk over, give himself up, and be treated. Since he seems to be breathing better with the hole in his chest wide open rather than closed, I cover it only with a very loose dressing and fill him up with sulfadiazine pills. He says his pain is not severe enough to require morphine.

The cave under the church is our home for the nights of October 6 and 7. Men of Headquarters Company occupy the basement and the rubble of the church itself. We have hot meals at night, kitchen trucks having caught up with us once again. At dusk on the night of October 7 the church receives a direct hit from an 88-mm shell. Four men are killed instantly and not another soul is scratched.

On October 8 we move out toward Rangolia, a small town two ridges to the northeast. As we vacate the church, our heavy artillery units move in. It is a foggy day and it is drizzling. I haven't been issued a map for several days and can't do anythning but follow Headquarters Company troops. By late afternoon we enter a small deserted village on the skyline. One of the undamaged houses has a large kitchen with fireplace, and we remain here for the night. We have no significant casualties. Fighting must be slackening off. The Germans are either moving out or the weather is too bad for us to advance.

On the afternoon of October 9 we receive orders to move to the left, toward the town of Sassoleone, capture the town, and cut the Sassoleone–Castel del Rio Road. We cut across country along the forward slopes of the mountains, the fog and rain giving us ample cover. We walk over deserted German positions; Jerry communications wires are scattered all over the slopes.

From the mountains Sassoleone looks like only a rock pile. All the houses are in shambles. Nevertheless, artillery shells keep pouring into the rubble. To approach the town we descend into a valley and follow a small road paralleling a creek.

This valley is strictly for the birds, for it is steadily pounded by mortars and artillery. Every few minutes the entire column hits the dirt. I'll never know why more of us are not killed, since we are completely exposed and even the mountain slopes are bare of all vegetation. There is no adequate cover for miles.

Frequently the narrow road crosses and recrosses the creek over small wooden bridges. These are usually demolished, and we cross the stream on debris strewn around them. I witness the entire battalion cross over one such obstacle, except for the last man, who is unfortunate enough to have his foot blown off by a shoe mine. How 450 men have crossed over the same path and avoided stepping on that mine is almost unbelievable!

Someone tells me that we are following the Sillaro River. One of our company is already in C. di Lesso, a small group of houses on a ridge before Sassoleone. I decide to move ahead to C. di Lesso and put my aid station directly behind the advance company. It is getting dark, and I must have cover for the night.

By 8:00 P.M. I am in a barn on a mountain ridge. There is no defilade, but at least I have a roof over my head. I wouldn't stay here if the weather were clear. Visibility today is only about two hundred yards, and if the Krauts want to shoot us up, they must do so by map. I am directly behind our troops, which are once again having a rough time. Progress is very slow. Sometimes they advance less than two hundred yards all day. Consequently, I remain here for three days. We treat at least fifty casualties per day. The arriving wounded are mud covered and rain soaked. The majority of wounds are gunshot and mortar shrapnel. Our station is constantly harassed by mortar fire, shells exploding outside both day and night. There are almost as many German wounded as GIs. One German noncommissioned officer is brought in with a palm-sized hole in his buttock. He had been lying in the woods for forty-eight hours. His wound is filled with leaves, sticks, and dirt. What he desires most is a swig of cognac. I offer him my canteen filled with whiskey, and he empties one-half of it without drawing a breath between gulps. I loosely suture his buttock together without any anesthesia. He never says "ouch."

On October 11 we are relieved by a battalion of troops from the 350th Regiment. We withdraw about two thousand yards to an old battered shack that leaks and is too small for both Headquarters Company and the aid station. I therefore decide to move one thousand yards to our left flank to Bell Isola. There's an old mill house, which I hear is still in good shape. Bell Isola is unprotected, and one of our anti-tank contact patrols has been captured here the night before; a comfortable house, however, is too good an attraction to pass up even at the risk of capture. Upon arrival, we find it warm and dry. We won't have a guard for the night but shall depend on our Red Cross flag, which we nail to the door.

In spite of our anxiety, nothing remarkable happens except for a slight disturbance at midnight. A hysterical Italian woman barges through the door crying and sobbing, stating that her house has just been shot up, her furniture burned, and her crippled father is still ly-ing in all that rubble. We can't help the poor soul, for we are only medics. I give her sodium amytal and sugar water, and she hyperventi-lates to exhaustion and falls asleep.

On the afternoon of October 12 we are ordered to reinforce our divi-sion's right flank. Our objective is a place called Di Gresso, a plateau on a hill mass, shaped like a bowl encircled by ridges. Our boys are to reinforce other troops presently attempting to take the ridges. We find upon arrival that the only site available as aid station is an old barn in the center of the bowl, completely unprotected and very ex-posed. Mortars drop all around the place. Luckily, the barn remains standing. Our battalion colonel, having gone forward with the lead troops, returns with a gunshot wound, a compound fracture of the humerus. His premonition of needing me some day has come to pass.

In the late afternoon the sun finally breaks through the clouds, and shortly thereafter the Rover Boys of the Air Corps roar over the hills, dropping their bombs. We are delighted but the next day hear that they bombed our own division troops by mistake.

Late that night our battalion, having completed its mission, is pulled back again. As we retreat, we watch our artillery plaster all surround-ing hill masses with phosphorus shells. We stumble about in dark-ness for six hours, finally returning to the banks of the Salleno River. Here we rest for four days.

It rains every day. Why we are resting and not chasing Krauts, I'll never know. The troops have pitched pup tents in deep mud. The Krauts are on high mountains several ridges to the north. On the high-est of these is an old castle that must be their OP, since our planes bomb it daily. The Krauts must surely see us, but we are behaving as though in a rest area. Our kitchen trucks serve us hot meals; we are finally issued winter uniforms. Every morning our boys do calis-thenics in the rain, and every now and then the Krauts lob in an artil-lery shell just to let us know that they are watching us. We are issued beer, write letters home, and candy and cigarettes are distributed dai-ly. All I can figure out is that our flanks are again lagging behind and we are sitting somewhere in the middle waiting for the division line to straighten out. I would much rather keep moving; the Po Valley is only about fourteen air miles to the north.

One unit of troops being relieved by another unit in the vicinity of Mount Altuzzo. U.S. Army Signal Corps photo, courtesy Lt. Col. (Ret.) William Konze.

Troops following fleeing Germans on a road in the vicinity of Castel del Rio.
U.S. Army Signal Corps photo, courtesy Lt. Col. (Ret.) William Konze.

Mud twelve inches deep on a road in the vicinity of Sassoleone. *Below:* Gen. Mark Clark visits battered San Clemente after the conquering infantry battalions move out. U.S. Army Signal Corps photo, courtesy Lt. Col. (Ret.) William Konze.

A mule train brings up supplies. Courtesy Lt. Col. (Ret.) William Konze, 88th Infantry Division historian and property custodian. *Below:* Relieving troops on a mountain in the Apennines. Courtesy Eugene Engelen, Park Ridge, Ill.

Soldier takes short nap in hole on front line north of the village of Manzuno.
U.S. Army Signal Corps photo, courtesy Lt. Col. (Ret.) William Konze.

The frequently shelled village of Loiano on Highway 6. U.S. Army Signal Corps photo, courtesy Lt. Col. (Ret.) William Konze. *Below:* Regimental assembly of the 349th Infantry in La Croce area, in the vicinity of Florence, before the Po Valley campaign. Courtesy U.S. Army Signal Corps.

A stroll between shellings; the town of Livergnano on the static winter line
north of Trasasso and Loiano on Highway 65, the road to Bologna. Courtesy
U.S. Army Signal Corps.

On October 16 we break camp. This, I hear, will be our last great offensive and effort to break into the Po Valley. We shall attempt to take the small towns of Frassineto, San Clemente, and then Mount Grande, the last highest hill mass before the Po Valley.

We set off at noon, take a mule trail over several ridges, then walk slowly and cautiously along the Sassoleone–San Clemente road. This road closely hugs the base of the Mount Grande hill mass, which looms dead ahead and is a semicircular ridge, high and rocky, its summit obscured by clouds. Its sheer cliffs would be a challenge to any professional mountain climber, and to the infantry men they look positively defiant and impossible. The only access to the top of Mount Grande is by way of narrow mule trails leading from the village of San Clemente. Consequently, San Clemente must be taken first. It will probably be costly. We can't take the town nor Mount Grande during the day; they must be taken at night when the Krauts can't see us coming. At either time, however, it will probably be slaughter on a grand scale. The casualties might possibly be less at night, I'll agree to that, but if the progress is slow and we are only halfway up the mountain by dawn, then we shall be trapped and the Krauts can really murder us. From their vantage points on the ridges, they can see our every move and position. They could even knock us off with rocks, let alone guns.

By nightfall on October 16, I am in a pig stable about three miles from San Clemente. The troops will attempt to drive along the road tonight and take the town. I wish them luck. I sleep very little that night. The aid station is filthy. Fleas, gnats, and flies abound, and the influx of casualties is heavy. The majority of the casualties have grenade-fragment and gun-shot wounds. To me this is always a bad omen. It means that the Krauts have been ordered to stand and die rather than yield ground. Enemy belonging to the 1st Parachute Division and the 90th Light Division are among wounded prisoners brought in to us. They are just as tired and confused as we are.

I feel lousy on the morning of October 16. I am feverish, and my eyes are swollen. My symptoms suggest those of sand fly fever. I won't mention this to anyone, however, since I would hate to be evacuated; it's really much safer in this pig stable than on the road outside. Shell fire outside, however, is not the only reason why I don't want to go to the rear. Once back in the division clearing station or in a hospital, you lose your outfit. Some joker might assign you to some other outfit when you are well again, and I certainly would not want to return to anyone else but my own bunch. Strange as it may seem, I have become very fond of my men in the aid station as well as those of battalion headquarters. They have become a part of me. I trust them. They are reliable. They are faithful. They have been true comrades in misery. With them, I shall always share unforgettable memories, of danger, of humor, and of desperation. A romance such as this would be a pity to lose. Therefore, sick as a dog, I shall try to stick it out.

Small-arms fire has now decreased, but enemy artillery activity is at its peak. The Krauts are pounding the San Clemente road relentlessly. We failed to take San Clemente last night, but our troops are on the outskirts of the town dug in and lying low, waiting to try again tonight. In the meantime, division artillery has taken over and is answering with heavy counterfire. Tanks are also brought forward to help us push into San Clemente. I wish they would not come up during daylight; they make such beautiful targets. When tanks are on the road and you happen to be caught near them, especially on foot, then watch out; your life is usually not worth a plug nickel.

Toward evening I must move two miles forward in order to remain closer behind the troops. I choose my next house by map; it appears to be one mile from San Clemente. I climb to the roof of the pig stable and look the situation over. The road is a mess. A horse-drawn Kraut supply train is strewn all over the road. Dead horses, loaves of bread, water cans, and corpses litter the shoulders.

At sundown I jump into my jeep and roar off. We race over the road at fifty miles per hour. Heavy shells explode on the road to our front and back. The Krauts are apparently after anything that moves. Being anxious not to lose my vehicle, I order the driver to halt and to let me off so that he can turn back while I proceed on foot. Walking along the road, however, is just as perilous as driving. While dodging the heavy stuff, I keep worrying about hidden mines. I recall Santa Maria Infante, where I was in the same predicament. I doubt if this road has been swept. I passed most of our troops, dug in off the road, several hundred yards back. I am really out front this time, and all on my own. My progress is very slow and uncertain, and when a recon car suddenly stops and offers me a ride, I gladly accept. The lieutenant informs me that as far as he knows this road has not yet been swept of mines. The recon car races faster than any jeep I have ever traveled in before. In a few minutes I am at my chosen farmhouse. The car stops only long enough to let me off, then races on. These guys deserve a medal. Just one mine would blow them to kingdom come.

The house is still in good shape. The ground floor is vacant. I hang my Red Cross flag on the door outside, then rest on the cement floor and await the arrival of my crew. Suddenly, I realize what a damn fool I am to venture ahead of the troops just for the sake of getting to a house first. What if the Krauts are still around or the place is booby trapped? Such thoughts never occur to you until it is too late to worry.

I sit and wait patiently for two hours. After sundown I hear the footsteps of troops on the road outside. Our men have started to move up with the purpose of taking San Clemente tonight. At the end of the column is my aid station group and jeep, and I am very happy to see them.

The night is full of uncertainty and commotion. The men are fighting for San Clemente and Frassineto and for the approaches to Mount Grande. Casualties, mostly gun-shot wounds, come drifting to us throughout the entire night.

The next morning, October 18, I hear that San Clemente is in our hands. Formidable and majestic Mount Grande is the next objective. Mount Grande swarms with Krauts. From its summit they can see everything, San Clemente and all its approaches. As a matter of fact, from an old castle on top of Mount Grande the Krauts can drop rocks directly on the houses of San Clemente. We know that that old castle is a Kraut fire-direction center, and are they taking advantage of it! We are really stalled! Our every move is watched. Our men, playing it smart, are silent and deeply holed up in the cellars of San Clemente. I hear only Kraut mortars and artillery, and our heavy artillery in turn keeps shooting at the Kraut castle. Occasionally an ammunition, communications, or water jeep races past us headed for San Clemente. Each vehicle draws a terrific amount of artillery, and I have often wondered if it ever reached the town. Shots aimed at racing vehicles always endanger the aid station.

In the early afternoon an 88-mm shell takes off one corner of my house. I think it's time to move. A smaller house fifty yards up the road looks more solid. One by one, at five-minute intervals, we dash to it. It's a fine house. It has a wine cellar, twelve feet by twelve feet, with walls a yard thick. Here we can treat casualties and won't have to worry about the roof caving in.

Soon, however, we run into more trouble. Heavy tanks are moving up. They are creeping over the road toward San Clemente. To make matters worse, they all stop in front of every house along the road seeking temporary cover. Once they are stopped, the Krauts shoot at them relentlessly. Soon 88s explode all around us. One shell tears up the entire second floor, and all the debris crashes down onto the first floor. Our wine cellar beneath it all remains solid. Moments later a casualty is brought in. It is a tanker. His head got in the way of the gun's recoil, and he is in a deep coma, with a lump on his forehead the size of a grapefruit. I can't feel a fracture beneath all the swelling, but I feel sure that he has a massive cerebral hemorrhage. We must wait until dark to evacuate him. When we finally ship him out three hours later, he is still unconscious and laboring to breathe. The tank, too, thank God, finally moves off under the cover of darkness.

On October 19, shortly after midnight, heavy fighting starts again. Again our men will be trying for Mount Grande. I can see streams of Kraut tracers shooting down the slopes. Our artillery in turn is blasting Grande with real heavy stuff. We work the entire night treating rain-soaked, mud-covered, shivering, and bleeding casualties, who have tried the impossible—to crawl up sheer cliffs in darkness, mud, and slime, fighting an enemy who is deeply entrenched and determined to die rather than be dislodged.

Throughout the entire day on the nineteenth, we continue treating casualties injured during the fighting of the previous night and just found. Our men are stopped on the slopes and are dug in. They will probably remain so for the rest of the day. Mount Grande can be taken only by night when the Krauts can't see.

On October 20 our men are almost on the top of Mount Grande, and I move my aid station into the village San Clemente. This village is now only a rubble heap. I seek refuge in the basement of a former four-story house. The basement is all that remains; our roof consists of the debris of the rest of the building. San Clemente is still very unhealthy. The Krauts keep pumping in 88s. Very few casualties are brought in to us, the litter bearers prudently waiting for cover of darkness to bring wounded down from the slopes. Only the dying are rushed in to us during lulls between mortar and artillery barrages. I spend the greater part of the day shooting crap with Catholic Chaplain Crowley. This at least takes my mind off the artillery falling outside.

Fighting is bitter and bloody during the morning hours of October 21. Even though victorious, my battalion is almost decimated. Large numbers are killed. The dead outnumber the wounded. Mount Grande, the key to the entire enemy defense line, finally falls. In a few days I hope to climb to the top of Mount Grande. I am told that on a clear day one can get a view of the Po Valley and Highway 9 to Bologna. Having crawled over nothing but mountains thus far, I doubt that there is any such flat land as the Po Valley.

On October 22 our sector is relatively quiet. Our troops are dug in on the top of Mount Grande and are not advancing. The reason for this does not become obvious to me for another week.

I move my aid station into a ravine about a quarter of a mile up the Mount Grande hill mass. I move into a farmhouse, of which two of the eight rooms are still intact. The rooms are cold, all windows broken, and the floors rain soaked. My head still hurts, my back aches, and my temperature runs a persistent 102 degrees. I still have sand fly fever.

We find an old ham the Germans lost in the woods. We hang it on the front door for everyone to help himself. This is the first meat we have had in weeks. The ham is quite moldy, but when fried it is delicious.

On October 24 I move further up Mount Grande into the small town of Frassineto. Our lead companies are trying to probe the terrain beyond and extend the spearhead. I move into another shack in a gully, which is worse than the one I just left. This one still has three rooms left, namely, a pig stable, a larger former kitchen, and a living room. This is a concrete house, but the walls are cracked and the roof leaks; the cement floor is covered with mud and water. Headquarters Company will occupy the rooms and allocates the pig stable to the medics. We clean out our ten-by-six-foot pig sty and convert it into an aid station. It never becomes very livable, however. Whenever it rains, water pours through the cracks in the walls and ceiling. All our bandages and food remain rain soaked. Muddy water seeps through the concrete floor and through the door. Every crevice and ditch on Mount Grande has turned into a muddy stream, and every stream engulfs all in its path. We usually have at least three inches of water on our aid station floor.

The next two weeks are a trying ordeal. Our troops are not advancing but are holding Mount Grande and patrolling the ridges. Patrols are sent nightly to the north to the town of Penzola. I lose another good friend, Lieutenant Galliart, killed on patrol. We are waiting for replacements that never come. Most companies are down to less than half strength, and one company has only forty men left. The men are all weary, their morale is low, their temper razor sharp, and their nerves exhausted. In order to break into the Po Valley, we need fresh troops. We sit and wait. The days drag on but no replacements show up. Fifth Army has apparently run out of reserves. My battalion alone needs about five hundred men.

The casualties during this period of waiting and holding the line are a sorry and pitiful lot. They have had a dog's life. They look thin and haggard, unshaven and unkempt, soaked to the skin and covered with grime. All their physical ailments are magnified since they are tired and exhausted dogfaces. Any unintentional unsympathetic word often sends a man into a rage of temper. The few replacements that drift in are absolutely of no help. They are forty-year-old men with flat feet and aching backs that have spent the past two years in rear areas serving as cooks, orderlies, or messengers and have been sent up to us in desperation. None of these last longer than a week at the most before they are ill with either bronchitis or pneumonia. I take one look at these fever-racked, coughing, and shaking miserable creatures and tag them for evacuation.

My greatest personal enemy during this time, other than the weather, is boredom. My chief occupation is looking for food and thinking up some new menus. There isn't too much you can prepare in a pig stable. For several days my diet consists of only dehydrated egg yolks and apple flakes. Whenever a PX ration arrives, I partake of nothing but peanuts and beer until that supply is exhausted. I've eaten all the other stuff so long that it nauseates me. One day a loaf of bread is received but in our eagerness unwrapping it, we allow it to fall into the water on the floor, and it is wasted. Whenever I receive a quart of whiskey, I mix it with lemon juice powder, sugar, and water, and live on nothing but whiskey sours for another two days. On November 1 one of the men in Headquarters Company spots a cow lost on the hillside. He fells it with a bullet from his carbine. It is butchered and divided. On November 3 I eat steak fried in Barbasol shaving cream; on November 4 I have fried liver followed by a week's session of diarrhea. I will be glad when all the meat is out of my sight.

The men begin to annoy one another. Everyone is grouchy and in a bad mood. Everyone is sick and tired of wet feet, damp clothes, and early morning rheumatism. Everyone has heard the other fellow's funny story a hundred times before. No one thinks that anything is funny anymore. Even the company sergeant's famous last warning words to the nightly outgoing patrol is no longer humorous, but he nevertheless persists in saying, "Now, any of you guys that owe me money be careful and don't get killed."

I never retire before 2:00 A.M. I read the *Stars and Stripes* paper several times and do geometry and algebra from an old textbook I have found among the rubble. The flickering candlelight raises hell with my eyes. The only time I turn in before midnight is when the candles run out.

Everyone itches from scabies. No one has had a bath for weeks. Because of the dampness we wear our heavy jackets throughout the day and sleep in them as well during the night.

I am completely stagnating medically. I treat nothing but common colds and evacuate several combat fatigue cases daily. Most of the time I just sit and think, but even my thoughts are no longer intelligent.

Every day we receive several rounds of harassing mortar fire. No one pays any attention to it. Small counterattacks occur nightly on the mountain, but we, being one thousand yards below, sleep through it all. During the day, however, our artillery is very active. Our OP can now direct our artillery to pound any movement in the Po Valley below.

The only real exciting event is the ration train, which carries supplies to the rifle companies every day at dusk and passes by our door. The mules are loaded with food and ammunition. We always wonder how many mules will come down again. The mud on the trail is so deep that some of the animals sink down to their necks in mud, and when they can't be extracted there is nothing left to do but to shoot them.

On November 5 we have exciting visitors. A British lieutenant and sergeant, on an advance reconnaissance mission, stop in to look over our house. They intend to relieve us in several days. Now, this is good news! The relievers will be the 11th Lancashire Fuseliers.

During the next three days our troops are gradually relieved by the British, and we have an excellent opportunity to observe their actions and manners. They are indeed different from us. Walking in battle column, the men appear chubby and pink cheeked; one fellow smokes a pipe, the other carries a cane; the next man looks quite scholarly wearing horn-rimmed glasses, and carefully scrutinizes all the surrounding scenery. All seem very nonchalant and unconcerned, yet all appear very solid. The ever-present white enameled tea cup dangles from the corner of every man's field pack.

Jeeps follow the rear of the column. The British will ride in jeeps as long as possible, no matter how horrible the trail. The vehicles are loaded to the roof with equipment; nor is seven men to a jeep an uncommon sight. Contrary to our rules and regulations in a battle zone, the roofs and windshields of the vehicles are all up. No one seems to care. The jeeps always seem to get stuck. They are either being driven off the road or into a creek, where they just remain standing upended, all four wheels off the ground. Some day they will retrieve them.

The British officers are all well groomed. Their faces are clean and their mustaches waxed. They are never without a necktie.

Indian colonials handle their mule trains, and they do a magnificent job. The small African donkeys receive excellent care. Once a donkey has been relieved of its heavy supply burden, the Indian leads it to a creek and washes it down from head to foot, then rubs it dry and covers it with burlap blankets. The Indians seem to be a happy lot as well. While leading a group of mules they suddenly burst forth with a shrilling whoop, then flourish into a song.

The carefree attitude of the British continues to amaze me. At night they strike matches, build fires, or sing. They will stop their vehicles in the middle of the road in broad daylight and have a spot of tea with the Krauts watching them.

They never seem to be in a hurry. They admit that war is just another big game that may last either one year or four. It makes no difference how long it takes, as long as you win.

On November 8 we are all finally relieved. A sergeant walks up to my aid station and says, "I have nineteen bloody blokes I must find lodging for. Think I'll put them in here and my cookhouse next door. I'm putting a sign on this house, that means I just occupied it. You chaps leave tonight."

As far as I'm concerned, he's very welcome to my house. It seems hard to believe that we shall finally rest after forty-four days and nights of fighting. We have fought in the worst of terrain and weather. The Germans were convinced we would never get through the Apennine passes; it still seems impossible that our vehicles ever managed to travel through so much mud and slime. The desperate Krauts never dreamed that we could crack their concrete defenses. Our division has done so, however, but has left about six thousand casualties on this Apennine front. Every man has done his best, but apparently it has not been good enough. We have not crashed through into the Po Valley, our main objective. We are nine miles short. The weather has been against us from the beginning. I think of all the time we wasted during August, sitting in pup tents just south of Florence doing nothing when the weather was dry, sunny, and ideal for mountain warfare. Had we started our push then, we would now be in the Alps instead of the Apennines. Somebody has goofed, and it has not been GI Joe.

Early that evening our troops come trudging down the mountain and pile into trucks waiting near San Clemente. As soon as one truck is full, it leaves for the rear area. I follow the last truck in my jeep piled high with equipment. A light snow covers the ground. Artificial moonlight helps my driver to see a little better. After driving for about two miles, I finally see how this light is created. Huge batteries of searchlights are set up and focused on low-hanging clouds over the entire front line. Some light is thus reflected down upon the troops. The Germans do not even bother to knock these lights out.

We drive over bumpy secondary dirt roads for about two hours in total blackout, then switch on our headlights. After another two hours we arrive in Montecatini, the Italian counterpart of America's Saratoga Springs.

Rome Revisited and Montecatini

NOVEMBER 8, 1944–APRIL 15, 1945

It is 2:00 A.M. Montecatini is partially blacked out. A guide directs me to a narrow three-story house in the center of town. I am told to sleep in any room on the second floor. I choose a front room in which cots have been set up. There is no heat nor light. The walls are of tile and the floors of terrazzo. Chaplain Hayes is my roommate. We break out our bedrolls, spread them out on the cots, and sleep in heavenly peace, away from mud, rain, and guns.

We orient ourselves the next morning. Our house is a small hotel. Almost every other house is a hotel of some sort. Troops are quartered in every one of them. On the ground floor of my hotel my sergeants have set up the aid station.

No one appears for sick call that first morning. We are in Montecatini and no one is ill. Even if a guy had a temperature of 105 degrees, I doubt if he would show up.

I pick up my PX ration, which consists of twenty-four cans of Ruppert's beer and four fifths of whiskey. After several stiff drinks I proceed to a bath house.

Montecatini is famous for its sulfur baths. I walk into a building where every room is a bathroom. For fifty cents, an Italian attendant fills up a tub full of hot water in which you just sit and soak. The water stinks of hydrogen sulfide or rotten eggs. You don't use soap but just soak. The only reason I am enjoying this bath is because the attendant says Field Marshal Rommel also bathed here several months ago. At least I'll have something to talk about. After thirty minutes of soaking in stinking sulfur water, I dress and walk to a GI shower for a real bath with soap and a change of clothes.

For the next several days my duties consist of getting the men of my battalion back in shape. I treat chronic colds and backaches and give booster injections of all previous shots. Boils and impetigo secondary to chronic scabies are the chief complaints.

I spend my evenings writing letters home and killing those four fifths of whiskey and twenty-four cans of beer. I usually retire inebriated and sleep like an angel between sheets. The latter have been issued us as a surprise.

One evening we spend at a civilian home. Many civilians earn their living serving home-cooked meals to military personnel. Montecatini has always been a tourist town, and the major part of the population has always depended on tourist trade. The past few years, however, the only visitors have been soldiers. All that is necessary to obtain a good meal is to make arrangements the day before. This evening four of us are invited to a house. We sit at a large, round table in the kitchen. Only Mama and Papa are home. Chaplain Hayes and I have a feast. We eat spaghetti, broiled pork chops, fried potatoes, lettuce and water cress, and a fruit salad. The beverage is white wine. The dessert is chocolate layer cake. We pay for the dinner what we think it was worth. To us it was worth ten dollars apiece.

Following this delicious meal, the chaplain and I walk to the officer's club, where the atmosphere is relatively dead. I drink a few cognacs, then return to my quarters.

On another evening I visit a small restaurant, one of many in the town. It looks just like one of our ice cream parlors with bare floor and furnished with a jukebox, a counter, and six bare tables. We buy local champagne for $4.50 a bottle. I'm sure that we are getting nothing more than carbonated wine on which somebody is making a good profit. I have several dances with one of the stag girls in the place, but the lady is not interesting enough to follow up. It is a rather boring place.

On November 14 I receive a three-day pass to Rome. Chaplain Hayes is also on pass. We again stay at the good old Hotel Excelsior. Since the chaplain is with me, I really see something of Rome other than the hotel. We spend one entire day just sightseeing and inspecting in detail the Forum Romanum, the Church of San Clemente, San Giovanni in Laterno, and San Pietro in Vaticano, the Colosseum, and the Catacombs. We window shop in the center of town, where silk stockings cost $12.00 a pair, a silk slip $45.00, shoes $18.00, and an Arrow shirt $20.00

My other two days are taken up with Marguerete. Marguerete is a new acquaintance. I meet her in the lobby of the Hotel Excelsior. I am introduced to her as the friend of another officer's girl friend. She is without an escort, and I cannot understand why. Marguerete is stunning. She has raven-black hair, sparkling black eyes, a glowing olive complexion, a beautiful smile, and delicately cut sharp features. This girl is a walking dream. We dance and dine, or just sit in a cozy corner of the bar sipping rum cokes. Marguerete lives in an apartment house in town with her mother. At midnight I take her home, the chaplain lending me his jeep. Her goodnight kisses are warm and responsive, and I leave her with high expectations for the next day.

I pick up Marguerete early the next morning. She is dressed beautifully in a close-fitting black suit. Two silver fox fur pieces thrown loosely over her shoulders make her look still more stunning. We tour Rome, visiting wine shops, coffee shops, a motion picture at the Red Cross center, and wind up for dinner at the Hotel Excelsior. We attend the nightly dance and floor show. Marguerete has a way with men—she makes you feel that you are the only one she has ever enjoyed being with. She at least gives me that impression, and it is a very gratifying feeling. During the evening's conversation I learn that Marguerete has a three-year-old child; she never discusses her husband and I don't press the subject. I enjoy her company very much. I take Marguerete home at 2:00 A.M. We both deplore that my leave ends tonight. She assures me that on my next visit to Rome, she will be waiting. I am to look her up as soon as I arrive in the city.

On November 19 I am back in Montecatini. Early the next morning we pack to move back up to the front. We ride in trucks until noon, then walk. We are in the mountains just east of Highway 65. At least twelve inches of snow cover the ground. We are wearing shoe-pacs, fur caps, and white lined parkas. The latter blend with the snow and are good camouflage. We walk along the ridges of mountains all afternoon. We can risk doing this since fog is so dense that visibility is less than one hundred yards. We rest briefly whenever we pass some peasant's mountain shack. I, however, am usually besieged with sick civilians who have not seen a physician for many months and have all sorts of ailments. An old man shows me a bone felon that has been bothering him for several weeks. His thumb is swollen to triple the usual size. He is in terrific pain. He wants his thumb cut off, and wants me to do anything even without anesthesia just so he gets relief. I do not carry novocaine. I apply a tourniquet around the base of his thumb and wait fifteen minutes until his thumb is practically black. With a knife blade previously dipped in iodine I make a large fish-mouth incision, splitting the end of his thumb in half; to keep the incision open I cut a strip of rubber from a bicycle tire one inch wide and six inches long—boil it for three minutes in a tin can—and insert it as a drain to keep the split portions of the thumb apart. The old man is most grateful. He offers me a cane, which I am sure took him several months to carve and which I naturally refuse.

A woman with a sore breast is in the same shack. Again without anesthesia I open her abscess, which contains at least a half-pint of pus. Just to see her suffering relieved is reward enough.

Toward evening we are close to the front. I still can't see farther than one hundred yards because of the dense fog. We are approaching territory held by a division of our colored troops. A house rather exposed on one side and sitting on the edge of a cliff is my aid station to be. We approach it cautiously. When we are only about fifty yards from it, a shell tears off one corner of the roof. Ten seconds later two colored boys, completely bare except for shorts and helmets, dash from the house, up the trail past us, through the snow and into the hills, never stopping to say hello. I shall probably never see them again.

The aid station is comfortable. It is a solid two-story house. The boys who just left so hurriedly were apparently artillery observers, because their maps, shirts with insignia, and binoculars are still here. I can now also understand why they were shelled. They were frying bacon over a fireplace on the second floor, and the Krauts apparently saw a shower of sparks coming from the chimney in spite of the fog. We leave the bacon for the rats to feed on.

We remain here for six days. No casualties occur. I play chess to pass the time away. The snow is too deep and the fog too thick for either side to become aggressive.

On November 27 we are relieved by our 2d Battalion and ordered to a "front line rest center" about six miles behind enemy lines in the hamlet of Di Lavaccia of about ten houses, which lies in a valley a little farther to our left but still east of Highway 65. I can see very little of the terrain because of the fog. I set up my aid station in a former grocery store. Troops sleep in tents. This time we have no defilade, so all our windows and doorways are heavily sandbagged. Little light enters the house, and life is rather dismal. The Krauts occasionally throw a long-range shell into the valley, but we are never hit. I do nothing in the line of medicine except treat a few head colds and evacuate many cases of hepatitis. The rest of the time I practice card tricks, play solitaire, and study Italian from a GI-issued booklet so that I can do better in Rome the next time I am on leave. At night I visit a house several yards down the road where the officers of Headquarters Company are quartered. Here, I play poker until midnight. I then retire to the second floor of my house, where the chaplain and I have set up cots. For another hour we discuss religion and all sorts of problems and finally doze off to sleep listening to the tunes of Bed Check Charlie's motor, who is still cruising about overhead dropping an occasional antipersonnel bomb wherever he sees a light.

On November 30 I drive five miles to the rear to the regimental area. I must see a dentist, as one of my molars has been killing me for the past few days. An 88-mm shell barely misses my jeep on this trip. The regimental dentist pulls my tooth, and I thus sustain my first real physical insult of this war to date. I sure could have had more serious ones by this time. In the regimental area I am told that Clare Boothe Luce is somewhere around saying hello to the men. My trip back to the battalion is uneventful.

December 3 is a big day. The Army-Navy game will be rebroadcast to us tonight. We wait all day for this event. When it is finally on the air, the static is so bad that we can't understand a damn thing. I bet on Navy, lose ten dollars to Colonel Henderson, but have a good evening at poker and wind up thirty-five bucks ahead.

Life is very boring. I can't find out why we are sitting in this valley so long. I really think nobody knows. Even three hot meals a day are no compensation for the utter boredom.

On December 10 we are told to pack up and get ready to move out.

It's back into the hills for us, farther up front. It will be about a four-hour hike. I just follow the troops over a mule trail that winds end-lessly over and around more mountains. Fog persists, and a steady rain is melting the snow, making the trail slippery and hazardous. By dark we are about three-fourths up a formidable mountain, and our path takes us halfway around it. Below us is a long, narrow valley. At approximately one-hundred-yard intervals along this path, the British have set up machine guns that spurt tracers into the valley at inter-vals. I wonder what they are shooting at. Fog and rain obscure my view. Furthermore, what are the British doing here? I can't figure out the entire situation. A couple of weeks ago colored troops were in our sector; now British troops are around. Perhaps we are trying to con-fuse enemy intelligence. Who knows? The machine guns make one hell of a noise, and echoes bounce back and forth, accentuating the racket. At a point just before the trail veers onto the northern slope stands a house, built right into the mountain. It's an ideal house for our aid station. It is protected from all sides except its front, which faces the valley below. The troops will be about a mile ahead of us, entrenched in preprepared foxholes protected by mine fields and barbed wire. We are told that during daylight the Krauts will have direct ob-servation, so keep your heads indoors. We are not to go outside unless it is dark or there is dense fog. Well, this will be another boring run with nothing to do all day. The chaplain is contemplating teaching me to play dominoes.

We remain here for six long days and nights. I never arise until 11:00 A.M. My recently issued feather-lined sleeping bag is most com-fortable. After a leisurely breakfast I play cards with my sergeants. In the afternoon I take a prolonged nap. From 7:00 P.M. to 11:00 P.M. there is some activity. During this time the men up front can leave their foxholes and come to us for treatment of their minor ailments. Head colds, bronchitis, diarrhea, athlete's foot, backaches, scabies, and hepatitis is about all their ailments amount to. In less than an hour my medical services are completed.

The nightly mule train with rations arrives around 9:00 P.M. Pack-ages from home are the big morale booster. All food parcels are shared. We feast on innumerable delicacies such as dill pickles, mustard on canned pumpernickel, caviar on crackers, lobster and mayonnaise, canned shrimp, and Bismarck herring. We read all letters received at least ten times. At 3:00 A.M. we usually turn in for the night. By that time any patrols sent out for the night have returned and all excite-ment is over.

My most faithful and most interesting patient during all this time is a stray cat that visits us nightly around supper time. Its entire back is afflicted with a secondarily infected fungus disease. After feeding it a hearty meal of powdered milk and C ration hash, I scrub its back with tincture of green soap, then apply sulfathiazole ointment. In five days the infection has cleared. Another five days of salicylic acid ointment and the patient is cured, fur is coming back, and the animal is fat and contented. It looks as though I am of some use after all.

One very foggy afternoon with visibility practically zero we start a fire in our pot-bellied stove. We can risk having a hot supper for a change. Too many turns in our crudely constructed chimney, however, cause the stove to backfire, and black smoke and soot fill the entire room. Our supper is ruined, all our equipment is covered with grime, and we all look like chimney sweeps. It takes us two hours to clean up the whole mess. Even the cat has hauled off. I shall probably never see it again.

On December 16 we move again, to the village of Gagliano about fifteen miles north of Florence. Gagliano is a small village of only about eight houses. It certainly is cozy and picturesque. We are surrounded by snow-covered mountains, and the snow is over a foot deep just outside our door. This year I know I shall have a white Christmas.

My aid station is in a former greenhouse. I, however, sleep in the farmer's house, which is a most intriguing place. Downstairs is a spacious, although very bare living room with a fireplace so big you can walk into it and sit on benches right next to the fire. A baking oven is built into the brick wall, heated by dried twigs that crackle as they burn. The smell of freshly baked bread revives memories of country life twenty-five years ago. At the head of the steps on the second floor is a toilet, a two-holer affair. The casing drops at least twenty feet, and this latrine will take a long time to fill up.

The three upstairs rooms are bare except for feather beds. The farmer and his family occupy two of the rooms, the chaplain and I the other. We prefer cots to the feather beds, however, since we have had too much experience with bed bugs in the past. None of the rooms are heated, and each night we are offered clay pots containing glowing ashes, which are put under the covers to heat up the beds prior to retiring.

On December 21 we celebrate Christmas, since our length of stay in unpredictable. All troops have the afternoon off. Our dinner consists of beef stew and eggnog made with wine instead of whiskey. Cookies and chocolate are served for dessert.

That evening we have an officers' party. In an upstairs room of Headquarters Company's house a long table is erected. Every officer of the battalion contributes his liquor and beer ration and any food he has received in packages from home. We have a tremendous feast on sardines, olives, pickles, assorted cheeses, tuna fish, and plum pudding. Liquor flows freely, and everyone is soon plastered. A big crap game follows the "buffet supper." Stakes are high, and gambling mania is at its peak. A warrant officer from division is here to pay us a visit. He is so loaded he must support himself with one hand resting on the table in order to roll the dice with the other. Whenever he is really drunk, he takes out his teeth. At this moment both upper and lower plates are in his pocket. He has already spent twenty-nine years in this man's army and still doesn't have cirrhosis of the liver. He now holds the dice. Four hundred bucks are in the pot. He shoots and rolls snake eyes. He looks at me and says, "Lend me four hundred bucks." I give him four hundred dollars and picture wings on every bill. He is so drunk he will never remember that I have lent him the money. He rolls again and shoots a seven. He takes another drink and passes out. I do not see or speak to him again for eight months. Then I suddenly receive a letter through message center without remarks but containing four hundred dollars. Ever since then, I have had a steadfast faith in Army regulars.

There is only one depressing feature that bothers me throughout the party. Of the thirty officers present, I can recall only four who started out with me from Texas. The others are all new, replacing those either dead, injured, or rotated to the States.

Lieutenant Gray, Distinguished Service Cross winner, is here. During the course of the party he casually mentions a lump in his groin that is bothering him. I glance at him and find a prominent inguinal hernia. I tell him that he better let me write him a ticket to the rear. For a while he even protests! Some guys don't know when they have had enough.

On December 22 we experience another treat, courtesy of Special Service. Leo "Lippy" Durocher and several of his boys present an hour-long baseball program. I even get a chance to give Leo some ammonium chloride lozenges for his laryngitis, another step for me toward immortal fame.

On December 23 I shoot into the rear end of all battalion officers 10 cc of immune serum globulin as prophylaxis against hepatitis. Somebody thinks it might do some good. I also receive a package from a girl friend from home containing everything I get over here—cigarettes, hard candy, shaving cream, and so forth.

On December 24 we celebrate Christmas again, since we are still around and not yet alerted to move back up front. A recreation tent has been erected on a field. News has been sent to all the farms within a fifteen-mile radius that there will be a party for kids. The entire battalion again gets the afternoon off. At 2:00 P.M. dinner is served in the barn. We have turkey with filling. Also ice cream. At 3:00 P.M. the kids from all the surrounding farms arrive. There are about twenty of them. The men of the battalion put on a show in the recreation tent. We hear a group singing Christmas carols, then a banjo player, a harmonica player, and several vocal duets. One fellow demonstrates card tricks and a few tell jokes. The kids enjoy the music but understand nothing else. When the show is over, a table loaded with cookies, candies, and chocolate from pooled home packages is uncovered for all the kids to feast on. Whatever they can't eat, they put in paper bags to take home. They all leave happy and contented.

That evening we all remain sober, having drunk up everything two days ago.

On December 29 we are alerted to go back to the front. We ride on trucks through slush and snow. Two miles from our destination we detruck and hike up a steep mountain. We are relieving troops of the 92d Division. This time my aid station is together with battalion headquarters in the only house in the vicinity. It stands alone on the highest point of Mount Fano. The Krauts must be saving their ammunition; otherwise, they would have shot it up long ago. Since the snow is four feet deep there is no combat. I do nothing except fight boredom. Folks at home think that I am saving lives every day. Instead of that, I am sitting in a cellar and am working on a small still, which I hope will change rubbing alcohol into a form fit for consumption.

December 31, New Year's Eve, is a memorable one. We are drinking beer and whiskey in the command post. All is quiet. For the lack of something else to do, I volunteer answering the battalion telephone, taking the hourly report from the rifle companies. At 11:50 P.M. M Company reports seeing a red flare over the Kraut lines. Soon thereafter I, K, and L companies report other flares. At twelve midnight the companies report the sky aflame. We step outside to have a look. The sky over what must be the Po Valley is illuminated with flares, rockets, and a hail of tracer bullets. The Krauts are only celebrating New Year's Eve with a dazzling display of fireworks over their own lines. At 1:00 A.M. the show is over and everything is again very quiet.

On January 10 I receive another five-day pass to Rome. I leave the front and drive sixteen hours in an open jeep. I drive all night through sleet, snow, and rain. I arrive in Rome very tired and cold. Hotel Excelsior is still as comfortable as ever. I have a hot tub bath, call for room service, have several rum cokes in bed, then take a six-hour nap.

The first night Lieutenant McFarland asks me to go on a double date with a pair of Air Corps nurses staying at the hotel. I do so against my better judgment, still having an aversion to female Army personnel. We have a pleasant dinner and dance afterward, then settle down for some serious drinking. The girls retire at midnight, but we close the bar at 2:00 A.M.

The Hotel Excelsior has changed. Civilian girls are no longer permitted in the rooms upstairs. It seems as though the place has become too wild, the Air Corps on one occasion tossing a girl out of a second-story window, thus ending the practice of taking girls to your room. MPs are now stationed at all stairways.

The next morning I call Marguerete to meet me at the hotel that evening. We are delighted to see each other. We have a lot of fun that evening just talking over the events of the past few weeks. Marguerete needs neither music nor a floor show to be content—she seems to live only for your company. On the way to her home that night she tells me to find a date for a girl friend of hers for tomorrow, who has an apartment where we can stay if we want to. I am only too happy to accept her invitation.

I sleep late on the morning of January 13. I want to be well rested for tonight. I spend most of the afternoon playing Ping-Pong with Colonel Henderson for five bucks a game.

Marguerete arrives at the hotel for supper. She looks positively ravishing tonight. Her girl friend is very pretty too, and my buddy, another lieutenant of Headquarters Company, is very favorably impressed. Everything is just perfect tonight—the dinner is excellent, the music very good, and the floor show clever and amusing. Around midnight we leave the hotel and drive to a large modern apartment house near the Forum d'Italia. We climb three flights of stone steps to a third-floor apartment with living room, kitchenette, bathroom, and two bedrooms. No one is interested in a midnight snack nor any prolonged conversation. We practically behave like long-married couples. With instinctive silent and complete understanding we retire to the bedrooms immediately. These girls are ready to sleep with us tonight, so why waste time on small talk? A very sensible attitude. The nights are too short anyway, so you might as well enjoy every minute fully and not just halfway.

Marguerete prefers to undress in the dark. She walks softly over to the bed and gently nestles herself close to me. As she presses her body against mine, I notice that she is completely naked except for her brassiere. No amount of persuasion can induce her to also take off this article of clothing. Her breasts are apparently only for her husband to enjoy—a peculiarity of thinking I have never run across before in my limited experience with women. To all other stimuli, however, Marguerete is exuberant in her response. Never before have I enjoyed so little sleep. As soon as I stir, Marguerete is awake also.

Tonight my desires are endless, and to my very pleasant surprise Marguerete shares all of them with me with genuine passion and sincerity. I am now convinced more than ever that Marguerete is not just another whore; she does not accept my love with the sullen submission and faked enthusiasm of a street walker. As a matter of fact, at this moment, just thinking of her as a possible whore is suddenly very repulsive to me. Marguerete is a woman not afraid to show her love, and since it is sincere, her emotional release is uninhibited, natural, and instinctive. I am fonder of her in the morning than I was the night before. That feeling, too, is completely foreign to me. Usually, once satisfied, I have always been anxious to leave. With Marguerete, however, I could have stayed forever. I offer Marguerete money before I leave, not as just payment for a night's pleasure but as a genuine gesture to help her financially. She is hurt; I can see it right away, and I feel like a heel. I finally manage to persuade her that my intentions were meant to be anything but insulting. I really felt all along, however, that she knew this from the beginning. No two people could have spent such a wonderful night together and still feel far apart. Marguerete is a jewel. Her love is genuine even if not forever. War has its compensations.

Late on January 14 I leave Rome. That sixteen-hour jeep ride is just as grueling going back up to the front as it was leaving it. Approaching the division area, I am informed that our troops have been pulled back again and are in another rest area, a muddy field dotted with the usual pyramidal tents. The closest village is supposedly Formiche.

Being in a rest area again, I go about the routine of catching up with world news. Nobody talks about what is going on on all the other fronts. The Italian front interests them the most, but information is always scarce. Again, I get my information from back issues of the *Stars and Stripes* and from what Marguerete told me in Rome and from some officers who seem to get around. The news is very encouraging. Our forces on the Ligurian Sea in the west are still about twenty miles north of Pisa. We are bogged down in the middle of Italy about twenty miles south of Bologna. The British and Canadians on our right have done well and are ahead of us. The Canadians on the Adriatic are on the southern tip of Lake Comacchio only sixty miles south of Venice.

In western Europe the Allies are only about forty-five miles from Düsseldorf in Germany, almost in Bonn farther in the south, and almost seventy miles from Coblenz, and still farther south the Ardennes campaign is still in full swing. Either the fighting is easier on the western front, or troops are more than we have in Italy.

News about the Russians and Japanese is scarce. The Russians are about to enter Warsaw in Poland and Budapest in Hungary. All I learned about the Japanese was that the Leyte campaign in the Philippines was difficult and is going strong.

On January 17 we are sent to the front again. We walk for hours along the floor of a ravine, then finally climb its western slope and move into a valley of about six houses, all nestled deeply into the contours of the hill mass. The scenery is great. I love this spot. As a tourist I would never have found it. Every house must be over two hundred years old, built of solid stone, and without any modern conveniences. A light snow covers the ground and roofs. The freshly fallen snow muffles all sound, and everything is very peaceful. My aid station is on the ground floor of a grain mill. The smell of flour and wheat is most pleasant. We use all the barrels as stands to support our litters. We even have room to set up cots on which to unfold our bedrolls. This is a warm aid station with plenty of room and an agreeable odor. This nice little village is called Gabbiano. The troops ahead of us are just north of the town of Manzuno. Loiano lies across a deep valley to our right on Highway 65.

Rats and mice are our only enemies. We should have anticipated these in a granary. The rats are the biggest and most brazen I have ever seen. At night they scurry back and forth, jumping from beam to beam. Sometimes they lose their footing and fall on your cot. My nights are thus constantly disturbed. I request barium sulfite with my next medical supply order and receive it. We make dough balls out of wheat and water and load them with barium, then distribute this bait in all corners and onto all rafters in the place. Soon all the pregnant rats abort with squeaking and commotion. In five days the rat population is reduced by at least seventy-five percent, and we all get some sleep. Some of the wiser rats never touch the bait.

All of us receive many packages from home. Most of these are delayed Christmas packages arriving one month late. We eat all the food quickly lest the rats beat us to it.

My evenings I spend mostly at the battalion command post, located in the warm kitchen of another snug house. Here we drink beer and sing songs. We play poker and blackjack. One evening I win four hundred dollars.

During the day I do very little. There is no enemy activity except artillery duels. Our troops are dug in about one mile to our north, behind barbed-wire defenses. There are no battle casualties. A few cases of head colds, trench feet, and hepatitis is about all I treat.

Civilians call upon me more often. They come to the aid station and lead me for miles over the mountains to some sick relative's shack. I am really confronted with problems. I catheterize one old man with chronic prostatic obstruction who must not have voided for over one week. His bladder is distended to above his navel. I leave him with the catheter taped in place; I wonder when he will have it taken out. As gratitude he offers me one of his goats, for which I naturally have no use whatsoever.

Among other fascinating civilian cases in outlying mountain shacks are grandmothers in heart failure, babies with scurvy and rickets, and a few young fellows with chancroids, bubos, and gonorrhea. I help all of them as best I can and am richly rewarded with eggs, vino, and mostly with a very sincere thank-you.

On February 7 we move again. We are shifted a little more to the right and more to the north. I haven't seen a map for several weeks. My best estimate is that we are somewhere between Highway 64 and 65, roads to Bologna. I'll never know why we are shifted so often. The only explanation I can think of is that we are still trying to confuse enemy intelligence.

On February 7 I am in a large farmhouse with a walled-in courtyard on a mountain ridge about a mile behind the front troops. This farmhouse is a sort of ranch-type affair. It reminds me of a Mexican hacienda. There are enough rooms to accommodate the aid station, battalion headquarters kitchen, battalion command post, and Headquarters Company's communication platoon. The nearest village is about a mile up a narrow cart trail. This house has been hit several times, and gaping shell holes mar the courtyard walls. Ahead of us lies Mount Adone.

I really loaf here for three weeks. All day I have nothing to do, since troops can come to me only at night when the enemy has no observation. Consequently, my daytime hours are filled with boredom. Just for the sake of something to do, I take apart our oil stove and clean it; I rig up another still to purify rubbing alcohol for drinking purposes but never get it perfected; I practice more card tricks; I drink whiskey and Coca-Cola; in the command post I study all the aerial photographs taken of enemy positions and help plan the next offensive or at least put in my two-cents' worth.

I inspect the battalion kitchen twice daily, not because of regulations but because the mess sergeant has time to make pies and pastries, which he always lets me taste first.

Nights I devote to my medical practice. The boys crawl out of their foxholes and trudge back to see me. Scabies, impetigo, and skin diseases due to lack of bathing are all I see. For one week an epidemic of gonorrhea sweeps through one platoon. It stops when a lady is found in a front-line cave. She is dirty and unkempt but well fed and torpedoed.

We are experiencing the mildest February in years. At times the temperature is 70 degrees. Some of the men just back from pass are singing a song, "Meet Me in St. Louis, Louis—Meet Me at the Fair." It has a very catchy tune. I am getting spring fever.

On February 17 we receive the startling news that cameramen from Warner Brothers are coming up to take some pictures of our life up front. We all shave and clean up a little, but no one ever shows up.

On February 20 I walk two miles to the rear to the village of Manzuno, where Regiment is quartered. A motion picture will be shown here. We are all seated in the basement of a farmhouse waiting for the show to begin when a Kraut shell knocks out the generator and the movie can't start. We all go back to our quarters.

On February 24 I receive orders to further my medical education. I am to report to the division area the next day for a medical lecture. In broad daylight and under direct enemy observation, I take my jeep over a twisting and turning mountain road running from Manzuno down a long slope, then up the other slope to Loiano. Airbursts and some really heavy stuff miss my jeep. Arriving at division area, I listen to a lecture on VD control I have heard at least twenty times and have often given myself. My trip back to the front is just as hazardous. The Krauts are peppering us with plenty of 88s. I arrive back at the aid station a physical wreck. I've risked my life all morning and haven't heard a damn thing new. However, I suppose I'm just as expendable as the next guy.

Early in March we are relieved and sent back to La Croce, close to Florence, where we pitch a camp of pyramidal tents along the Florence-Pistoia-Lucca road. Many replacements are sent to us. We are apparently bringing our battalion up to full strength for our spring offensive.

On March 10 I drive to Lucca. The Rome Opera Company and the Lucca orchestra are presenting "Madame Butterfly" to the American troops. The opera house is cold and damp. Both performers and spectators are chilly. The performance, however, even though crude, is a pleasant reminder of civilization.

I also have a brief chance to drive around Lucca and Pistoia, both flourishing cities as far back as the twelfth century. In Lucca the church of San Frediano, built in 1147, is still standing. Lucca's ancient city wall is also still relatively well preserved. Pistoia is pretty well shot up except for the ancient churches. I would love to leisurely roam through these ancient cities, but unfortunately they are declared "off limits."

On March 15 I am back in the Apennines. Our move to the front is rather mysterious. All identification markers are removed from all our vehicles. We are told to remove our blue clover-leaf division patches. In other words, we are blacked out.

I am now on Highway 65 about three miles behind the front lines and in Trasasso. We are probably in reserve position. Headquarters Company and the aid station are in a former small hospital, its walls riddled with shell holes. Our main body of troops is quartered in tents on a field just behind us.

Spring is definitely here. Fields are a refreshing green, apple blossoms have burst forth, and I feel lazy and moody. I drive or walk to the surrounding mountains, visit each company in turn, and give the boys their necessary booster shots. I draw these trips out as long as possible, and treat many civilians on these rounds, stopping in at stables, climbing to the attics of ruins, or just crawl into a goat hut to ease some old man's complaint. After doing the best possible under the circumstances, I usually sit on the doorstep of their humble dwellings, light my pipe, and listen to the Italian family expound on stories of peace and beauty of this area—the Apennines in the spring, where there is peace on earth and romance in people's hearts. I love this part of the country. I cannot feast my eyes enough on the explosive beauty of erupting trees and flowers.

By midafternoon I usually return to the aid station. There my daydreaming ends. The Krauts are throwing airbursts over the road, our building, and tents. On one occasion they shoot us up a little with long-range artillery. Five tents and a latrine fly through the air. Ten men are wounded. One poor fellow's scrotum and penis are torn away completely, the only radical injury of this type I encountered during the entire war. After two hours' work, the casualties are all patched up and evacuated. We haven't had a casualty for over two weeks, now suddenly ten at one time. I can't figure out the Kraut's shooting schedule; they certainly have seen us long before this time, but only now are they beginning to harass us.

On March 22 I am offered another pass to Rome. I accept with pleasure. A hell of a lot of us are suddenly receiving passes, a bad omen, for someone wants to let us have a brief fling before we are led into another slaughter. But back to Rome I fly in an open jeep, over dusty roads, a fifteen-hour trip.

Five days at the Hotel Excelsior seem like only twenty-four hours. Spirits run high at the hotel, almost too high to seem real. Everyone seems to sense that this may be his last chance for happiness before that fatal bullet. Everything is overdone; everyone drinks to excess, sleeps very little, is very boisterous, throws away his money recklessly, and sleeps with the first whore who propositions him.

Marguerete is my steady companion. She remains at the hotel until 2:00 A.M. every morning, and we genuinely enjoy every dance until the night's activities cease with the strains of "Auld Lang Syne." I, too, drink more heavily than usual. Under the heavy influence of alcohol, my evenings with Marguerete seem more like a dream than a reality. My mind is hazy, my disposition moody, and I pour all my sentiments out to Marguerete. I admire this girl, and I have a profound respect for her, so profound that in spite of my desire to spend each night with her, I send her home in a taxi instead and, after a final drink at the bar, retire alone, my last thoughts still with Marguerete before succumbing to a deep, drugged slumber.

My first thoughts in the morning are of Marguerete, and I count each hour until nightfall when I shall see her again. Marguerete is really quite a girl. She makes me feel proud. Taking her to the dining room or any place in Rome is like showing off an ornament and saying, "Look what I have; isn't this something?" Marguerete's life is much less complicated than Maria's. Marguerete is divorced. She knows that I am not married, so no matter what we do together—no wife at home is getting hurt. Because of my being single, Marguerete is outgoing and uninhibited but in a socially accepted manner, being so only when we are alone.

Marguerete would be the ideal picturesque type of female for a six-foot-tall, broad-shouldered cigarette "ad"-type hunk of a male, but for one reason or another she pays attention to only me. Marguerete is therefore a morale booster and instills in me more self-confidence. The only assets I have that can possibly attract her are that I am a fairly decent conversationalist, that I have shown that I respect her, that I can dance well, and that I have some brains or else I could not have become a doctor; being one, I probably will also never be a bum.

Marguerete is always the same, vivacious, exuberant, beautiful, loving, and understanding. I know that this will be my last trip to Rome, and I am relieved, for I am falling in love with Marguerete. She never makes any remarks to suggest that she wants to start a lasting relationship. With my experiences in the vicinity of Volterra and Mount Grande and with the Po Valley campaign coming up, I feel it to be unfair to promise Marguerete anything. A woman like her does not deserve her lover returning from the war with legs missing or crippled from the waist down. I try not to let Marguerete suspect my love for her and am artifically gay and happy-go-lucky. Marguerete, however, is not easily duped—her eyes often speak more than words could express. Every night parting becomes more difficult, and my final hour at the bar alone more morose. I can now sleep only under the influence of alcohol. I drink just enough for it to act as a hypnotic; too much makes me sick, and therefore I will never become an alcoholic. When with Marguerete, I drink only enough to feel relaxed. Were I to drink more I would lose self-control and propose to her.

I know that my last night with Marguerete is my final one, but I believe she thinks that I will see her again tomorrow. However, I promise nothing. To know that Marguerete would be waiting for me after the war would give me a tremendous boost and a will to survive at any cost. For her sake, however, I make up my mind never to see her again. My future is too uncertain. I might even be sent to the South Pacific should I remain healthy, and the Japanese are not yet defeated. Marguerete deserves all the chances for earlier happiness. The confidence Marguerete has given me will be permanent. In the past I was always afraid of beautiful women. I no longer am, and this will be an asset when someday I choose a wife.

I must be a sentimental person to fall in love repeatedly. All the women I have encountered thus far I respected and loved in one way or another, and had I been in a situation to afford it would have asked any one of them to marry me at the time of our relationship. Only three times did I have sex for the sake of sex only; once in a whorehouse in Cuba, once with a girl while interning, and once with Lillie in Rome. Even then, I thought that all three were rather cute and not just sexpots.

On March 31 I am back in Trasasso. Easter, April 1, 1945, is a beautiful day. My thoughts, however, are still confused, and I perform my duties methodically and without emotion. This damn war creates too many problems.

I have received a few letters from home. The last time I wrote home I asked to be informed as much as possible on what is happening elsewhere in the world because we over here in Italy get very little news and for me to keep up to date I have to scrounge around.

I learn that on the western front in Europe things are going well. Two weeks ago we were only about seventy-five miles from Berlin and about two hundred miles from Munich but still about four hundred miles from Vienna, which the Russians are about to enter. The Russians are just a little farther from Berlin than we are and will probably soon take Prague in Czechoslovakia. The Italian Alps look as though they could be the final refuge of the German Army, and we could therefore be in for a really tougher campaign than all the others have been. This is a rather pessimistic outlook because I have become pessimistic.

In the Pacific things are apparently a little tougher. Iwo Jima fell in March, but fighting is still fierce in Central Luzon in the Philippines, but the south of Okinawa has been invaded. The war with the

Japanese worries me. Once the war is finished over here, unmarried doctors have a good chance of being reassigned to the Pacific theater of operations.

Our Italian front starts about twenty miles north of Pisa in the west. The line then passes about twelve miles south of Bologna and then through the city of Imola on Highway 9; from there it runs northeast to the northern shores of Lake Comacchio on the Adriatic Sea.

On April 14, 1945, we get the big news we have been expecting. We are ordered to move into jump-off positions just north of Manzuno. Ahead lies the Monterumici Hill Mass. We shall attack tomorrow—April 15, 1945.

Slaughter in the Po Valley

APRIL 15, 1945–MAY 3, 1945

April 15, 1945, is a clear, warm, and sunny day. We are just west of Highway 65. A majestic boot-shaped, bare, but rocky hill mass lies ahead and to the right. It is the Monterumici Hill Mass. On our left flank is the 6th South African Division; ahead of it is a huge pyramidal-shaped mountain called Mount Sole; 91st Division troops are on our right flank, straddling Highway 65; to their right in turn is the 34th Division.

By 10:00 A.M. our planes are active. They are bombing Highway 64 and 65. "Rover Pete," a fast group of low-flying monoplanes, dives frequently with machine guns wide open, apparently raking everything it sees moving on either highway.

At 4:30 P.M. dive bombers are active on our left flank. Large numbers of these swoop down on Mount Sole dropping phosphorus bombs. Clouds of smoke and many fires soon cover the entire forward slope of this mountain.

At 10:30 P.M. our artillery lets loose with one of its hour-long barrages. The dark sky is heavy with flying steel. Huge flashes like distant lightning occur every second, but the crash of thunder is replaced by the steady roar of cannons.

At 11:00 P.M. our lead company moves out toward a formidable ridge that forms the foot of the boot-shaped Monterumici Hill Mass. This ridge is known as Furcoli Ridge. We have been looking at it for months. It is dotted with caves occupied by heavily armed machine-gun and mortar crews. Mine fields cover all approaches to this ridge. It is an almost impossible objective to take. Mount Adone, farther north, towers above Monterumici.

At 6:00 A.M. our battalion is stopped at the foot of a ridge near a hamlet called Ca Valla and a hill mass called only K-12 on my small map. I am behind the ruins of a farmhouse on a small knoll about a thousand yards from Furcoli. Casualties are heavy. We treat wounds of every description—blown-off feet, machine-gun wounds, mortar and bayonet wounds. We treat out in the open but behind the shattered walls of the house. The inside of the house is too full of debris and much too unsafe.

I am much too busy to keep up with the strategy of the raging battle. I judge progress from what I hear from the wounded. They relate tales of confusion. One company after the other fails to take the ridge. Occasionally, one platoon reaches it and drives beyond, then is suddenly surrounded by enemy, cut off from retreat, and annihilated. Colonels from regiment and division volunteer to join the attacking companies, hoping to find some break in the approaches to the ridge. These men all prove themselves heroes. One colonel digs out mines with his bare hands and tosses them at the Krauts. Another destroys several machine-gun nests by tossing hand grenades like baseballs.

By late afternoon of April 16 we have tried everything and failed. Tanks are brought up to shoot up the caves, but most hit antitank mines and are abandoned. Men with flame-throwers crawl up to the caves but are only partially successful before being forced back by mortar barrages and criss-crossing machine-gun fire.

By nightfall the men are dog tired and parched from thirst. They are covered with dust and blood. Their eyes are red from hate and fatigue. We have lost over 25 percent of our men and still there is no hope of a breakthrough.

Fighting continues during the night. I do not sleep. Wounded keep pouring in. Other than rapidly applying splints and giving morphine, we do very little. I can't use light out in the open and therefore am unable to give plasma. Since we are not very far off Highway 65, rapid evacuation is possible and of tremendous help.

Throughout April 17 and the dark morning hours of April 18 the battle rages on. Again and again we try to blast the Krauts out of their deep holes and solid caves by using tank fire, phosphorus shells, and finally direct assault. With every attack we lose more men. At 10:00 A.M. on April 18, after fifty-five hours of fighting and advancing only four thousand yards, things finally begin to loosen and the Krauts show less signs of resisting. Our battalion finally clears the small town of Vado and also the well-defended Nuzzano ridges. We suddenly receive orders to stop our assault, since troops on both of our flanks have been able to achieve a breakthrough and stubborn Furcoli Ridge can now be given up and bypassed. The resisting Krauts can be left holed up where they are, since they are now cut off from their supplies and must eventually surrender anyway. It is useless to fight them longer. Even though enemy, we must admit that they have been excellent soldiers.

Why do the Krauts keep on fighting so fiercely? I think they are fighting for a different cause than we are. They are now near their homeland. Their backs are almost against a wall. They are no longer fighting for a principle, but to keep strangers from crossing their border. We, on the other hand, are just fighting to get it over with—to get back home. We are fighting on Italian soil far from home, and who of us cares who lives on the soil over here?

My battalion rapidly assembles, and in our usual column of ducks we move out on the double heading northwest over the hills toward the town of Vergato on Highway 64, which has fallen to the troops of the IV Corps, among them the 85th Division, 1st Armored Division, and 10th Mountain Division. We shall exploit this breakthrough and follow Highway 64 into the Po Valley.

We fail to reach Highway 64 by nightfall. We sleep in an old schoolhouse in a small village near Vergato. We have met no resistance since abandoning Furcoli Ridge except sniper fire from an occasional group of Krauts who must not know where they are and how the battle has been going. We are very cautious in entering houses in the dark. Sometimes bypassed or lost Krauts are still in them; all could also well be booby trapped. With poles we shove open the doors, expecting everything we touch to explode. Tonight we are lucky again, for the schoolhouse contains neither booby traps nor time bombs. I don't know if any of our troops are already in the Po Valley or not. No one seems to know anything. Our artillery keeps shooting over our heads all night long.

On the morning of April 19 we move on toward Highway 64. Once on the highway, we are ordered to halt and await orders. All battle plans apparently have gone snafu in the hurry to break into the Po Valley. The 85th Division and the 10th Mountain Division, all belonging to the IV Corps and on our left flank, have fouled things up a little. The 10th Mountain Division, instead of heading due north, has headed diagonally northeast and has forced the 85th Division on its right flank to conform to this diagonal and to also head northeast. Thus two divisions slightly ahead of us and pushing northeast instead of due north cause our division, the 88th, to be pinched out.* Now this mess must be straightened out. We are therefore sitting on High-

---

*I did not know that our delay in advancing was because of the existing confusion and the remedy that was planned until I read the explanation in

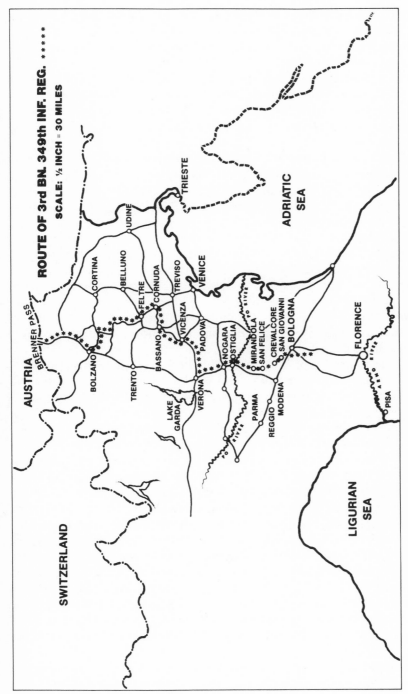

5 The Po Valley Campaign: Route of the 3d Battalion into the Po Valley and the Alps

way 64 and waiting. Our 351st Regiment has already jumped off and
is moving north along the highway. We are to follow. We are detained,
however, since the 351st Regiment is having all sorts of trouble. Since
the 10th Mountain and 85th Division units are still cutting across
their path, this regiment in its advance runs into both friendly units
as well as bypassed pockets of the enemy. At night they do not know
whom they are fighting; this mess is finally straightened out when
it is agreed that 88th units will relieve in place all 85th units as they
are overtaken.

While the 351st Regiment is thus having its troubles and is slowly
overtaking troops of the 85th Division, we of the 349th Regiment are
just biding time. I am safely holed up in a former Kraut cave along
the highway. It is quite a layout, cut into a roadside bank with at least
twenty feet of dirt as a roof. The cave's narrow entrance leads to a
narrow hallway, from which branch off four rooms, all about eight
by eight feet square. This is like a small house, only deeply underground. The floors are covered with neatly spaced and neatly cut tree
branches so that your feet remain dry. Kraut communication wires
and radios are in every room. I have seldom spent a night in a safer
place. This cave must have taken many months to build. No wonder
the Krauts always have remained no matter how severe our bombing
or strafing. Even a direct bomb hit could not destroy this lair.

On the morning of April 20 we shove off to catch up with the 351st
Regiment, move abreast of it, and head north into the Po Valley. All
divisions of the II and IV Corps are now apparently straightened out
and will once again push forward abreast and due north, each assigned
to a definite sector. Only the 34th Division will leave us; it will mop
up and garrison Bologna.

My battalion follows Highway 64 for several hours. It seems strange
to be walking along a highway instead of climbing over mountains.
All of a sudden we go downhill. This, too, is a strange experience for
us, since during the past year all our journeys have been uphill. The
mountains ahead of us seem to be lower and lower, and finally we
get a glimpse of an endless plain stretching out for miles below us.
This is certainly a welcome sight. We can hardly believe that we have
finally made it. Light resistance thus far, too, makes us feel pretty
good. Tanks of the 1st Armored Division roll over the road and pass
our column. We halt only occasionally to weed out pockets of snipers.

Just before entering the Po Valley we leave Highway 64 and proceed
cross-country. We see the buildings of Bologna far off to our right. We

1947 in *The Blue Devils in Italy* by John P. Delany (Washington, D.C.: Infantry
Journal Press, 1947), pp. 203–204.

Monterumici Hill Mass with Furcoli Ridge in the foreground. Courtesy U.S. Army Signal Corps.

Monterumici Hill Mass with Mount Adone in the background. Courtesy U.S. Army Signal Corps.

A litter case being borne to Highway 65 after the casualty was treated in the aid station on Monterumici. U.S. Army Signal Corps photo, courtesy Lt. Col. (Ret.) William Konze.

One cave on Furcoli Ridge finally captured by 88th troops. U.S. Army Signal Corps photo, courtesy Lt. Col. (Ret.) William Konze. *Below:* Surrendered Germans on Monterumici Hill Mass. Courtesy U.S. Army Signal Corps.

Moving off the Monterumici Hill Mass and toward Highway 64 on the way to Bologna. U.S. Army Signal Corps photo, courtesy Lt. Col. (Ret.) William Konze.

Heading downhill from the mountains into the Po Valley. Courtesy U.S. Army Signal Corps.

Captured Germans marching to the rear in the Po Valley. Courtesy Eugene
Engelen, Park Ridge, Ill.

Crossing the Po River in ducks. Courtesy U.S. Army Signal Corps. *Below:* Captured Germans who had passed through the town of Cornuda the night before. Courtesy Eugene Engelen, Park Ridge, Ill.

Site of our bivouac in the vicinity of Mezzano the morning peace was declared. Courtesy Eugene Engelen, Park Ridge, Ill.

shall bypass this city, head through the fields, and remain off most of the roads, since these are usually the best defended. We are to advance as swiftly as possible, day and night.

In the early afternoon of April 21 we are just east of San Giovanni. The terrain is flat. Roads are numerous. Suddenly I feel hedged in even though on flat country. I have become accustomed to seeing for miles from mountain tops. The Po Valley's lush vegetation obstructs your view, and one can see for only several hundred yards; thus, you never know just what is lurking directly ahead.

We move forward in single file through vineyards, gardens, pastures, and orchards. We cross many irrigation ditches, all about twelve feet wide and filled with water to a depth of about two to three feet. These are a nuisance; your clothes and feet never dry out, and soon my feet are a mass of blisters caused by the rubbing of wet socks and shoes.

Our planes are all over the skies, dive bombing the retreating Krauts, most of whom are fleeing in vehicles on the main roads. By moving rapidly through the fields and not taking to the roads, we bypass great numbers of them. Krauts caught between two of our advancing columns winding across the fields abreast about a mile apart often number into the hundreds. Many are smart enough to realize that they are trapped and then just sit down on the road and wait to be marched to the rear.

Hedgerows and isolated farmhouses offer us the most resistance. One Kraut machine-gun nest or mortar crew can hold up our entire column for hours. I doubt if these isolated groups of diehards know what they are tackling. Entire regiments of Krauts have been bypassed, and these small units must surely have lost communication with their main body of troops and know nothing of the disposition of their own forces. They are fighting not knowing that they have been left behind, are cut off, and are dead ducks unless they surrender. Most fight on to the bitter end.

The roar of our dive-bombing planes overhead is augmented by our steady artillery fire. Having finally good roads to move on and flat terrain, the artillery boys are in their prime. They are right behind us and shooting constantly. It is a miracle that their shells do not hit our own low-flying planes, which are hedge-hopping and swooping over the whole valley, shooting up anything which looks German. Since we have bypassed so many German units and are often ahead of many of their fleeing columns, our strafing planes become a hazard even to us. They must first come down low to look us over and see if we are friend or foe. I don't particularly care for all this uncertainty. To end this confusion, all our vehicles the next day are protected with bright orange hood covers so that the fly boys can tell which vehicles belong to us.

Our casualties are few, since we are purposely avoiding contact and are chiefly intent on gaining ground by bypassing as many enemy units as possible. My worst casualties this afternoon are a forward group of artillery observers who even far ahead of us have been shelled by our own guns. The old church in which I find their bodies is in total ruins. One officer's entire chest is shot away; only a rim of tissue connecting the head with his abdomen remains. A large-caliber shell must have hit him directly. I have never seen a more mutilating wound. The others in his group are all dead too, but their wounds even though mortal are much less extensive. All I can do with these poor fellows is tag them.

We are moving so fast that I have little time to figure out our location at definite times. I am not issued a map and can only guess where we are by listening to conversation carried on at the battalion command post. At 11:00 P.M. we are somewhere near the village of Crevalcore. In a small shack just off a secondary road, I try to get a few hours sleep. The troops sleep in a field outside. A burning Kraut half-track sits on the road a hundred yards away and every few minutes another one of its shells explodes. It is an eerie night all around. Bypassed and lost German outfits roam about the countryside, and when someone suddenly pops out of the darkness you never know if it is friend or foe.

At 3:00 A.M. we are on the move again. The burning Kraut half-track is still sputtering and exploding. We proceed toward the village of San Felice, bypass it at noon, and head toward San Martino. On April 22 at 3:00 P.M. halfway between San Felice and San Martino one of our fighter planes high above us bursts into flames. I can see the pilot bail out but his chute never opens. He falls and falls, gathering speed with every second. Later, about a mile away, I come upon his shattered body in a field. He has made an imprint in the ground about a foot deep. His pockets have already been ransacked and his watch is missing. The thieves are civilians, peeking from a farmhouse about a hundred yards away. They plead innocence when questioned. As soon as I leave, they will probably be battling each other for his parachute. However, they have left the dog tags hanging about the poor fellow's broken neck. I pull out my tag book, make out my routine slip, jotting down the coordinates where he plunged to his death. I abandon his body for the rear troops to find.

Pockets of German rear guards continue giving us plenty of trouble. Small groups are holed up in clusters of farmhouses. Some of these units just won't give up. Men of our lead company must then resort to hand-to-hand fighting in order to root them out of the buildings.

The "Rover Boys" above us have been flying all day. They are massacring the Krauts. We are walking through the fields and parallel to Highway 12. For short stretches we often cross it or even walk along it; then we see the devastating results the strafing planes have accomplished. Dead Krauts, charred enemy vehicles of every description, and innumerable dead horses litter the highway for many miles. The Po Valley has been one big graveyard for the enemy. I am disgusted to see so many dead, even though they have been my enemies.

Here's a picture to remember. It's that of a dead German. His grimaced face is bloated and his head lies in a pile of dust. His leg wound stinks and crawls with flies and maggots. What a degrading sight. No one seems to give a damn. How calloused we have all become! Our men don't even give this guy a second look, but just walk over him. He will only be remembered by his loved ones back home. For many years they probably gave unselfishly and unstintingly their time, effort, love, and money to raise him from infancy to manhood. Who knows how much more they may have sacrificed to give him a good education? Now he lies dead — one lousy bomb fragment put an end to it all. His parents will probably receive a notice that he died a glorious death. You never die in any other way in telegrams or war reports. They will picture him dying nobly in one way or another, but here their imagination stops, and it's a good thing too; could they see him now they would never sleep again.

At approximately 10:00 P.M. on April 22 we are in Magnacavello. Here a secondary highway joins a better one. We are not far from the Po River. Confusion and traffic jams exist on all roads. Half-tracks, tanks, trucks, jeeps, and weapon carriers flash by in the moonlight, all racing toward the Po River. We stay off the pavement lest we be run down. The drivers of all these speeding vehicles can't possibly see more than twenty yards ahead. I rub my eyes in disbelief when I see German trucks roll by — closely following ours. These are really lost. In darkness and by mistake they simply follow the vehicles ahead of them, and usually these turn out to be ours. This is certainly a crazy mixed-up night.

By midnight we limp into a village still closer to the banks of the Po River. It has been a long walk. There are many farmhouses available for quarters. I have visions of a good night's rest. Captain Bellmont tells me to walk into any house I want and use it for an aid station. It seems as though all the Krauts have fled across the Po River. Our lead scouts are at this moment scouting the river's banks for a good place to cross in the morning. Until then, we can rest.

I can hear small-arms fire on the other side of the river but on our side it is quiet. All the houses are dark and appear deserted. I am scouting about alone. I come upon a lone house surrounded by a small orchard. This place looks cozy and is very much to my liking. I open the front door and walk into a dark room. I catch a glimpse of light coming from an adjoining room and walk toward it. I also hear subdued voices. The inhabitants of this house must still be up—perhaps they are awaiting us. Softly I walk toward the light and peek into another room. About a table illuminated by one lone flickering candle sit only Krauts. They have their helmets on and their guns rest beside them. They are drinking wine and are eating their rations. Had I not seen their helmets, I would have taken them for Americans. I have never experienced such an empty feeling in my stomach. A lump comes up in my throat and for a few seconds I am too damned scared to move. My only weapon is a shovel, which would not be of much use anyway. As quietly as a mouse I very slowly do an about-face, tip-toe back out of the house, then run like hell back to the battalion command post. Here I relate my story. Captain Bellmont immediately sends a squad of riflemen to the house. The boys return with a dozen startled Krauts. They had been unaware that we were already upon them. They were not expecting us for another twenty-four hours. Episodes like this would happen all night long along this "fluid" front.

After my chosen house is cleaned out of Krauts, we make ourselves comfortable. The farmer and his wife make noodle soup for us and serve us wine. They are beaming with joy; for them, the war is over. They offer us their feather beds to sleep in. I sleep like a baby. I awake the next morning chewed up by bed bugs all over again.

At 9:00 A.M. on April 25 we head for the shores of the Po River. Now to put to use all I have learned about river crossings. Many long nights I have spent mastering the technique essential for this type of tactical operation. But lo and behold, the Army engineers are waiting for us at the banks with "ducks." Quickly we are shuttled across the stream. I have practiced river crossings at least fifty times, yet still have to cross one on foot. Something always seems to happen at the last minute to save me from disaster. I can't figure out what has happened to the Krauts.

At 11:00 A.M. we bypass Ostiglia and march along the highway toward Nogara. For the first time I am strafed by a Kraut plane but am not hit. After splattering us, he chases one of our artillery Cubs; the latter, however, just drops sharply out of the sky and hops over the tree tops. The fast Kraut plane is outmaneuvered and misses his target. I am sure that the Kraut pilot is either lost or is contemplating suicide. In a few minutes "Rover Pete" will probably shoot him down. We bypass Nogara on our left and go cross-country to Ronco and the

Adige River, reaching the point on April 26. I hear that the Adige River Line is strongly fortified, for it is to this line that the enemy has planned to withdraw for a last stand in the Po Valley. We have moved too fast, however, for the Krauts to get there. Most of the gun emplacements are unmanned, and only the largest of the guns point south and east. We have no trouble crossing this river, first because there is little resistance and second because there is no water in the river bed. It has not rained since the start of our Po Valley push, and the riverbed is bone dry. My last big river crossing is again successful, or a flop—it all depends how you look at it.

By nightfall we are walking along railroad tracks that run parallel to Highway 11, a good road running east-west between Verona and Vicenza. We encounter sporadic and erratic mortar fire throughout our march; otherwise, resistance is light. We are chiefly intent on gaining ground and cutting Kraut communication and supply routes while our planes and artillery do most of the annihilating behind us. At 2:00 A.M. we rest on a farm near San Bonifacio. We post guards all around our camp, for no one knows where the Krauts are. A regiment of enemy coming from the south and moving north could readily pass through us at any time.

I set up my aid station in a three-room stone house about a quarter-mile from battalion headquarters. As usual, we hang a Red Cross flag on the door. We spend about an hour patching up a few walking wounded, then bed down for the night. Suddenly, without warning, six strangers enter. A half-dozen Kraut soldiers have walked in on us. For a few minutes I can't say anything. No one speaks. The Krauts just stand and stare too. When I finally regain my composure, my knowledge of German again comes in mighty handy. I inform the Germans that this is an aid station and that we are unarmed. They reply that they are aware of this fact, having seen the flag on our door. They desire to surrender, since they are lost and fully aware of being surrounded by Americans. An aid station was the best place to come to in the dark in order to surrender, instead of surrendering to a group of riflemen and being shot up a little first during the process. They affirm their sincerity by not having brought their weapons into my station; instead, they stacked them neatly outside before entering. We offer them some of our rations, then send a messenger to battalion headquarters informing it that we have six prisoners. A couple of riflemen shortly relieve us of our captives. The rest of the night is uneventful.

At 8:00 A.M. on April 28 we are already on Highway 11 heading for Vicenza. We are on an excellent road. Tanks and heavy artillery carriers move along with us. It seems strange to be marching east instead of due north. Today, anything can happen. We are cutting directly across the path of any fleeing Krauts that are coming up from the south. Fortunately, our plane support is very good, and the Krauts are not moving during the hours of daylight; they are waiting for the cover of darkness to avoid strafing.

By midafternoon we are on the outskirts of Vicenza. Here we meet stiff resistance. A tank battle rages just ahead of us. When it quiets down, we move in. Snipers shoot at us from roof tops and windows. Two such characters hold us up for at least an hour before they are finally picked off.

Vicenza is a rough place. I'll never forget it. I cross a public square. A fountain spewing spurts of water stands in the center. About two dozen civilians have just been lined up here moments before and shot. Their crumpled bodies lie in one large pool of blood. They have been shot by their own countrymen without a trial but only on suspicion of having collaborated with the Nazis. Their murderers with red 'kerchiefs around their necks are pacing back and forth, gesturing with flailing arms, jabbering and shouting, proud of the deed they have just performed. Just as I pass by, the shoes of the corpses are being distributed to the bystanders.

We rush through the streets ducking into every doorway for cover until finally through town. On the northern outskirts we rest on Highway 46 leading to an airport. Here larger German pockets are fiercely resisting capture. Prisoners captured are from the 1st Parachute Division, a do-or-die outfit. The battle for the airport lasts all afternoon. A German field hospital supposedly lies beyond the airport. We receive word that its commanding officer desires to surrender. Here is my chance to become a hero, go there, and accept the surrender. All I need do is drive a jeep through a few isolated pockets of Krauts and I'm there. The colonel, however, says no to my suggestion. I think about it, and the more I think the more absurd seem my ambitions; I then promptly drop my plan. Captain Mullins is sent instead. He and I had a great time together on our last leave in Rome. Captain Mullins never reaches the hospital. A half-mile from it a sniper gets him. In a half-hour his jeep returns. His dead body is draped over the hood. He has a bullet through his brain. The corpse could have been I. A macabre thought runs through my mind: had I been killed, my obituary would have stated that I died on my birthday. Our troops capture the airport during the night. I never find out who accepted the surrender of the hospital.

On April 29 we cross the Brenda River near Bassano. On April 30 we are moving in single file again to the northeast. We were hoping that it would be southeast to Venice, but no such luck. It's to the northeast toward the highest mountains in all of Italy—the Alps. There are now rumors that our next objective will be Innsbruck in Austria. The weather is good, the sky clear, and it is sunny. We are making excellent time. We are on a paved road and hitching rides on tanks and trucks. Some GIs are riding liberated bicycles. We move along at a rapid pace, never resting, intent on gaining as much ground as possible during daylight when the Krauts don't dare move. We pass through Bassano, and about sixteen miles east of Bassano take a secondary road to the town of Cornuda, which we reach by late afternoon. The Alps are clearly visible to the north.

Cornuda is only a small town, and the east-west road and north-south roads cross in the town's center, a spacious square. A watering fountain for horses is at this intersection. The town's houses are grouped around the square. We shall remain in Cornuda for the night. We post guards along all the roads leading to and from the town. Furthermore, a tank is stationed at each one of the four corners of the square. My aid station is in an abandoned haberdashery and dry cleaning store. My jeep is parked in an alley just beside the shop. We have a little backyard and are lying in the grass just loafing, waiting for sundown.

I just lie back and relax. I feel tired and lazy. It has been a long war and I have had many a close shave. I'll be satisfied to come out of this mess alive. I have no ambitions to become a hero, nor do I want to be a coward; I just want to make it, that's all. I have tagged many a dead "hero" and have felt extremely sorry for each one. I have often wondered what suddenly compels a guy to gamble on his life. Is he sane at the moment he attacks machine-gun nests alone or throws himself at the enemy? I think he becomes temporarily insane from sheer madness and hate against those who have forced him into a temporary life not too remote from that of an animal; in addition to this, he is compelled to be a murderer or be murdered himself. He concentrates so intensely on what lies ahead of him that he completely forgets himself. It is then that he becomes a reckless, insane gambler. If he comes out alive, he is a hero. He was lucky. He won against immeasurable odds. The ones I have talked to seldom have remembered the details of their exploits. Others, such as buddies for example, describe the details of our hero's fantastic feats later, and then the commanding officer makes the necessary recommendations for that big, shiny medal. If our hero was perfectly sane, why does he need someone else to recall his deeds for him? What about the poor guy who isn't so lucky and stops a bullet? He just has goofed. He will be nothing. One or two good buddies might mourn over him for a few weeks; the rest of the boys forget him in a few days. His hometown paper might write a story about him, but that is about all. His loved ones might remember him forever, but even the fervor of this memory gradually cools off. He has died for his country. These are noble words indeed, but they are really untrue and just good propaganda. He only died because his luck ran out. Those really responsible for his death are the politicians and diplomats on both sides. They are the ones who would like to see their names perpetuated. A declaration of war is their admission of defeat—they just didn't have the brains to avoid conflict. Through a propaganda of hate, they stir up your emotions and work you up into such a rage against your fellow men that you gladly go to war and kill others just as innocent as you are. The ensuing confusion is the politician's gain. We forget all about their boners —something they have wanted us to do all along.

I think of past Memorial Days. What were my thoughts during the ceremony? I don't think that my heart really ever bled for anyone in particular. All I ever thought of was, "It's a damn shame so many died and I hope it doesn't happen again." Did I mourn over the guy who ran straight toward a machine-gun nest tossing grenades until he was finally mowed down? Hell, no! No one remembered him. Everyone just prays for his own hide. If our dead heroes once believed that they would ever be remembered individually, then they were really wrong. Now, they just belong to a group of dead, a very impersonal group, a group mentioned once a year when everyone gets a day off so that he can go on a picnic. That's not worth dying for.

I am now determined to come out alive. Like any old soldier, I shall be cautious. Old soldiers still exist because they were cautious. This by no means implies cowardice. Being cautious is being smart. You can also call it adaptation to your environment, where the development of a certain additional sense keeps you out of trouble.

In spite of all this feeling of wanting to survive, I really, in a strange sort of way, have enjoyed danger when I have escaped with an unscathed hide, and look forward to other dangers still to come. Why? I can't explain it. For some peculiar reason I have enjoyed cheating death.

But be that as it may, I have said before I am now determined to come out alive. I'll gamble on anything but my life. I'll keep my head down, keep my damn helmet on, probe carefully for mines along my path, keep digging my holes deep, and look for cover as I run. I'll think about each situation first, then face it as planned. No show-off stuff for me. I'll obey all orders to the letter and do nothing more. My instinct for self-preservation is deep seated. Most of the boys I started with in Texas are long dead and buried. My obedience to the principles of basic training have thus far paid off very well. I am alive and healthy. I've tried to be a good doctor. I haven't demonstrated much of my medical knowledge to date—but that is just the point—you don't have an opportunity to do so in the infantry. During almost two years with my battalion I have learned nothing new and am two years behind in my profession. If I come out of this war alive, I will only have gained composure in the face of disaster. No injury, no matter how grotesque or mutilating, will ever startle me. I have seen the entire guts spilled out of an abdomen, heads blown off, half of a face missing, holes in chests big enough to put your fist through, hands ripped off at the wrist, feet imbedded with mud and metal splinters and dangling only on a single tendon, eyes pierced by bullets or grenade fragments, bloody heads with brains oozing out, and corpses flattened by tanks. I have seen the worst and managed to stay calm. Perhaps this is an asset.

A sudden explosion brings me to my feet. In the square of the town lies a critically injured American soldier. He had been trying to pry apart a Kraut bazooka shell, just to take home as a souvenir. The shell exploded in his hand. I recognize the fellow; he is the man from M Company, the same fellow who knifed his buddy in San Antonio while we were waiting in line to take the train to the port of embarkation. It has taken a long time for his foolishness to catch up with him, but it finally has.

Thereafter until about 12:00 P.M. all is quiet, then all hell breaks loose. Every tank in the market square suddenly fires. Grenades and mortars explode. Men are shouting in both German and English. We are overrun by Krauts. We push chairs and cabinets against our doors so that no one can enter. Only when wounded pound on the door do we open up. The story I hear is fantastic. It seems as though shortly after midnight the advance company of a battalion of Krauts quietly walks into the town. They must have stayed off the road, walking through alleys and backyards instead. When a horse-drawn vehicle passes one of our guards, however, and stops at the fountain to let the horses drink, the guard becomes leery, for only the Krauts have horses. When the drivers of the horse team start jabbering away in German, there is no longer any doubt, and he fires a warning shot. The nearest tank also opens fire, and the rest immediately follow suit. Now, everyone is in action. The remainder of the Kraut battalion is now pushing into the town on the road coming up from the south. The Krauts don't know we are in town, and we at first think troops of our division are passing through. In the darkness no one can distinguish friend from foe. The Krauts can be recognized only by the noise their hobnailed shoes make on the cobblestones of the street. Our men in the houses along the crossroad are having the worst time. As Krauts enter the first floor, our men run up to the second. Grenades are tossed down stairs and through windows to the street below. The Krauts fire their bazookas into the ground floors and toss their potato mashers upstairs. This is a real nightmare! Now some damn fool is shooting mortars, and one explodes in our backyard, breaking all our windows and knocking one of the doors off its hinges. I step outside momentarily to retrieve the fallen door and hear Krauts jabbering only a few feet away. I drop to the ground and crawl back into the station, and hide behind the counter. Several shots from a machine pistol hit the cash register, and the drawer of that damn contraption flies open with a loud ring. Suddenly everything is quiet. The shouting stops and all gunfire ceases. We wait fifteen minutes, then peek outside. All Krauts are gone. Strange as it may seem, we have only about ten wounded to treat, and none of these is seriously hurt. About twenty more, however, are dead and not brought in. Kraut casualties are much heavier. They leave at least fifty dead behind. We don't sleep much the rest of the night—we have had just a little too much excitement.

On the morning of May 1 we are on our way to Feltre. We walk along a good road and just before noon capture without resistance what is left of the tired and hungry Kraut battalion that passed through us the night before. They are resting just off the road on the banks of the Piave River.

In the late afternoon we are in the foothills of the Alps. We already see mountains five thousand feet high. I just don't think I am going to be able to climb those damn things. There are no trails, but only one main road. Just one Kraut machine gun zeroed in on a single point in the road could stop us for hours. Fortunately, we never encounter more than a few craters in the road, which hold up only our tanks and jeeps. We hike on and on, the mountains becoming higher and higher. At midnight we are in Feltre, grab a few hours' sleep, and at dawn are on the move again.

On May 2 we are walking up Highway 50. The scenery is absolutely beautiful. No Krauts are to be seen. I am becoming convinced that we have bypassed all the Krauts in the Po Valley. The suspense of whether we will be suddenly ambushed is the only thing that bothers me. The mountains are becoming higher and higher. I just hope that we are not walking into a trap. The mountains on either side of the road are sheer cliffs and impossible to climb. The road is the only way forward and also the only way of retreat. All the Krauts need do is to let us pass, have one roadblock up ahead, and sneak one cannon into position behind us, and that would be our death sentence. I think of Hannibal, who also tried to cross the Alps, and what a damn fool he was. However, we run into neither roadblock nor organized resistance. Our lead scouts shoot occasionally, but I can't find out at what. We reach a small village near Mezzano late that night.

I am exhausted from walking. We shall rest here for the night. The air is cool and fresh. I am in a farmhouse; a lush meadow is all around us, and in the moonlight the Alps look like jagged hulks almost reaching the stars.

The highest mountains are yet to be conquered. I am told that during the night our tanks will be scouting the road ahead of us, seeking enemy contact.

I am awakened at dawn on May 3, 1945 by crowing roosters. A heavy blanket of fog hugs the meadow. The sun is not yet visible, but its red glow vividly outlines the highest ridges of the Alps. A messenger comes to us from battalion headquarters. We are not to move but are to await further orders. The battalion radio crackles with static and unintelligible phrases mentioning the word surrender, which holds all listeners spellbound. At 10:00 A.M. we receive an original communication from Regiment. The war was over yesterday, May 2, at 6:00 P.M. to be exact.

That the war is over is hard to believe. I am sure that I am not dreaming, for everything is too real. I have lived for this moment for three long years, and suddenly it is here without any fanfare or celebration. The brief message from regimental headquarters will now give me a new lease on life. I am still alive. Again I have a future ahead of me and can make plans. However, I am totally broke. Not expecting to come out alive, I have spent every dollar earned either while on leave or by playing poker. This, however, is really a minor problem. Not even ever being injured or having become psychotic is really something to be thankful for. I can be productive again. I almost forgot to pray, something I had promised myself I would do as soon as the Germans would surrender. I pray in German because I never learned a prayer in English. The village in which I was born lies just ahead of us over a few Alps in Bavaria. Had I not emigrated to the United States in 1926, I would now probably be a dead German on the Russian front like every one of my relatives of comparable age. Instead, I managed to evade the shells and bullets of my former countrymen. How lucky can you get?

Epilogue

I was born April 28, 1916, in Thansau, Bavaria, a village of five houses in a valley, forty miles southeast of Munich, fifteen miles north of Kufstein, Austria, and as the crow flies fifty-five miles north of the Brenner Pass. From Thansau the Austrian Alps are clearly visible six miles to the south.

I can remember at the age of three bringing a small bucket of water to cavalry troops bivouacked in a meadow next to our house. The troops were remnants of the Kaiser's Army and were waiting to be disbanded. In 1920, at the age of four, I recall sitting on the handlebars of my mother's bicycle riding from farm to farm scrounging to buy food, which was very scarce. In winter I would go ice skating on a large lake called the Chiem See, about ten miles east of Thansau. Transportation was either on foot, by bicycle, or by horse and carriage.

In 1921 the family moved to Eisenach in Thuringia in central Germany, where my father had accepted a position with the German chemical giant I. G. Farben. Eisenach is now two miles within the Russian zone of occupation.

In Eisenach during the years 1921 to 1926 the chief recreational activity was hiking. Sundays, holidays, and during vacations the family hiked through forests from village to village, staying overnight in farm houses or small inns. In the fall we hiked through the forests at night, to listen to deer locking their horns in their struggle over females. In the winter we hiked on skis or ice skated on one of the many ponds in Eisenach constructed just for that purpose. On Sunday mornings a military band would play waltzes to which people skated. In Eisenach I also spent many days in the Wartburg castle in which Martin Luther once took refuge and threw his inkwell against a wall on which he had seen the devil.

In 1926 at election time I recall seeing men in brown shirts wearing swastika arm bands riding about in 2½-ton trucks and handing out leaflets. Nobody paid much attention to them. People talked more about communists. I also saw young boys in groups, wearing white shirts and black pants marching in Army cadence while going on camping trips. We were told that these boys belonged to the Hitler Youth Movement. Some politician named Hitler had just gotten out of jail in 1925 and was not permitted to give any speeches. That is all I knew of Hitler as a child; little did I realize then the impact this man would have on my life in the future.

In 1924 my father had accepted a position as chemist in the United States and had gone to Philadelphia. He sent for us to join him in December, 1926. We arrived in the U.S.A. on December 24, 1926. Although I had been in the fifth grade in Germany, in Philadelphia I was demoted to first grade because the teacher assumed that anyone who could not speak English was stupid. I was enrolled on a Friday. I reported to school on Saturday, but all the doors were closed. Nobody had told me that in the United States there was no school on Saturdays. First grade in grade school was too humiliating, and so was the teacher. She started my education by attempting to show me how to hold a pencil. This was the last straw; I quit and was sent instead to a German Lutheran Church School, where after two years I was proficient in English and ready for transfer to an American school into grade six.

In May, 1934, while a student at West Philadelphia High School having just turned eighteen, I received a notice from the draft board — in Berlin, not Washington, D.C. I was asked to return to Germany and sign up for duty for two years. I was to pay the expenses for the trip back to Germany. I asked for deferment and rapidly put in my claim for derivative citizenship. I obtained my U.S. citizenship on April 10, 1935. I now notified Berlin that they could forget about me since I was no longer a German citizen. I was in the clear with Germany and was not considered a draft dodger since I had asked for deferment for one year and had received it.

I was graduated from the West Philadelphia High School in January, 1935, in the "meritorious group." I entered the College of the University of Pennsylvania in February. During my college years I had summer jobs in the Pocono Mountains as bartender, gigolo, and so on. I was active in sports, track, cross-country meets, and tennis.

During the summer of 1938 I worked on a German tanker flying the swastika. I had very interesting political discussions with the crew, all of whom were 100 percent for Hitler. The captain of the ship was a very intelligent man, and he had serious doubts about Hitler. These he confided to me, but of his doubts the crew had no knowledge. Germany was saving money even in 1938. Butter and sugar on the tanker were already rationed. The sailors received only four dollars per week spending money. The rest was kept for them until they got back to Hamburg.

I was graduated from the College of the University of Pennsylvania in June, 1938, and was awarded a Phi Beta Kappa Key, which was my entrance ticket to the Medical School. I entered the University of Pennsylvania Medical School in September, 1938, and joined the Medical ROTC in October. I attended the Medical Field Service School in Carlisle, Pennsylvania, in August, 1940, for six weeks.

In September, 1940, my family moved from Philadelphia to Elkton, Maryland, where my father was to be chief chemist of the Triumph Explosives Company. The company made detonators, 20- and 40-mm antiaircraft shells and the very sensitive explosive pentolite.

During the summer of 1941 I took a three-month junior internship in the Lankenau Hospital in Philadelphia. I was graduated from the University of Pennsylvania Medical School on June 2, 1942, and was commissioned a 1st Lieutenant U.S. Army Medical Corps Reserve the same day.

Between 1939 and 1942 I was reported to the FBI three times, twice by some medical fraternity brothers, who were overzealous patriots and seized with war hysteria. The first accusation was that I had a swastika button in my possession while at the Medical Field Service School in the summer of 1942. Investigation showed that the so-called swastika button had been no more than a match packet containing three condoms, issued to me by the company sergeant before I went on pass. The match packet had a big red X on a white background, which, at a hurried glance, might have looked like a swastika button. The second accusation was that my roommate, a Hungarian by birth, and I, while living on the third floor of our medical fraternity house, were often listening to a short-wave radio and were receiving messages from Nazi Germany. Investigation showed that our radio had been homemade, that it had many impressive dials, none of which were working, and that it had a receiving distance of only about five miles. The third accusation was that I had committed a criminal act by having a photostatic copy of my citizenship paper made. I had done so because Washington, D.C., had asked to see my citizenship paper before giving me my commission. That I make a photostatic copy was suggested by the Army colonel in charge of our ROTC. Investigation showed that the colonel was at fault since he had given me the wrong instructions. A fine of five thousand dollars and a jail sentence of two years were cancelled, and in the presence of the colonel I shredded the photostatic copy, and he then wrote an affidavit attesting to the copy's destruction.

I interned at Lankenau Hospital in Philadelphia from August, 1942, to May, 1943. Starting in May, 1943, I awaited orders to be called to active duty. Until I received such orders I took a temporary job as physician in the hospital of the Triumph Explosives plant in Elkton, very close to the new home the company had built for my parents on a nearby meadow. In charge of this small hospital was the only surgeon in the county. After I had gained his confidence, he left me in charge of the place all day while he attended to his private practice. I had three well-equipped emergency rooms, a four-bed ward, and three registered nurses. Trauma requiring minor surgery occurred all day long and I had a field day reconstructing fingers and doing skin grafts and other minor surgery. I could take my time and had good help. The two months spent at Triumph were a valuable experience for my duties in the Army in the future.

I was called to active duty on July 30, 1943. From August 2 to September 9, 1943, I spent another five weeks in the Medical Field Service School in Carlisle, Pennsylvania. I reported for active duty with the 88th Infantry Division in San Antonio, Texas, on September 15, 1943.

I met Margaret Luise Nuber, first lieutenant Army Nurse Corps, in October, 1945, in the hospital in Foggia. In December, 1945, on a two-week leave in Switzerland, I proposed marriage after our Army service. To my astonishment she accepted.

The 61st Station Hospital moved from Foggia to Leghorn in December, 1945. Lt. Margaret Nuber left Leghorn for home that same month. I received my orders for home on February 22, 1946, and reentered the United States on April 1, 1946. Margaret Nuber and I were married in New Orleans on April 25, 1946. I was discharged from active duty in June of that year.

I started private practice in North East, Maryland, in May, in association with the only surgeon in the county, who had supervised me while I had been working at Triumph Explosives before my Army service. Karl Huebner was born on September 20, 1951. In 1954 after assisting my associate surgeon for eight years I built my own office in North East.

By May of 1963 I had delivered approximately fifteen hundred babies and had been having office hours almost daily from 8:00 A.M. to late at nights. Margie and I needed a change of pace.

In late June, 1963, I decided to close my office for two years. I accepted a position in Pago Pago on Tutuila Island in American Samoa for a two-year hitch. American Samoa was under the jurisdiction of the Department of the Interior, which asked for volunteers to help treat the native population at a salary just basic enough to meet expenses. I was interviewed in Washington for the job by the governor of American Samoa and was hired.

From July 1, 1963, to June 30, 1965, I was chief of the Out-Patient Department in the small hospital of American Samoa. Medical care was given to some twenty-five thousand natives and about five hundred Caucasians. In the Out-Patient Department we would see about 180 patients per day, of whom I myself treated about 50. I gained valuable experience treating such diseases, new to me, as filariasis, yaws, dengue, fungus diseases, leprosy, tropical eosinophilia, intestinal parasites, and infections with protozoa and nematodes.

Tutuila Island was only forty-six square miles large. Recreation consisted of hiking through the forests and jungles of the interior, riding a moped over the few existing roads, attending almost nightly beach parties, and snorkeling off the reefs. Medical trips to outlying islands were an adventure. I wrote a book about my experiences in Samoa, then filed it away in a foot locker in our attic and have never given it to anyone to read.

Upon leaving Samoa in July, 1965, Margie, Karl, and I spent a couple of months traveling around the rest of the world, staying about a week in each of the following countries: Fiji, Australia, Singapore, Thailand, India, Turkey, and Greece. In Rome I took delivery of a new VW from Germany. In it we drove through Italy, and I found every "aid station" I had been in between Rome and Florence. We also drove through sections of Austria and Switzerland and visited the town of my birth, Thansau, Bavaria, which still had only five houses. We then drove through Germany to Holland and back to Bremen, which we made our headquarters and from which we visited Berlin. Finally we put ourselves and the VW on the 8,000-ton German freighter the *Tannstein* of the North German Lloyd line and after a leisurely two-week ocean voyage landed in New York, unloaded the VW, and drove to Maryland, where I reopened my office and resumed general practice.

In 1967 Margie and I decided to see a little more of the world and took a two-week cruise on the flagship of the North German Lloyd the *Bremen*. We visited St. Thomas in the Virgin Islands, Barbados, Guadalupe, Trinidad, Haiti, and Jamaica. Other brief vacations while I was in general practice included golfing vacations on Prince Edward Island and Cape Breton Island in Canada, in Fort Lauderdale, and at the Cloisters in Georgia, as well as fishing trips to Maine or on the East Coast.

In October, 1968, I closed the office again and signed up for a two-year hitch in the Canal Zone in the Coco Solo Hospital operated by the Army. I went to work in the General Practice Clinic. I wanted to see more tropical medicine, and the rat race in North East had again become overpowering. In Panama I saw cases of leptospirosis, tympanosomiasis, cutaneous leishmaniasis, malaria, a few snake bites, and lots of VD. On one tour of annual leave in Panama we managed to spend one week each in Colombia, Ecuador, Peru, Bolivia, Chile, Brazil, and Argentina. We went to Machu Pichu, Cuzco, and Lake

Titicaca in Bolivia. I had hauled a sixteen-foot outboard motor boat to New Orleans and from there had it shipped to me in Panama. In it we explored the tropical Chagras River. With an Indian guide I also made excursions in a dugout canoe up the Chepo-Bayano River into the Darion jungle between Panama and Colombia.

In August, 1970, Margie and I set out for home. Karl had already left Panama and was attending Duke University. Margie and I decided to drive home in our 1965 VW, which already had eighty thousand miles on it and retread tires. Deciding to take the Pan-American Highway, we loaded up with Army rations and five-gallon cans of drinking water. We spent about a week each driving through Costa Rica, Nicaragua, Honduras, El Salvador, Guatemala, and Mexico.

We arrived in New Orleans in September, 1970, and from there drove home to North East. This time I went into practice on the internal medicine service of the Veterans Hospital in Perry Point, Maryland. In 1972 I took and passed a Board examination in the newly established specialty of Family Medicine.

In April, 1985, my old army buddy Ted Bellmont, of Houston, renewed his acquaintance and encouraged me to submit the diary of my war experiences for publication. When I retired from the V.A. on January 19, 1986, I began working to do just that.

Index

Abbey on Monte Cassino, 48
Adige River, 190
Adige River Line, 190
Adone, Mount, 167, 172
Adriatic Sea, 107, 172
Aetna, Mount, 31
aidmen, of infantry company, xv, 18,
    23, 49, 115, 137
airbursts, 66, 69, 82, 168, 169
Albano, Italy, 98, 99, 104, 107
Albano, Lake, 99
Algeria, 14
Algiers, Algeria, 31
Alpini troops, 38
Alps, 192, 195, 196
Alto, Mount, 78, 81
Altuzzo, Mount, 122
Amaseno River, 83, 84
Amaseno River Valley, 82, 83
Ancona, Italy, 107
Anzio, Italy, 60, 82, 84, 86
Apennines, 124, 168, 169
Arabs, 12, 13, 14, 15, 24
Army Transportation Corps, 10
Arno River, 108, 116, 117, 122
artificial respiration, 4
Atlas Mountains, 16, 17
Augusta harbor, Sicily, 31
Aurunci Mountains, 71
"Axis Sally" of Berlin, 51, 54

Bagnoli, 32, 33
Bailey bridge, 122
Bassano, Italy, 191, 192
battalion aid station, xiii, xv; to Arno
    River, 110, 114, 115; on Garigliano
    River front, 42; to Gothic Line, 125,
    133, 135, 136, 137, 139, 148, 150,
    151; in north Apennines, 160, 166,
    167; in Po Valley, 190, 192; during
    push on Rome, 72, 74, 76, 78, 80,
    82, 88

Battalion Headquarters Company, xiv
battalion medical detachment, xv
battalion rifle companies, xiv
battalion surgeon, xiv, 3
bazooka, xiv, 71, 83
bed bugs, 72, 189
"Bed Check Charlie," 37, 159
Bell Isola, 139
Bellmont, Capt. Ted, 13, 44, 54, 56,
    100, 108, 188, 189, 202
Bernadini, Mount, 136
Bizerte, Tunisia, 31
Blue Devils in Italy (John P. Delaney),
    57n
Bologna, 124, 151, 172, 176
Bon, Tunisia, Cape, 31
Brazilian Expeditionary Force, 121
Brenda River, 191
British Army units: Canadians, 60, 165;
    commandos, 60; Eighth Army, 84,
    107; 11th Lancashire Fuseliers, 154;
    Indians, 60; New Zealanders, 48, 60;
    Poles, 60; 6th South African Divi-
    sion, 172
Bronze Star medal, 112
Browning automatic rifle (BAR), 4, 52,
    58, 76
Bucciano, Italy, 116

Callahan, Lieutenant, 28
Camp Bullis, Texas, 4
Camp Cibalo, Texas, 4
Camp Don B. Passage, Morocco, 12, 13,
    14
Camp Patrick Henry, Virginia, 7, 8, 9
Casablanca, Morocco, 12, 13
Casanova, Italy, 54, 57
Casbah, Casablanca, 13
Cassino, Italy, 36, 40, 48, 60
Castel del Rio, Italy, 133, 135, 136
Castel del Rio–Sassoleone road, 138
Castelforte, Italy, 48, 49, 53, 57, 62

cat hole, 4, 15
Ca Valla, Italy, 173
Cave, Italy, 86
C. di Lesso, Italy, 139
Cecina, Italy, 108
Cecina River, 107
Ceracoli, Mount, 58
Cevitavecchia, Italy, 104
Cima Del Monte, Mount, 76, 78
Civita, Mount, 65, 68
Clark, Lt. Gen. Mark W., 60, 61, 105
Coco Solo Hospital, Canal Zone, 201
collecting company, medical, 50, 68
Collegio Costanza Ciano, 32
Comacchio, Lake, 165, 172
Cori, Italy, 84, 86
Cornuda, Italy, 192
C-rations, 13, 15, 27, 33, 34, 39, 78, 124, 136
Crawford, Colonel, 57, 105
Crevalcore, Italy, 187
Crowley, Chaplain, 33, 34, 151

DDT powder, 36
Di Gresso, Italy, 140
Di Lavaccia, Italy, 159
Distinguished Service Cross, 59, 162
division clearing station, 105
Dorocher, Leo "Lippy", 162
draft board, German, 198

88-mm shellings, 57, 65, 67, 74, 77, 78, 80, 110, 115, 138, 150, 151, 159
88th Infantry Division, 3, 108, 121, 174, 200; 350th Regiment, xiv, 61, 108, 139; 351st Regiment, xiv, 61, 62, 63, 65, 136, 176; 349th Regiment, xiv, 108, 176; 1st Battalion 349th Regiment, 61, 132; 2d Battalion 349th Regiment, 61, 132, 159; 3d Battalion 349th Regiment, 3, 16, 55, 61, 64, 108, 109, 123, 175
emergency medical tag (EMT), 66, 79, 90
Empress of Scotland (American ship), 10, 11, 12

Fano, Mount, 163
Feltre, Italy, 195
Felts, Capt. "Pappy," 9, 11, 13, 24, 59, 65, 78

Fertig, Sergeant, 23, 125
Fez, Morocco, 14, 15
Firenzuola, Italy, 126, 127
Firenzuola–Castel del Rio road, 126
first aid demonstrations, 4, 17
Fitzsimmons, T/3 Sergeant, 36
Florence, Italy, 107, 108, 116, 122, 124
Florence-Pistoia-Lucca road, 168
fly control, 4
Fondi, Italy, 71, 74, 75
Formia, Italy, 69
Formiche, Italy, 165
Fort Sam Houston, Texas, 3, 4, 5
40-and-8s (French boxcars), 15, 27
Forum Mussolini, 118, 119, 120
Foss, Lieutenant, 108
Frassineto, 148, 150, 152
French colonial troops, 60, 61, 81, 83, 84, 90
Furcoli Ridge, 172, 173
Futa Pass, 124

Gabbiano, Italy, 166
Gaeta, Italy, 69
Gagliano, Italy, 161
Galliart, Lieutenant, 152
garbage pit construction, 4
Garigliano River, 41
Garigliano River Valley, 48, 54, 59, 60
German Army units: 1st Parachute Division, 98, 148, 191; Hermann Goering Division, 88, 89, 90; 90th Light Division, 148; 94th Infantry Division, 58; Poles, conscripted, 58; 71st Division, 58
Gioa, 36
goldbrick, 4, 9, 36
gonorrhea, 4, 102, 121, 167
Gothic Line, 124
Goums, 62, 76, 81, 82
Grande, Mount, 148, 150, 151, 152
graves registration detail, 49
Gray, Lieutenant, 162
grease trap construction, 4
Grosseto, Italy, 107
Gulf of Gaeta, 48
Gulf of Naples, 31
Gulf of Salerno, 31
Gustav Line, 62
Guzeman, 2d Lieutenant, 7

Hampton Roads, Virginia, 7, 9
Hayes, Chaplain, 156, 157
Heavy Weapons Company, xiv
Henderson, Lieutenant Colonel, 44,
    159, 164
hepatitis, 16, 159, 160, 162, 166
Hess, Colonel, 121, 140
Highway 11, 190
Highway 50, 195
Highway 46, 191
Highway 9, 151
Highway 1, 107
Highway 7 (Via Appia), 40, 69, 71, 72,
    74, 78, 83, 84
Highway 6, 48, 78, 83, 86, 88, 89, 90
Highway 65, 124, 125, 158, 159, 166,
    167, 169, 172, 173
Highway 64, 167, 172, 174, 176
Highway 12, 188
Highway 2, 97, 98
Hill 44, 108, 111, 112
Hitler Line, 74
Hollis, Lieutenant, 24, 30
Hotel Excelsior, 101, 102, 103, 118, 157,
    163, 164, 169
Huebner, Capt. Klaus, 44, 94, 112
Huebner, Karl, 200
Hurley, Private First Class, 36

Imola, Italy, 172
infantry battalions, xiv
infantry division, components of, xiv
Isle of Capri, 31
Itri, Italy, 69, 71, 72
Itri-Pico road, 69, 71

jeep drivers, 66, 74
Jenkins, Lieutenant, 105
Jones, Capt. Charlie, 59

Kielty, Colonel, 8
King's Palace in Caserta (Palazzo Reale),
    54, 56, 57
Knox, Major, 44
Konze, Lt. William, 108
K-rations, 33, 82, 132, 133, 136
K-12 hill mass, 173

La Croce, Italy, 168
La Fine, Mount, 129, 130, 131, 132

Lankenau Hospital, Philadelphia, 22,
    199
Larderello, Italy, 108
latrines, 4, 17, 51
Leghorn, Italy, 108
Liebenstein, Lieutenant, 58
Ligurian Sea, 165
Lillie, 119, 120
litter bearers, xv, 18, 49, 80, 87, 111, 137,
    151
Loiano, Italy, 166, 168
long toms, 122
lorries, 41
louse control, 4
Lucca, Italy, 168
Luce, Clare Boothe, 159
Lyster bag, 15, 24, 27

McFarland, Lieutenant, 163
machine pistols, 52, 58, 76, 77, 98, 125,
    128, 129
Maddaloni, Italy, 54
Mae West belts, 10, 11, 30
Magenta, Algeria, 16, 26
Magenta-Bedeau area, Algeria, 14
Magnacavello, Italy, 188
malaria prevention, 4
Manzuno, Italy, 166, 168, 172
Marceau, T/3 Sergeant, 36, 79
Marguerete, 157, 164, 165, 170, 171
Maria, 100–101, 102, 103, 104, 105–106,
    107
Mazzano Romano, Italy, 98
Mazzola, Italy, 108
Medical Administrative Corps officer
    (MAC), 118
Medical Field Service School, Carlisle,
    Pa., 23, 199, 200
medical illnesses, treatment of: in
    American soldiers, 4, 7, 8, 11, 16, 23,
    26, 30, 36, 80, 82, 133, 152, 153,
    156, 159, 160, 166, 167; in Italian
    civilians, 83, 113, 116, 140, 158, 166,
    167
Mediterranean Sea, 28, 31
Melcher, Lieutenant, 13, 39
mess kit sanitation, 4
Mezzano, Italy, 196
Milvio Bridges, 97
Minturno, Italy, 48, 69
Minturno–Santa Maria Infante road, 63

Montecatini, Italy, 155, 156, 158
Monterumici Hill Mass, 172
Monti Aurunci Ridge, 69
moonlight, artificial, 155
"Moose," the (Lieutenant Moss), 13, 28
mosquito control, 4
mountain climbing, 17, 39; and disease,
    18; school for, 37
mule pack artillery, 71
mule pack trains, 39, 79, 80, 82, 126,
    133, 154, 160
mules, for aid station, 18, 69
Mullins, Captain, 191
mutton, 30

Naples harbor, 31, 32
Nebelwerfers (screaming meemies), 89,
    110
Neuralia (British ship), 29, 30, 31
Nogara, Italy, 189
North East, Maryland, 200
Nuber, 1st Lt. Margaret Luise, 200
Nuzzano ridges, 173

observation post (OP), 53, 58, 140
olive drab (OD), 6, 27
Oran, Algeria, 27, 28, 29, 31
Ostiglia, Italy, 189

Pago Pago (American Samoa), 200
Palaia, Italy, 114, 115
Palestrina, Italy, 86, 89
paper cutters, 52. *See also* machine
    pistols
Passignano, Mount, 75
patrols, 52, 54, 58, 152
Peterson, Lieutenant/Captain, 7, 44, 53
Pezzola, 137
phosphorus shells, 62, 70, 84, 173
Piave River, 195
Piedmonte d'Alife, Italy, 36, 37, 38
Pierson, Lieutenant, 7, 80
Pincio Gardens, 97
Pisa, Italy, 107, 108, 172
Pisterza, Italy, 82, 83
Pistoia, Italy, 168
Pomerance, Italy, 107
Pompeii, Italy, 31
Po River, 188, 189
Potter, Captain, 30

Po Valley, 124, 140, 151, 155, 163, 174,
    176, 186, 188, 190
Priverno, Italy, 78
Priverno-Prossedi road, 82, 83, 84
prophylactic (pro) kits, 40
Prossedi, 78

Rabat, Morocco, 14, 15
Radicosa Pass, 124
Rangolia, Italy, 138
regimental commander, 8, 16, 23, 24,
    57
Reinboth, Chaplain Oscar, 59
Reserve Officers' Training Corps, medi-
    cal, 3, 23, 199
Rome, Italy, 82, 86, 90, 97, 99, 101, 102,
    103, 104, 118, 163, 169, 170
Rommel, Field Marshal, 156
Ronco, Italy, 189
Rotundo, Mount, 78, 81
"Rover Boys," 140, 188
"Rover Pete," 172, 189

Sacco River Valley, 78, 83
Salleno River, 140
San Antonio, Texas, 3, 6
San Bonifacio, Italy, 190
San Clemente, Italy, 148, 149, 150, 151,
    155
San Clemente road, 149
San Felice, Italy, 187
San Giovanni, Italy, 186
San Martino, Italy, 187
San Miniato, Italy, 116
Santa Maria Infante, Italy, 62, 63, 66,
    69
Sassoleone, Italy, 135, 139
Sassoleone–Castel del Rio road, 138
Sassoleone–San Clemente road, 148
Savage, Lieutenant, 9
Scandicci, Italy, 120
Schockman, Lieutenant, 7
screaming meemies, 89, 110
Section 8 discharge, xiv, 5
Section 10 discharge, 5
short-arm inspection, 6
Shutzky, Major, 11
Sicily, 31
Sidi Bel Abbès, Algeria, 25, 26
Siena, Italy, 108
Sillaro River, 139

64th Station Hospital, 26
Sloan, General, 10, 120
Sole, Mount, 172
Stars and Stripes, 17, 60, 153, 165
Straits of Messina, 31
sulfadiazine, 105, 120, 136, 138
sulfanilamide, 50

tank destroyers (TDs), 53, 58
Tarquinia, 104, 105, 107
Texas, 3
Thansau, Bavaria, 197
38th Evacuation Hospital, 40
Thompson, Lieutenant, 68
Tiber River, 97
Todd, Lieutenant, 44
Torres, Sergeant, 36, 52, 79, 134
train surgeon, 6
Trassasso, Italy, 169, 171
Tufo, Italy, 62, 63
Tutuila, American Samoa, 200
Tyrrhenian Sea, 31

United States Army units: 85th Infantry Division, 54, 59, 61, 69, 70, 86, 121, 124, 125, 126, 127, 174, 176; 82nd Airborne Division, 60; Fifth Army, 121, 152; 1st Armored Division, 60, 108, 174, 176; 45th Infantry Division, 60, 121; 442nd Japanese-American Regimental Combat Team, 120, 121; IV corps, Fifth Army, 174, 176; 91st Infantry Division, 117, 121, 172; II Corps, Fifth Army, 84, 176; 10th Mountain Division, 174, 176; 3d Infantry Division, 60, 84, 86, 87, 97, 121; 34th Infantry

United States Army units (*cont.*)
    Division, 121, 172, 176; 36th Infantry Division, 121. *See also* 88th Infantry Division
University of Pennsylvania, 21, 198; medical school of, 22, 199

Vado, Italy, 173
Valmontone, 86
val-pack, 6
venereal disease (VD) control, 4, 168
Vergato, Italy, 174
Verona, Italy, 190
Vesuvius, Mount, 31
Veterans Administration Hospital, Perry Point, Md., 202
Vicenza, Italy, 190, 191
Vichy French, 28
Villamagna, Italy, 113, 114, 117, 120
Volkswagens, 74
Volterra, Italy, 107, 108, 111

war gases, 4
war wounds, self-inflicted, 50
war wounds, treated: in American soldiers, 50, 52, 63, 65, 66, 68, 70, 73, 75, 77, 79, 80, 81, 87, 88, 110, 111, 113, 115, 127, 131, 139, 148, 150, 169, 173, 187; in German soldiers, 76, 88, 89, 90, 98, 113, 125, 129, 138, 139; in Italian civilians, 50, 70, 81
water purification, 4
Williams, Lt. Charlie, 38, 39

Yeager, Colonel, 108, 121
Young, Captain, 7

Long Walk Through War was composed into type on a Compugraphic digital phototypesetter in ten point Trump Mediaeval with two points of spacing between the lines. Friz Quadrata was selected for display. The book was designed by Jim Billingsley, typeset by Metricomp, Inc., printed offset by Thomson-Shore, Inc., and bound by John H. Dekker & Sons. The paper on which this book is printed bears acid-free characteristics for an effective life of at least three hundred years.

TEXAS A&M UNIVERSITY PRESS : COLLEGE STATION